Teaching Augustine

Edited by

Scott McGinnis and Christopher Metress

This book is a reprint of the special issue that appeared in the online open access journal
Religions (ISSN 2077-1444) in 2015 (available at:
http://www.mdpi.com/journal/religions/special_issues/teaching-augustine).

Guest Editors
Scott McGinnis
Religion Department, Howard College of Arts and Sciences
Samford University
800 Lakeshore Drive
Birmingham, AL 35229
USA

Christopher Metress
Samford University
800 Lakeshore Drive
Birmingham, AL 35229
USA

Editorial Office
MDPI AG
Klybeckstrasse 64
Basel, Switzerland

Publisher
Shu-Kun Lin

Assistant Editor
Jie Gu

1. Edition 2015

MDPI • Basel • Beijing • Wuhan

ISBN 978-3-03842-115-3 (Hbk)
ISBN 978-3-03842-116-0 (PDF)

© 2015 by the authors; licensee MDPI, Basel, Switzerland. All articles in this volume are Open Access distributed under the Creative Commons Attribution 4.0 license (http://creativecommons.org/licenses/by/4.0/), which allows users to download, copy and build upon published articles even for commercial purposes, as long as the author and publisher are properly credited, which ensures maximum dissemination and a wider impact of our publications. However, the dissemination and distribution of copies of this book as a whole is restricted to MDPI, Basel, Switzerland.

Table of Contents

List of Contributors VII

About the Guest Editors.. XI

Preface XIII

Acknowledgments XV

Introduction XVII

Section I. Keynote Addresses

Peter Iver Kaufman
Deposito Diademate: Augustine's Emperors
Reprinted from: *Religions* **2015**, *6*(2), 317-327
http://www.mdpi.com/2077-1444/6/2/317 3

Kristen Deede Johnson
The Justice Game: Augustine, Disordered Loves, and the Temptation to Change the World
Reprinted from: *Religions* **2015**, *6*(2), 409-418
http://www.mdpi.com/2077-1444/6/2/409 14

Section II. Pedagogical Contexts

Allan Fitzgerald
Naming the Mystery: An Augustinian Ideal
Reprinted from: *Religions* **2015**, *6*(1), 204-210
http://www.mdpi.com/2077-1444/6/1/204 27

J. Caleb Clanton
Teaching Socrates, Aristotle, and Augustine on *Akrasia*
Reprinted from: *Religions* **2015**, *6*(2), 419-433
http://www.mdpi.com/2077-1444/6/2/419 34

Ian Clausen
Seeking the Place of Conscience in Higher Education: An Augustinian View
Reprinted from: *Religions* **2015**, *6*(2), 286-298
http://www.mdpi.com/2077-1444/6/2/286 49

Peter Busch
Modern Restlessness, from Hobbes to Augustine
Reprinted from: *Religions* **2015**, *6*(2), 626-637
http://www.mdpi.com/2077-1444/6/2/626 62

Section III. Rarely Read Augustine

Daniel E. Burns
Augustine's Introduction to Political Philosophy: Teaching *De Libero Arbitrio*, Book I
Reprinted from: *Religions* **2015**, *6*(1), 82-91
http://www.mdpi.com/2077-1444/6/1/82 77

Robert D. Anderson
Teaching Augustine's *On the Teacher*
Reprinted from: *Religions* **2015**, *6*(2), 404-408
http://www.mdpi.com/2077-1444/6/2/404 87

John MacInnis
Augustine's *De Musica* in the 21st Century Music Classroom
Reprinted from: *Religions* **2015**, *6*(1), 211-220
http://www.mdpi.com/2077-1444/6/1/211 92

Section IV. Exemplary Assignments

Bryan J. Whitfield
Teaching Augustine's *Confessions* in the Context of Mercer's Great Books Program
Reprinted from: *Religions* **2015**, *6*(1), 107-112
http://www.mdpi.com/2077-1444/6/1/107 103

Mark S. M. Scott
Augustine and Autobiography: *Confessions* as a Roadmap for Self-Reflection
Reprinted from: *Religions* **2015**, *6*(1), 139-145
http://www.mdpi.com/2077-1444/6/1/139 109

Maria Poggi Johnson
Augustine, Addiction and Lent: A Pedagogic Exercise
Reprinted from: *Religions* **2015**, *6*(1), 113-121
http://www.mdpi.com/2077-1444/6/1/113 115

Section V. Augustine in the Core Curriculum and Beyond

Michael Chiariello
Augustine's *Confessions*: Interiority at the Core of the Core Curriculum
Reprinted from: *Religions* **2015**, *6*(3), 755-762
http://www.mdpi.com/2077-1444/6/3/755 125

Thomas Nordlund
The Physics of Augustine: The Matter of Time, Change and an Unchanging God
Reprinted from: *Religions* **2015**, *6*(1), 221-244
http://www.mdpi.com/2077-1444/6/1/221 133

List of Contributors

Robert Anderson is Professor of Philosophy at St. Anselm College.

Daniel Burns is Assistant Professor of Politics at the University of Dallas. He received his doctorate in political philosophy from Boston College in 2012 with a dissertation entitled "St. Augustine on the Nature and Limits of Human Law." He studies the relationship between religion and politics in a range of authors, including Augustine, Locke, Rousseau, Leo Strauss, and Joseph Ratzinger. He is a member of the Neuer Schülerkreis Joseph Ratzinger/Benedikt XVI., a Germany-based group of scholars dedicated to furthering Ratzinger's intellectual legacy.

Peter Busch is a Gallen Teaching Fellow in the Augustine and Culture Seminar Program at Villanova University, where he is in his fourteenth year of teaching. His interests range from Homer to Nietzsche and most things between, but he is currently writing on Augustine's critique of political philosophy in the *City of God*.

Michael Chiariello is professor of philosophy, and former dean of Clare College, at St. Bonaventure University. Currently, he serves as director of The Franciscan Heritage Semester Study Abroad Program in Perugia, Italy. Recent publications include "Bob Dylan's Truth," in *Philosophy and Bob Dylan* (Open Court, 2005) and "Umberto Eco's Name of the Rose: Teaching the Franciscan Intellectual Tradition to Postmodern Undergraduates," in *Postscript to the Middle Ages* (Syracuse Univ. Press 2010).

J. Caleb Clanton is University Research Professor and associate professor of philosophy at Lipscomb University. His research centers on issues in philosophy of religion, moral philosophy, and the history of philosophy. His most recent book, *Philosophy of Religion in the Classical American Tradition*, is forthcoming with The University of Tennessee Press.

Ian Clausen is a Lilly Postdoctoral Fellow at Valparaiso University. As a British Marshall scholar, he earned his MTh and PhD in Theology and Ethics from the University of Edinburgh. He holds the Research Associate post at the Kirby Laing Institute for Christian Ethics, and is a Fellow of the Paul Ramsey Institute. His published work can be found in journals such as *Augustinian Studies*, *Religions*, *Expository Times*, and *Radical Orthodoxy*. His first book, under contract with Bloomsbury Publishing, will bear the title *The Long Surrender: Augustine's Moral Self*.

Fr. Allan Fitzgerald, O.S.A, is the director of the Augustinian Institute at Villanova University as well as professor in the Department of Theology and Religious Studies. Editor of *Augustine Through the Ages: an Encyclopedia* and editor emeritus of the journal, *Augustinian Studies*, his research also includes numerous studies on Ambrose of Milan and on the history of Christian penance.

Kristen Deede Johnson is Associate Professor of Theology and Christian Formation at Western Theological Seminary in Holland, Michigan. Previously, she served as the founding director of the Studies in Ministry Minor and the Center for Ministry Studies at Hope College, programs dedicated to upholding the significance of theological formation, spiritual growth, cultural engagement, and vocational discernment. She is the author of *Theology, Political Theory, and Pluralism: Beyond Tolerance and Difference* (Cambridge University Press, 2007), a number of articles and chapters related to theology, culture, and political theory, and a forthcoming book with Bethany Hanke Hoang of International Justice Mission titled *The Justice Calling: Where Passion Meets Perseverance* (Brazos Press).

Maria Poggi Johnson was educated at the Oxford University and the University of Virginia. She is a Professor of Theology at the University of Scranton, where she has taught since 1996. She is the editor of *John Keble, Sermons for the Christian Year* (Eerdmans, 2006) and the author of *Strangers and Neighbors: What I Have Learned about Christianity by Living Among Orthodox Jews* (Thomas Nelson, 2006) and *Making a Welcome: Christian Life and the Practice of Hospitality* (Wipf and Stock, 2011).

Peter Iver Kaufman is Professor Emeritus, University of North Carolina at Chapel Hill and George Matthews and, from 2008, Virginia Brinkley Modlin Professor at the University of Richmond. His publications on Augustine include *Incorrectly Political: Augustine and Thomas More* and articles in, inter alia, *Journal Of Late Antiquity*, *Augustinian Studies*, *Church History*, *Journal Of Religious Ethics*, and *History Of Political Thought*. His most recent book, *Religion Around Shakespeare* was published in 2013.

John MacInnis is Assistant Professor of Music and Department Co-Chair at Dordt College (Sioux Center, IA), where he teaches Music History and Music Theory. His dissertation (Florida State University, 2014) traces the use and influence of music as a liberal art throughout the writings of John Scottus Eriugena, a ninth-century philosopher. Other research interests for MacInnis include the place of music in Neoplatonic philosophy in late Antiquity and the Middle Ages as well as the history and philosophy of church music. As a keyboardist, MacInnis enjoys performing in chamber ensembles, in addition to his work as a church musician.

Thomas M. Nordlund is Associate Professor of Physics at the University of Alabama at Birmingham. His publications focused for 35 years on biophysics. Recently he began writing Physics education research papers and physics textbooks, including s *Quantitative Understanding of Biosystem* (2011) and *Physical Theology* (in preparation), for "nonstandard" students. His interest in Augustine as a physicist was sparked when a lively philosophical classroom discussion on Augustine's *Confessions* ground quietly to a halt when the text suddenly addressed the author's frustrations with understanding the nature of time, the most fundamental parameter of physical understanding.

Mark Scott is an Arthur J. Ennis Postdoctoral Fellow in the Augustine and Culture Seminar Program at Villanova University. He is the author of *Pathways in Theodicy: An Introduction to the Problem of Evil* (Fortress Press, 2015) and *Journey Back to God: Origen on the Problem of Evil* (OUP, 2012). His articles have appeared in *Harvard Theological Review*, *Journal of Religion*, *Journal of Early Christian Studies*, *Theology Today*, *Teaching Theology and Religion*, and elsewhere. He is the recipient of five Certificates of Distinction in Teaching from Harvard College and the Purple Chalk Teaching Award from the University of Missouri.

Bryan J. Whitfield is an associate professor in the Columbus Roberts Department of Christianity in the College of Liberal Arts of Mercer University in Macon, Georgia. He also teaches in Mercer's Great Books Program, an alternative general education program of seven courses focused on the intellectual history of the West. He is the author of *Joshua Traditions and the Argument of Hebrews 3 and 4* (Berlin: De Gruyter, 2013) as well as articles on Hebrews and Jude.

About the Guest Editors

Scott McGinnis is Associate Professor of Religion at Samford University, where he teaches courses in history, theology, and the critical study of religion. He regularly teaches general education courses as well as the western intellectual history sequence in the university's honor program. He is the author of *George Gifford and the Reformation of the Common Sort: Puritan Priorities in Elizabethan Religious Life*. His articles and reviews reflect his interests in religion in early modern England, popular religion, and the history of religious dissent and toleration.

Christopher Metress is University Professor and Associate Provost for Academics at Samford University, where he teaches courses in literature, film, and western intellectual history. His publications have appeared in such journals as *Studies in the Novel*, *African American Review*, and *Southern Quarterly*, and he is the co-editor of a forthcoming volume entitled *Memory, Invention, Delivery: Transmitting and Transforming Knowledge and Culture in Liberal Arts Education*.

Preface

The role of the humanities in university curricula has been the topic of much national debate, with politicians predicting the imminent demise of liberal learning, a fate feared by some and perhaps welcomed by others. Even if one stops short of such apocalyptic scenarios, core and general education courses that promote a humanities-based liberal arts education are under tremendous pressure to justify themselves in an environment where dollars are tight and professionalization is all the rage. Concurrently, humanities departments feel a similar push, urged by their administrations to pitch their disciplines more for the skills they develop than the dispositions they cultivate, or the questions they inspire. In this context, it is more important than ever that liberal arts courses not only be taught, but taught well.

In October 2014, Samford University, with generous support from the Lilly Fellows Program, hosted a conference entitled *Teaching the Christian Intellectual Tradition: Augustine Across the Curriculum*. The first in a planned series of conferences focusing on commonly taught figures and movements from the Christian intellectual heritage, the meeting was designed to help non-specialists teach the writings of Augustine more effectively in undergraduate core and general education classes. The papers gathered in this volume include the two keynote addresses and a selection from the more than fifty papers presented at this conference.

The organizers of the *Teaching the Christian Intellectual Tradition (TCIT)* conference series are committed to the liberal arts as both a foundation for and a unifying force of degree programs across the university, and we assume that general education and core courses are the key locations where this integrative learning will take place. This strategy, however, faces several difficult challenges. For instance, core courses at institutions similar to Samford often draw faculty who are asked to teach outside of their disciplines and areas of expertise. Specialists in Romanticism find themselves pondering with their students Luther's theology of justification in the context of the late medieval church; theologians struggle to offer historically informed readings of post-colonial fiction; and Latin American historians edge their way cautiously into the foreign world of the drawing rooms of English nobility. The challenge can be daunting, particularly for younger faculty. Having emerged recently from specialized graduate training, they are now called upon to teach, and teach well, texts they may not have read since their undergraduate years, or ever.

A somewhat different problem emerges in general education courses. Here, faculty move more comfortably within their own disciplines. However, professional training and disciplinary pressures often marginalize the great works of the Christian intellectual tradition, resulting in general education courses that, whether by intention or benign neglect, fail to draw to upon the rich insights of that tradition. What emerges are survey or introductory courses that perpetuate the notion that the concerns and positions of the faithful have no place in the disciplines. Finally, for those faculty fully committed to the Christian intellectual tradition, there remains the further challenge of finding a way to promote a creative, constructive, and critical engagement with that tradition without lapsing into either hagiography or shallow presentism. Just as simply teaching the humanities is not enough, teaching the Christian intellectual tradition is not enough. It must be taught well, and that means creatively and critically, with a mind toward how that tradition, through its own long and contested engagement with the deepest questions, enriches every discipline and, by extension, every curriculum.

The *TCIT* conferences are designed to address these challenges in academic professional training by providing venues for non-specialists to gather and exchange ideas and strategies for engaging in productive classroom discussions of key writers and, ultimately, the fundamental questions of human existence and flourishing: Who are we? Why are we here? How does one live purposefully and morally with others? Given that such questions transcend any university degree program or discipline, and given that the Christian intellectual tradition provides an array of influential answers to these questions, it is appropriate that such discussions both within and across the disciplines be made available to all. It is with this intent that the following volume is offered.

Scott McGinnis and Christopher Metress
Guest Editors

Acknowledgments

The editors wish to acknowledge a generous grant from the Lilly Fellows Program that helped underwrite the conference at which the following essays were first presented.

Introduction

Why Augustine? For many teachers a more appropriate question may be "Who else?" Living as he did in the twilight of Roman imperial power, and standing as he does at the headwaters of the Western Christian tradition, Augustine has long been the standard source for offering students a quick summary of late ancient Christian attitudes. On topics ranging from politics to predestination, sexuality to music theory, his shadow looms large. It goes without saying that Augustine would not have imagined himself in this position; his world was filled with unresolved theological and political conflicts. Manichees, Donatists, and Pelagians offered strong alternatives to Augustine's Christianity, and it was not a foregone conclusion that his brand would survive and thrive. But thrive it did, in no small part to his own contributions. Like Augustine or not, a historian wishing to argue for an inconsequential Augustine would have an uphill climb indeed.

Yet it is hardly surprising that freshmen, bombarded as they are with cultural messages that privilege the present and future over the past, might question the relevance of dusty tomes written by a North African bishop sixteen centuries ago. In high school they were told to structure their interests and activities to become suitably competitive for college. Now having arrived, and even before taking their first class, they are encouraged think beyond graduation towards employment and professional life. Education, they are told, is valuable not for the experience it provides but for the outcome it produces: a job. Are we surprised, then, that so many students fail to appreciate college as a time to contemplate life's deepest questions, much less still as an opportunity to engage in a sustained critique of education as nothing more than the acquisition of skill sets?

Fortunately, such an instrumental understanding of education cannot fully kill the spirit. Many students quickly discern that they can orient those skill sets toward lofty goals, and they maintain a hearty optimism that the world they are inheriting might become a better place—more humane, more sustainable, more just—and that they might help to make it so. Before long, though, consideration of the messy mechanics of world-changing leads to a more fundamental question. Can governments and the politicians that direct them make the world a better place? Or to reduce the abstract to the existential, should undergraduates, struggling with what Kristen Deede Johnson suggestively labels the "*temptation* to change the world" (emphasis added), pursue a career in politics or a similar avenue of power running parallel to the political? Alternatively, do they take a left (or right) turn, avoiding entangling alliances with worldly powers, and seek to change the culture by focusing their energies outside, against, or in spite of those powers? It is here that Augustine can enter the conversation, the first of many ways in which he can enrich a student's experience across the curriculum.

Augustine's view of the utility of political power is the question that yokes together the two keynote addresses in the first section of this volume, and each address argues in its own way for the continuing relevance of Augustine's political thought. As Peter Iver Kaufman observes, Augustine was no stranger to the pressures of careerism faced by the modern undergraduate. As Augustine pondered his own turn from politics and rhetoric toward a contemplative life, he offered much in the way of raw material for subsequent thinkers who have struggled with a similar predicament. Kaufman's Augustine might have been neck-deep in the political struggles of North Africa as he worked to establish his brand of Christianity against rival Donatists and pagans, and he was certainly not hesitant to call upon local officials to aid his cause. Yet Kaufman suggests that behind Augustine's tactical maneuvering lay a more fundamental concern with the nature of the political life, which was controlled by what Augustine deemed the "lust to be first" (*libido principandi*) and the "lust to dominate" (*libido dominandi*). Indeed, these broken desires were so foundational to political life in the city of man that even a celebrated Christian leader such as Constantine is discussed by Augustine with a relatively dispassionate tone. He takes note of Constantine's political accomplishments, yet Augustine reserves his highest praise in the *City of God* for the emperor Theodosius, and precisely for the virtue that Augustine judged to be lacking in so many leaders: humility. To put it another way, Theodosius was at his best when he was at his weakest, politically speaking: on his knees as a repentant sinner begging Bishop Ambrose for forgiveness for his transgressions as a leader.

What use, then, should moderns make of Augustine's emperors? Kaufman rejects those who use Augustine as a clarion call for a remade political order, one purged of lusts for power. Find enough pious and humble leaders, such proponents argue, and the city of man might begin to take on a heavenly glow. Similarly misguided, Kaufman avers, are those who employ Augustine to establish secular power and influence for the church over the state. Instead, Kaufman argues for an Augustine who models the twin attitudes of "recoil and reorientation," recoil from the status quo of the powerful always striving for more power, and reorientation of one's interests in the context of communities shaped by the "virtues of humility, compassion, and forgiveness." It is this Augustine who speaks to the modern condition and provides a way forward.

Whereas Kaufman resurrects Augustine's emperors to explore questions of political order, Kristen Johnson turns to Augustine's writings on justice to engage students with "the difficult questions that arise as they face the reality of injustice and ponder what it means to change the world." She orients her argument around the twin poles of justice and power. Both are from God and hence good, but humans must pay close attention to the proper ordering of these two goods. Perfect possessor of both, God nevertheless chose justice rather than power to defeat evil in the world. Herein lies the rub, according to Johnson. In Augustine's view, humans are so fatally flawed that they cannot overcome their own desires in order to imitate the divine. Their loves are fundamentally disordered, with the love of power swallowing up the love of justice. Power, and a corrupted power at that, thus takes pride of place in the city of man, and true justice is found only in the city of God. On earth, it appears, might does indeed make for right. Or does it? Johnson finds a limited redemption in Augustine's thoughts on the nature of peace, a type of which he allows is attainable in the earthly city since people in their own self-interest tend to prefer peace to war. This type of peace may be but a shadow of the true peace of the city of God, but Christians may rightly view it as a "good suitable to the temporal life and a good they seek to foster."

Alongside her reading of Augustine "the idealizer," Johnson turns to Augustine's letters to find evidence of a political theorist who subverts his own idealizations. Taking the example of slavery, she finds that Augustine's understanding of justice "as an eschatological reality does not prevent him from working towards a form of what we would call justice in this earthly city, nor from finding in the tension between [the two cities] ... aspirations for just outcomes." She concludes by suggesting that students might invoke as muse both Augustine the idealizer and Augustine the subverter; the former to provide a standard by which to judge the world's brokenness while reassuring them that they are not responsible for the eschtatological remedy, and the latter as a prod to avoid despair as they seek the good in and for their communities.

The remaining essays collected in this volume complement the larger questions raised by Kaufman and Johnson, and draw us toward particular contexts, questions, works, and classroom assignments. For instance, in Section II each essay reflects on how studying Augustine's writings raises important contextual issues for undergraduates. In the opening essay, Allan Fitzgerald argues that introducing Augustine to undergraduates often requires us to point to those moments when Augustine insists on the deeper, unknowable mystery of things, a turn that helps many students to move past their resistance to Augustine as a dogmatic, orthodox theologian. For Fitzgerald, it is important present Augustine as "fully human before discussing the issues that are often seen in controversial terms," and focusing on Augustine's intellectual humility provides one way to do so. In the two essays that follow, Caleb Clanton and Ian Clausen alert professors to other fruitful contexts, with Clanton placing Augustine in conversation with Plato and Aristotle on the nature of *akrasia* and the will, and Clausen situating Augustine in a larger discussion of conscience in higher education. Clanton acknowledges that his approach to Augustine may generate more questions than answers and does not fully settle the issue of whether Augustine's account of wrongdoing is fully distinct from his Greek predecessors; still, Augustine's "sufficiently different" approach to the question is helpful for core curriculum teachers who want to broaden the discussion of Socratic and Aristotelian *akrasia*, which many students find "counterintuitive." For Clausen, a key question for professors should be, "Does conscience have a place in liberal arts higher education?"—and, if so, "What kind of 'place' does it refer to or designate, and why does it matter?" Although Augustine's writings cannot answer the more ambitious, two-fold question as to "what extent conscience operates in the Academy, and what are the conditions for its retrieval and flourishing," his works can "shed light on the process by which human beings *become* agents in the morally relevant sense," thereby helping teachers to understand that the education of our students "can only be anticipated not achieved or controlled for—and ... for the simple reason that it involves the work of conscience." Finally, Peter Busch examines the perennial philosophical question of happiness to contrast Augustine with the modern age, which Busch argues is heavily indebted to a Hobbesian understanding of happiness as a restless and endless search for that which satisfies. However, Hobbes' definition can leave students dissatisfied and, Busch argues, better prepared for an encounter with Augustine's account in the *Confessions* of a restless heart that reaches its final goal in the ultimate good that is God.

In the next section, the authors turn from standard texts such as the *Confessions* and *City of God* to consider what might be gained by teaching the less commonly read works of Augustine. For Daniel Burns, Book I of *De Libero Arbitrio* is an ideal text for introductory courses on political thought and the theology of social life, providing students an entry point for considering the intimate connection between political citizenship and moral philosophy. "Wonderfully compact," this work presents fewer pedagogical difficulties than the more ambitious and, for students, more daunting *City of God*, and it shows, through the struggles of Evodius, a less dogmatic and confrontational Augustine grappling with our "elementary moral experiences as individuals and citizens." For Robert Anderson, *On the Teacher* serves multiple ends. In addition to being an underutilized introduction to Augustine's thought in general, this work helps students to better understand their own intellectual journeys, highlighting such virtues as persistence, interest, and conversation as vital to both the student and the teacher. Ultimately, however, this work drives students to see that "genuine education is an activity in which [they] are always the primary agents," a journey that is often "mysterious" as it moves from "external conversation" to "internal dialogue." John MacInnis makes a similar plea for *De Musica* as useful for generating student reflection about the goals of education, noting how the work emphasizes the spiritual benefit of academic study and praises the cultivation of music for promoting Neo-platonic insights into the created order and higher realities of the cosmos. Employing *De Musica* in both music history and literature courses, MacInnis has introduced his students to rich insights into art and aesthetics, as well as truth, beauty, and goodness.

In the fourth section, the essays outline specific assignments that help students to engage in substantive reflection on Augustine. In his contribution, Bryan Whitfield situates the *Confessions* in the third semester of Mercer University's seven-semester Great Books Program. By their third semester, Whitfield's students have read four Platonic dialogues (*Euthyphro*, *Apology*, *Meno*, and the *Republic*), as well as *Nicomachean Ethics* and the *Aeneid*. They begin the term with significant portions of the Old and New Testament before spending two or three weeks with the *Confessions*. In his essay, Whitfield describes a series of questions he uses at the beginning of class to connect the *Confessions* to these earlier works, prompting his students, for instance, to compare "the relationship between God and human beings" in the first five chapters of Augustine's autobiography and Psalm 139, or to reflect on how Aristotle would evaluate Augustine's friendships. Mark Scott offers us a different strategy for teaching the *Confessions*, focusing not on how to guide students through the work, but on how to help them absorb the meaning of the full work by assigning them the task of composing their own "confessions" or life narratives. The purpose of the assignment is twofold: first, to help students to "overcome their resistance" to Augustine and to "view him more as a fellow quester after truth rather than as a moralizer," and, second, to facilitate a "heightened sense of self-knowledge" by engaging students with the course's guiding question: "Who am I?" Because the *Confessions* contains various and "subtle strategies for self-reflection," students can borrow from those strategies, be encouraged to develop their own new strategies, and, finally, learn how to cultivate a sophisticated self-awareness. In the section's concluding essay, Maria Poggi Johnson describes a series of exercises focused on addiction and silence. Frustrated by her students' repeated complaints that Augustine was "not relatable," Johnson developed her exercises to address this problem, seeking a way for her students to make an "explicit personal connection" to the text. These exercises, which required students to wrestle with their own weaknesses and shortcomings, helped them to understand themselves as a collection of "variously flawed, confused, [and] conflicted" individuals, who, like Augustine, "are mysteries to [them]selves." In the end, this exercise not only deepened her students' appreciation of the

Confessions, but also helped them to move toward a better understanding of their own difficult quests for self-knowledge.

The fifth section concludes the volume by examining the place of Augustine in two very different curricular locations, one familiar and one foreign. Michael Chiariello steps back from his position as developer and administrator of a core curriculum program at a Catholic university to consider how the writings of Augustine have fared within the program over the past two decades. Chiariello's observations highlight the difficulties of maintaining a coherent narrative in a core curriculum as different faculty cycle through in the program. Nevertheless, he maintains that Augustine can offer a model for integrating the personal, spiritual, and intellectual growth that occurs during the undergraduate years. Finally, Thomas Nordlund uses his background as a physicist to explore how Augustine's reflections on time might provide a useful entrée into the sciences for religion and theology students. His proposal touches on topics ranging from the philosophy of science to the nature of time and space. By doing so, he reminds readers that the disciplinary divides of today's academy were not present in Augustine's world and so provides a fitting conclusion to a volume dedicated to promoting cross-disciplinary conversation and innovation.

Scott McGinnis and Christopher Metress
Guest Editors

Section I.
Keynote Addresses

Deposito Diademate: Augustine's Emperors

Peter Iver Kaufman

Abstract: To assist colleagues from other disciplines who teach Augustine's texts in their core courses, this contribution to the Lilly Colloquium discusses Augustine's assessments of Emperors Constantine and Theodosius. His presentations of their tenure in office and their virtues suggest that his position on political leadership corresponds with his general skepticism about political platforms and platitudes. Yet careful reading of his revision of Ambrose's account of Emperor Theodosius's public penance and reconsideration of the last five sections of his fifth book *City of God*—as well as a reappraisal of several of his sermons on the Psalms—suggest that he proposes a radical alternative to political conformity relevant to undergraduates' conventional expectations of society's progress and their parts in it.

> Reprinted from *Religions*. Cite as: Kaufman, P.I. *Deposito Diademate*: Augustine's Emperor. *Religions* **2015**, *6*, 317–327.

We should keep in mind, as we think about Augustine and political leaders, that he was on track to becoming one. But 386, in Milan, he gave up his career as orator—as what we might describe as a public relations operative, a post that helped other ambitious men make the kind of connections that led them to a provincial governorship. Instead, at Cassiciacum, near Milan, then at Thagaste, on his African estate, he presided over assorted friends contemplating more sublime or philosophical than political questions. He was traveling to establish a similar sort of countercultural, contemplative society when he was drawn into church leadership in Hippo Regius. He retained his disdain for what he perceived as a widespread "lust to be first" (*libido principandi*) and "lust to dominate" (*libido dominandi*), yet, as bishop of a bustling port from the late 390s, he had business with local magistrates and with statesmen governing Africa on behalf of Emperor Honorius to ensure that his brand of Christianity was well defended against rivals—Donatist Christians and pagans. Augustine, therefore, was both critical and acquiescent with respect to what we would regard as political life. We shall ask whether criticism trumped acquiescence.

The title of this plenary address, *deposito diademate*, refers to rulers setting aside their royal regalia when approaching the church. Augustine used the phrase sparingly, but, we shall see, the deference it signals was very much in his mind when he pondered the proper place of public service and the perils and impiety of political leadership ([1], 65.4, 86.8).[1] Yet, rather than begin with the piety and politics of his time, we shall explore his attitude towards power *in illo tempore*, with Moses, before we attend to Augustine's surprisingly infrequent comments on Rome's emperors,

---

[1] Citations in the text give the book, section, and/or chapter numbers used in editions of Augustine's work, the most accessible of which is on-line at [2] (http:www.Augustinus.it/latino/index.htm), drawn from volumes 32 to 45, *Patrologia cursus completus, ser. Latina*, edited by Jacques Paul Migne and published in Paris from 1844 to 1864. To translate, I have consulted variations cited in relevant volumes of the *Corpus scriptorum ecclesiasticorum latinorum* and the *Corpus Christianorum, series Latina*. The titles of Augustine's works appear in the reference section.

an infrequency that suggests the insignificance of politics as usual for him in the late fourth and early fifth centuries.

Moses was an embarrassment. The Manichees, with whom Augustine associated for nearly 10 years—and through a few books of his *Confessions*—found Moses dishonorable. He stole from the Egyptians. Yet Augustine grew disenchanted with Manichaean cosmology and distressed by the Manichees' contempt for the Hebrew Scriptures, whereupon he came to Moses' defense. Though, his defense has a patchy quality. At first he professed that God ordered Moses to have his people relieve the idolaters on the Nile of the gold they used to gild their idols. As the defense proceeded, however, Augustine tried another explanation. Perhaps, God allowed—not commanded—the Hebrews to grab and go. Moses simply relayed their license to steal. "Steal", Augustine then reconsidered, may be too strong a word, inasmuch as God would shortly, from Sinai, etch a "thou shall not" against larceny. Hence, continuing and concluding his anti-Manichaean exegesis, Augustine had the Hebrews expropriate Egyptians' wealth as wages for their work in captivity: back pay, not payback or ill-gotten gain. He granted that, had the idea originated with Moses, the exodus with Egyptian coin could ruin his reputation, as Manichees suggested; Moses would have been just as sinful as the people he delivered from bondage, in whom greed stirred as soon as God's orders (or permission) to plunder were relayed, as soon as they learned that they would not be departing empty-handed. (That sentiment shows Augustine was fretting, as he often did, about the inordinate desire to acquire.) Moses was exceptional; no guile or greed tainted his leadership. He had not coveted what he instructed (or allowed) others to take. Most important for Augustine, Moses had not disputed God's authority to punish the Egyptians, provision the Hebrews they enslaved, and—as it turned out—mystify the Manichees who mocked Old Testament stories. Moses understood that God's will, even when not instantaneously comprehensible, was always to be obeyed ([3], 22.71–72).

True, Moses did have a problem obeying God in the book of Numbers, and, as a result, was prohibited from entering the Promised Land. Also true, he prefigured the flinching of the faithful as he struggled to keep his arms aloft to ensure Israel's victory over the Amalekites in the Negev ([4], 352.6). Maybe the Manichees had some justification for radically distinguishing Old from New Testaments. Certainly there were flawed, even sinful leaders in the former. All rulers, whom the Hebrews' prophets berated, including the venerable King David, disappointed on occasion. Leaders in the New Testament were cut from different cloth. They were not to the manor born. They were proles—a fisherman, a carpenter from Galilee. Augustine suggested that God commissioned the powerless to shame the powerful. By the fifth century, it seemed to be working; princes flocked to Rome, kneeling at the tombs of saints Peter and Paul and setting aside their regalia, *deposito diademate*. They apparently trusted they might learn something significant for their souls' salvation ([1], 65.4).

We need to be mindful that scholars disagree about the extent of imperial power during Augustine's tenure as bishop. Adolf Lippold painstakingly accumulated material evidence of provincial householders' independence from Rome and Ravenna ([5], pp. 54–55). Recently, Yale University Press—possibly aiming to capture the supermarket market—let Adrian Goldsworthy subtitle his long convoy of arguments for the imperial government's diminished capacity, "The Death of a Superpower" ([6], p. 312). Yet, in Western parts of the empire, despite pressures from the Goths and Vandals, Emperors Theodosius I and his son Honorius still had appreciable say and sway. Augustine relied on them. What mattered to him was that his emperors continued to make what Peter Heather called "highly Christian noises" that kept their chanceries churning out edicts against Donatists, pagans, and pelagians. Augustine was aware and grateful that his emperors were capable "to exert a powerful pull on the allegiances and habits of [Rome's] provinces" ([7], pp. 126–28).

But let us look more closely at that "pull". Augustine, as a bishop from the 390s to 430, could hardly have been indifferent to privileged parishioners whose local "pull" depended on the central government's. Their attachments to things of this world—possessions, promotions, and reputations—were deeply rooted in their characters and culture. Very few rose above that desire to acquire. Most were ordinary and imperfect. Yet Augustine would not allow them to wallow in their imperfections. Both the imperfections and wallowing were among his principal pastoral concerns. He preached persistently to those unable to decathect from what he called "the business of Babylon" ([1], 44.25).

You can almost hear the sneer in his *Confessions*, when he referred to "the streets of Babylon", as if he were describing a city's sordid districts, a graphic novel's Gotham of greed and gore. Though, he referred similarly to unsavory practices around the imperial Court in Milan where, as orator for hire, he advanced his career, lacing with lies the eulogies he delivered to flatter the powerful while other ambitious place-seekers—knowing he lied—were nonetheless quick to praise him ([8], 2.3, 8; 6.6, 9). In his sermons, "Babylon" becomes a city (*civitas*) or state (*respublica*), so one may be excused for suspecting Augustine had what we call politics or statesmanship in mind when he preached about "the business of Babylon," extending his scorn to the politics of an empire, which he described as "aging and shriveling up" ([4], 51.6). That, after all, was what empires did. Conquest, oppression, and shriveling had not started with Rome or Carthage. The Assyrians were equally successful, equally cruel, equally conceited, yet eventually overtaken. No point trying to comprehend why God needed to reward Assyrians and Romans with their empires. The former never worshipped him; they and the latter persecuted those who did, yet still seemed sufficiently virtuous to warrant hegemony in time for a time. God's ways with this world often baffled onlookers, but, Augustine maintained, those ways were never unjust ([9], 5.15, 5.21).

When the time was right—in God's sight—God converted an emperor. Augustine was relatively dispassionate about Constantine's conversion. The few references to that emperor in his sermons and correspondence avoided celebration. In a long letter on the nature of faith, for example, Augustine argued that one need not see to believe that Constantine founded the city of Constantinople, but omitted mentioning what Constantine saw—specifically, the vision that brought him to the faith, dazzling him and dazzling generations of the faithful who dated their deliverance to that time ([10], ep. 286).

Tributes to Constantine and Theodosius surface at the end of the *City of God*'s fifth book, immediately after Augustine discusses what qualified as virtuous leadership. Rulers ought to be self-assured yet not arrogant, unmoved by flattery, slow to punish, inclined to pardon, devoted to taking command of themselves—and only then to commanding others. But the apsule on Constantine that follows this wish-list lands squarely on *none* of those qualities. One learns about Constantine's reign—that it was long and prosperous—not about Constantine's virtues ([9], 5.24–25; [11], pp. 556–59).

Elsewhere, Augustine defended Constantine (and Christianity) against accusations that the former's seemingly sudden disaffection and defection from Rome's old religions prompted the empire's fourth- and early fifth-century setbacks—frontiers crossed, battles lost, and cities sacked. Augustine touted Constantine's part in fulfilling God's promise, made in the Hebrews' psalms, which prophesied that the whole earth would hasten to believe in Jesus. *Ante oculos vestros*, "before your very eyes", he preached, "the pagans' idols were overthrown", proving that his faith's story was "promising", so to speak: Christianity's sacred texts foretold without stipulating precisely *where* or *when* the empire would turn to the new faith—foretold *that* it would turn, as Emperor Constantine had. It was all God's doing. God had seized the Roman Empire ([4], 62.1; [10], 1.14, 21). Numbers after commas designate sections in the original; traditional references for classical texts.

Though, then the empire seemed to seize up, and its western parts fell apart. Christians asked why. Augustine speculated that the reason was that many who professed the new faith, the not-so-faithful-faithful emperors among them, had not done their part. Their piety was, if not insincere, insubstantial. It proved no match for those lusts to be first, to dominate. Hence, the Christian empire got knocked about. The promises in the psalms were still relevant, but any political fulfillment was out of the question. The Christian empire's humiliation in and after 410 was neither a turning point nor a stopping point, but, Augustine proposed, the disappointment tested the faith of the faithful, tested, and reoriented it [12].

Augustine was relatively indifferent to much of fourth-century political history. He could not be bothered with Emperor Constantius II, the one son and heir of Constantine who survived the two their father left alive and who ruled alone for 11 years, nearly as long as his father. Augustine remembered that Valens, emperor in the East from 364–378, preferred the Arian or Homoian Christology, outlawed at Constantine's Council of Nicaea in 325, and that Valens had persecuted the Nicenes, but Augustine stopped short of denouncing Valens as angrily as had his Nicene colleagues. Ambrose, for one, attributed the empire's catastrophic defeat at Adrianople, where Valens died, to the defeated and deceased emperor's Arian sympathies. God's wrath; game over ([9], 18.52; [13], 2.16, 139).

Theodosius succeeded Valens in the East. His restraint impressed Augustine. Having rescued the young Valentinian II from one usurper and having intimidated other rivals in the West, he left the youngster enthroned, returned to Thessalonika and Constantinople, and put leading anti-Nicene prelates were at a decisive disadvantage ([14], pp. 220–21). That equally impressed Augustine, who favored the Nicene party. But Emperor Theodosius's record on paganism was uneven, too much so to please African bishops. True, his anti-pagan decrees seemed far-reaching and his victory, in 394, at the River Frigidus suppressed a regime that relied on—and reportedly cultivated—a revival of interest in paganism, but the circumstances were complicated. The Frigidus outcome nested in contemporary Christian chronicles as Christianity's victory over Rome's old gods. The emperor's prayers were said to have summoned the strong winds that prevented weapons hurled by his enemies from reaching their targets. Augustine condensed the story, kept the prayers and winds to document the effectiveness of Theodosius's piety, but kept the story very, very short ([9], 5.26). Perhaps Augustine was simply underscoring his insistence that Christians ought not to expect an uninterrupted series of military miracles from their Christian emperors. Perhaps he was reluctant to celebrate statesmen in arms—or politics—who fell far short of his ideal. Yet Augustine may also have abbreviated his account because some parts of the story were difficult to reconcile with the idea that the Frigidus was a whopping victory for Christianity. Eugenius, the would-be whom Theodosius defeated, was a Christian. Arguably, he and his accomplices had been compelled to seek support among pagans by the emperor's cavalier, condescending appointment of his nine-year old son Honorius to rule in the West. Possibly Augustine would also have been informed that Theodosius marched roughly as many pagan troops to the Frigidus as did his enemies ([15], pp. 94–95, 122–23). All told, the causes as well as combat, along with other available evidence of Theodosius's appointments and allies, suggest that he was relatively uninterested in evangelizing the empire. He was content, working with non-Christians—particularly with members of the aristocracy who remained resistant to Christianity yet who refrained from publicly protesting his regime's opposition to pagan sacrifices ([5], p. 134; [9], 5.26; [16], p. 187).

One encomiast, however, gives posterity a very different Theodosius, and Augustine would have known of both. Poet Prudentius alleged that the emperor had turned evangelist, urging pagans to give up their cults and to trade up to Christianity ([17], 1.423–24). Augustine said nothing about the oration that Prudentius remembered or invented to add a sensational aftermath in Rome to Theodosius's victory at the Frigidus (in Slovenia). But the poet's story (and Theodosius's resolve to convert pagans) must have acquired sturdy legs, because it required refutation before two hundred years passed. The sixth-century pagan Zosimus, referring to the oration, insisted that Roman pagans refused to take seriously either their emperor or his faith ([18], 4.59).

Augustine could no more have subscribed to Zosimus' reading of Theodosius's irrelevance than to Prudentius' messianic, majestic tiger-of-an-emperor. Indeed, Augustine was ill-at-ease with majesty or, to be precise, with poet-orators who, much as he once had in Rome and Milan, marketed majesty and trumpeted the virtues of statesmen. Early in the fifth century, he pilloried politicians who "love temporal power" and who "seek their own glory in the subjection of others" ([19], 19.31). Later, composing his *City of God*, he continued to deflate the residual optimism about Christian empire. He lost his faith in Rome's fate, as R. P. C. Hanson noticed. On reviewing its past and surveying its present, Augustine concluded that, in Hanson's words, "the empire must be condemned". "It had placed its whole hope and trust in success [in glory], and by that worldly standard it had at last failed, as it inevitably was destined in the end to fail" ([20], p. 276). Hanson's "at last" and "in the end" are telling. They reflect Augustine's take on government, leaving us with a question: what could be redeemed—what could he redeem—"in the end".

A Christian emperor's humility! That was a colossally important lesson for all creatures who coveted honor, status, and power. Of those, rulers were most tempted to court notoriety and to treasure titles. Hence, Theodosius was exceptional, a celebrated statesman who prized piety over celebrity. To Augustine, he looked to have learned not only to resist this wicked world's seductive rewards but also not to brag about his resistance ([9], 5.18). Conceivably, Augustine wrote his cameo account of Theodosius in the *City of God* to ensure that the emperor's subjects (Christians and pagans alike) perceived the challenges to be humble, acknowledge human frailty, and negotiate celebrity—when and if it comes—without fanfare. Emperors were useful, on their knees and with their regalia set aside—*desposito diademate*. Using Theodosius, Augustine, in effect, counselled the powerful to cultivate "a conception of themselves as repentant sinners"—and to conduct themselves accordingly. ([21], p. 153).

A number of Augustine's sermons, his *Confessions*, and his *City of God* identified repentance as the "sacrifice" that God expects. Repentance required creatures to acknowledge how far short of perfect righteousness they had fallen and to present their contrite hearts as an offering (*sacrificium contriti cordis*). Sacrifices of hearts "bruised" by scalding self-accusations (bear in mind the multiple confessions in Augustine's *Confessions*) alerted creatures to their dependence on their creator. The signs of same, from start to forever, were self-discipline, denunciation of self-deception, and an acknowledgment that contrite hearts were not only offerings to God but God's work, teaching and redeeming the penitent as well as onlookers. Repentance of this nature, Augustine insisted, echoing the apostle Paul, confirmed that the penitent were not conformed to this age ([9], 10.5–6).

No wonder, then, Augustine's tribute to Theodosius culminates with the penance required by Ambrose after the emperor ordered the slaughter of citizens in Thessalonica. Dodging the details, Augustine packed in just enough to exonerate Theodosius and incriminate his bloodier-minded partisans. What was meant to grab attention was the proclamation set at the start, where Augustine asserted that "nothing was more marvelous than religious humility". The emperor's self-abasement then sprawls across what follows. Augustine has Theodosius make explicit—and dramatic—that air, light, soil, the expanse of empire, as well as glory for expanding the last were given by God to the virtuous as well as to the wicked, although the devotion exhibited in a powerful man's penance is a gift reserved for the great, good, and faithful ([9], 5.26).

Augustine inflected what Bishop Ambrose reported about the emperor's disrobing before his public expressions of sorrow for sins: Theodosius so prostrated himself that he brought tears to the eyes of all who beheld his humility. Augustine editorialized to suggest that, at the grave, statesmen must relinquish their power, *deposito diademate*. From there, the righteous take only their righteousness with them ([9], 5.2; [22], section 34; [23], pp. 183–84).

Ambrose worked himself into the story as its chief protagonist, specifying that every priest's duty was to confront wrongdoers. God would almost certainly punish a timid bishop. Speaking truth to power, of course, was never easy. A bishop's truth-telling could have had terrible consequences for colleagues and their churches as the emperor's anger ricocheted around his realm. So Ambrose's audacity was all the more impressive ([24], 11.3–11). Still, Augustine dropped Ambrose from his narrative: "The discipline of the church" brought the emperor to his knees ([9], 5.26). Ambrose was missing as well from a sermon Augustine preached on penance, the point of which was to shame auditors too embarrassed to grieve publicly for their sins as the emperor had done ([4], 392.3). Arguably, Ambrose spooled his stories to promote the interests of the church, his alternative infrastructure—which was complementary to, yet somewhat independent of, the Court. Though, Augustine's interests diverged from those of his illustrious acquaintance.

Theodosius died in 395. Thereafter, the emperor to whom Augustine and his African colleagues appealed was his son Honorius, who ruled the West after his father's death until 423. Often, on his watch, Italy was overrun; Honorius's record on "state security" was abysmal ([16], p. 234). He and his brother Arcadius in Constantinople never ventured far from the safety of their courts, which prompted Bishop Synesius of Cyrene to argue that only emperors with first-hand knowledge of war knew how to preserve the peace ([25], section 16). Africa was remote from the frontiers where war-formed and warlike emperors were wanting. Augustine and his catholic colleagues appeared satisfied to have Emperor Honorius's support, especially his edicts against the Donatists. No reason to lionize Honorius, therefore, but no cause to censure him. Christians' enthusiasms for empire had ebbed. But the emperor and his representatives in Africa were still serviceable, while the faithful awaited a victory yet to come ([1], 123.4). For, as Augustine often said, the world was an unsettled, unsettling place, "an evil place"—*malus est mundus* ([4], 80.8); Christians' challenges were to retain hope in their ultimate, celestial victory, to restrain their basest desires, and to pay God's love forward, practicing compassion ([4], 105.8–9). Augustine's Theodosius helped inspire the faithful to meet those challenges. He was unaffected, uninfected by *ardor gloriae*, the passion for glory. Some other idealizations of the emperor studied by Jörg Ernesti, tugged him closer to figures around whom imperial cults had formed—a granite statue draped with archaic Roman virtues to appeal to senators who, Ernesti suggests, tilted toward nostalgia for paganism ([23], pp. 349–50). Christian idealizations were just as tendentious (as Prudentius showed us), and why not? Theodosius gave devotees of his faith what they "most wanted", as John Matthews noticed: piety, deference to bishops, partisan legislation. The emperor did signal on occasion that he preferred to suppress paganism ([26], p. 252). We know now, however, that a number of his appointments reflected a less than persistent antagonism and that Christianity's prospects were not as promising as Prudentius or Ambrose—but not as Augustine—had hoped. Augustine's hopes attached to the emperor's personality—not to his policy. Theodosius, he said, enjoyed his Christianity, happier being in church than ruling the world ([9], 5.26; [27], pp. 135–42).

A short summary is in order before we apply a few generalizations addressing issues that often surface when we teach or discuss what has been described as Augustine's political theology. Clearly, Augustine had difficulty warming to Constantine, whose virtues seemed to him political or pragmatic and insufficiently personal. Hence, he served them up chilled, with what Jean-Marie Salamito dubs *la froideur augustiniennes* ([11], pp. 561–62). Theodosius was better suited to Augustine's purposes. It was easier to lift him than to hoist Constantine from this world's sordid practices and to lower or humble him to make a case that was emblematic for Augustine from the 380s to his death, a case against "the lust to be first", *libido principandi* ([8], 3.8, 16). Now that is an extraordinary place to find a politician! Or might it have been (and still be) a summons for an extraordinary politician?

How, then, should we read Augustine's purposes in featuring the empire's leading fourth-century statesmen in his *City of God*? What might interest our faculty and student colleagues who come across parts of that *City* or a sample of his sermons or a cut from his *Confessions* in their core courses? I want to suggest two plausible and popular responses before endorsing a third, less popular at present but, I shall argue, more defensible.

Commonly among ethicists and a number of historical theologians [28–30], Augustine is taken to have added theological virtues to the political virtues he supposedly admired. The result is a renewed faith in political culture. Statesmen in the 21st century must learn from Augustine, colleagues subscribing to this first approach say, to extract from the squalid, seamy, side of their business "an order of love" or the lesson of humility that will help renew faith in what is both humane and politically possible, in what Eric Gregory calls "a morally robust Augustinian civic liberalism" ([28], p. 298). That would likely be uplifting, but it would not be Augustine.

A second interpretation was fashionable for decades after Henri Xavier Arquillière published his essay on political Augustinianism in the 1930s and credited Augustine with having motivated hierocratic theorists to assert the church's authority over secular governments. Debate swirled for some time thereafter around the extent to which Augustine would have sanctioned claims of that sort [31]. But the claims persisted. It was widely thought that, after Pope Gregory I (590–604) introduced several strategic tropes, popes and their apologists drew Augustine's *deposito diademate* into their arguments for papal supremacy, specifically for Rome's right to appoint and depose secular sovereigns.

A third approach emphasizes Augustine's recoil from politics and takes it to signal a dramatic reorientation. Emperors shed their regalia when they drew close to the shrines of Saints Peter and Paul, in Augustine's accounts, not because the church is superior to their "states" but because it is a wholly and holy other order.

Recoil and reorientation: speaking this morning to a convocation of freshmen and sophomores who participate in the college's core course, I deployed Augustine to underscore the value of both. I took the third approach to his positions on emperors, statesmanship, and political leadership to offer alternatives to the contagious careerism so many undergraduates bring to college and to the core—careerism that makes students impatient with instruction in the arts and humanities. Pre-professional programs in business or finance, journalism or law, are all the rage on campuses, notwithstanding a realization that unexpected socio-economic swerves play havoc with careers; they bloc some paths and open others. In effect, they put a premium on undergraduates' and graduates' agility—versatility. During Augustine's tenure, the "swerve" or crisis sped along the disintegration of the empire in the West. In 410 the Goths sacked Rome, and other incursions chased refugees across the Mediterranean. The capital and Roman portions of the European continent had been troubled before, but the fifth century's first decade deprived pagans and Christians alike of the faith that their empire would be—as Virgil's Jupiter (although not, as Augustine repeatedly pointed out, the Christians' God) had promised—without end, *sine fine* ([32], 1.279).

The crossbeams of our empire are hardly as sturdy as they once seemed, yet one need not speculate about political collapse to find Augustine's stirring call for recoil and reorientation relevant. Sections of the economy and the stability of local institutions are often in jeopardy, so the skills needed for reorientation, for changing the trajectory of one's interests and career are always in season. Augustine praised Theodosius because—whether he saw it or wanted to see it—the emperor subscribed to an alternative vision of what was preeminently important. And, removing their regalia, *deposito diademate*, the powerful self-consciously became prodigals and pilgrims as often as they honored the saints and sacraments, portals through which the sacred streams into the profane.

To one of the faithful who confided that he desired to surrender his military command to catch more of that stream by entering a monastery, Augustine wrote urging that he stay his course, do damage control (check the Vandal invasion), and periodically, through prayer, enter a better place. God placed that soldier—as well as emperors and magistrates—in their respective roles. Their relief—but not their release—was to decathect or disinvest ([9], 19.6). Civic piety and municipal morality might contribute to general wellbeing. But informed Christians knew that, *in hoc saeculo maligno*, in this wicked world, all was driven by self-love, *amor sui* ([9], 18.49). The best one could do was acknowledge imperfection and discover times and places and alternative communities where the virtues of humility, compassion, and forgiveness might prosper.

Negotio, the ordinary business of our lives, has us all in its grip. But *Deificari ... in otio* ([10], 10.2); in leisure (and Augustine accompanied leisure with friendships, contemplation, and conversation), the serious work of personal re-formation proceeds. Augustine trusted that an alternative love—compassion—and an alternative orientation—humility—would create and hold together alternative associations—convents and churches. Ideally, the social practices of those two would inspire the forgiveness that issued in reconciliations. A preternatural compassion breathed into the hearts of the faithful was the foundation of the peace that sustained the social practices of such communities ([33], 3.16, 21), where the faith, hope, and love were, Augustine insisted, different from those on offer in the terrestrial city.

Augustine was good at finding those places where the values and trajectories of this wicked world did not seem to apply. His efforts can contribute to the sentiments of students who find him in our core courses. Indeed, those places in our colleges may be the alternatives that will save them from the blowback occasioned by subsequent realizations that their guilds' skills inhibit their humanity. Perhaps, Augustine along with their exposure to the humanities in core courses will keep undergraduates from the revelation that moved attorneys to write the indictment I recycled this morning from Stanley Fish's suggestive essay on professionalism. It reflects the lawyers' lament that "mindless specialization" and competition rules out self- or social criticism in their practice. "We have become acculturated to an unnecessarily limiting way of seeing and experiencing law and lawyering", they complain,

> a way which can separate lawyers from their sense of humanity and their own values. When that separation occurs, the profession easily becomes experienced as only a job or role, and human problems as only legal issues. Care and responsibility then yield to exigencies and strategems; and legal education, instead of reflecting the aspiration and searching that embody law and lawyering, can all too easily become an exercise in attempted mastery and growing cynicism ([34], p. 217).

Augustine is not the antidote to acculturation of this sort, but his questioning cultural premises and the ambitions they foster illustrates how the humanities can take our students out of maintenance mode. Instead of teaching them how to perform in "the system", I want them to transform systems, to envision something wholly different from what could trap them in "a way of seeing and experiencing" to which they had been habituated. Augustine's pilgrims, prodigals, statesmen, and emperors help me help them. Whether you are convinced Augustine can make that difference or disinclined to think it should be part of an educator's task to inspire it or are unpersuaded that historical study of Augustine can support my deployment of him, permit me, again, to thank you for making Augustine part of our culture's core—and thank Augustine for demoting the desire to acquire, tucking away the lust to be first, and introducing perhaps frightening, yet potentially fulfilling alternatives to the robust civic humanisms that too often stymie (or completely confound) our chances to change the rules.

Critics of my work [35] say that I have replaced with pessimism Augustine's evangelical confidence in Christians' ability to respond to the grace of conversion. I say they misplaced their confidence in the receptivity of our various systems to conversion and displaced (or attenuated) Augustine's confidence in grace, which, for him, made radical rather than incremental changes.

The "grace of conversion" cannot bring heaven to earth—the celestial is still celestial—but it can make the new now and make the now new.

Conflicts of Interest

The author declares no conflict of interest.

References

1. Augustine. *Enarrationes in Psalmos*.
2. Opera Omnia di Sant'Agostino. Available online: http:www.Augustinus.it/latino/index.htm (accessed on 30 March 2015).
3. Augustine. *Contra Faustum*.
4. Augustine. *Sermons*.
5. Adolf Lippold. *Theodosius der Große und Seine Zeit.* Stuttgart: Kohlhammer Verlag, 1968.
6. Adrian Goldsworthy. *How Rome Fell: Death of a Superpower*. New Haven: Yale University Press, 2009.
7. Peter Heather. *The Fall of the Roman Empire: A New History of Rome and the Barbarians.* Oxford: Oxford University Press, 2006.
8. Augustine. *Confessiones*.
9. Augustine. *De Civitate Dei*.
10. Augustine. *Epistles*.
11. Jean-Marie Salamito. "Constantin vu par Augustin: Pour une relecture De Civ. 5.25." In *Costantino: Prima e dopo Costantino*. Edited by Girogio Bonamente, Noel Lenski and Rita Lizzi Testa. Bari: Edipuglia, 2012, pp. 549–62.
12. Augustine. *De excidio orbis Romae*.
13. Ambrose of Milan. "De fide ad Gratianum Augustum." In *Corpus Scriptorum Ecclesiasticorum Latinorum*. Edited by Otto Faller. Vienna: Akademie der Wissenschaften, 1962, vol. 78.
14. Robert Malcolm Errington. *Roman Imperial Policy from Julian to Theodosius.* Chapel Hill: University of North Carolina Press, 2006.
15. Alan Cameron. *The Last Pagans of Rome*. Oxford: Oxford University Press, 2011.
16. Hartmut Leppin. *Theodosius der Grosse*. Darmstadt: Primus Verlag, 2003.
17. Prudentius. *Contra Symmachum.* Edited by H. Tränkle. Turnhout: Brepols, 2008.
18. François Paschoud, ed. *Zosime: Histoire Nouvelle.* Paris: Les Belles Lettres, 1979, vol. 2.
19. Augustine. *De Catechezandis Rudibus*.
20. Richard Patrick Crosland Hanson. "The Reaction of the Church to the Collapse of the Western Empire in the Fifth Century." *Vigiliae Christianae* 26 (1972): 272–87.

21. Robert Dodaro. "Augustine's Revision of the Heroic Ideal." *Augustinian Studies* 36 (2005): 141–57.
22. Ambrose of Milan. *De obitu Theodosii*. Edited by Mary Dolorosa Mannix. Washington: Catholic University Press, 1925.
23. Jörg Ernesti. *Princeps Christianusn und Kaiser aller Römer: Theodosius der Gross im Lichte Zeitgenössischer Quellen.* Paderborn: Schoningh, 1998.
24. Ambrose of Milan. "Epistulae Extra Collectionem." In *Corpus Scriptorum Ecclesiasticorum Latinorum.* Edited by M. Zelzer. Vienna: Kaiserliche Akademie der Wissenschaften, 1983, vol. 82.3.
25. Synesius De Regno. *Synesii Cyrenensis Hymni et Opuscula.* Edited by Nicola Terzaghi. Rome: Typis Regiae Officinae Polygraphicae, 1944, vol. 2.
26. John Matthews. *Western Aristocracies and Imperial Court, AD 364–425*. Oxford: Oxford University Press, 1990.
27. Yves-Marie Duval. "L'éloge de Théodose dans le Cité de Dieu: Sa place, son sens et ses sources." *Recherches Augustiniennes* 4 (1966): 135–79.
28. Eric Gregory. *Politics and the Order of Love: An Augustinian Ethic of Democratic Citizenship*. Chicago: University of Chicago Press, 2008.
29. Robert Dodaro. *Christ and the Just Society in the Thought of Augustine.* Cambridge: Cambridge University Press, 2004.
30. Charles Mathewes. *The Republic of Grace: Augustinian Thoughts for Dark Times.* Grand Rapids: Eerdmans, 2010.
31. Henri Xavier Arquillière. *Augustinisme Politique: Essai sur la Formation des Théories Politiques du Moyen âge.* Paris: J. Vrin, 1933.
32. Publius Vergilius Maro (Virgil). "The Aeneid." In *Eclogues, Georgics, Aeneid: Books 1–6.* Edited by George Patrick Goold. Cambridge: Harvard University Press, 1916.
33. Augustine. *De baptismo Contra Donatistas.*
34. Stanley Fish. *Doing What Comes Naturally: Change, Rhetoric, and the Practice of Theory in Literary and Legal Studies*. Durham: Duke University Press, 1989.
35. Peter Iver Kaufman. *Incorrectly Political: Augustine and Thomas More.* Notre Dame: University of Notre Dame Press, 2007.

The Justice Game: Augustine, Disordered Loves, and the Temptation to Change the World

Kristen Deede Johnson

Abstract: Augustine's thought on justice offers enduring wisdom to today's undergraduates as they grapple with the difficult questions that arise when they ponder what it means to change the world in the light of the reality of injustice in this world. By juxtaposing Augustine's theological writings on the nature of justice and power within the earthly and heavenly cities with Augustine's letters that demonstrate his public engagement with injustice, we learn how Augustine thought about justice and how his convictions intersected with his practice. Through exposure to Augustine's life and thought, students can be encouraged to wrestle with the existence of injustice, their complicity in its existence, their understanding of justice, and what it takes to seek justice today.

Reprinted from *Religions*. Cite as: Johnson, K.D. The Justice Game: Augustine, Disordered Loves, and the Temptation to Change the World. *Religions* **2015**, *6*, 409–418.

1. Introduction

Not long ago, while I was still teaching at Hope College, I met with three college students in my office on the same day, all of whom articulated that they felt called to move to Africa. Each of these students had a longing to help those who did not have the same access to clean water, health care, and supportive parents that these students had had their whole lives. Each student wanted to do what she could to change the world. Each understood this as a way of seeking justice. Meeting with these three young, sweet, female Midwestern students back to back to back as they named this fairly dramatic desire to move across the world to, in their minds, pursue justice and help change the world, was striking.

I used my better judgment and refrained from handing to any of these students my copy of *City of God* or an excerpt from *The Trinity*. Yet, as our students think deeply about the brokenness of this world, as they become aware of its injustices, as they seek to understand where their deep gladness meets the world's deep hunger (as Frederick Buechner eloquently describes vocation [1]), Augustine can and ought to be one of their guides. But how are they to call upon him of whom they have not heard? How are they to hear without someone to teach him? We cannot assume that undergraduates will encounter the enduring wisdom of Augustine before they graduate, but if given the opportunity, we ought to do our best to bring the richness of Augustine's thinking before their eyes. With a body of writing as large as Augustine's, we could tap any of a number of veins and invite our students to wrestle with the insights that flow forth. Here, I invite us to focus on Augustine's thoughts on justice as a way to encourage our students to grapple with the difficult questions that arise as they face the reality of injustice and ponder what it means to change the world.

2. Augustine the Idealizer

Let us turn more directly to Augustine to assess the claim that Augustine has lasting wisdom to offer today's undergraduates as they seek justice in this world and navigate the temptation to save the world. I offer as a starting place one of my favorite passages from Augustine's corpus, found in *The Trinity*:

> The essential flaw of the devil's perversion made him a lover of power and a deserter and assailant of justice, which means that men imitate him all the more thoroughly the more they neglect or even detest justice and studiously devote themselves to power, rejoicing at the possession of it or inflamed with the desire for it. So it pleased God to deliver man from the devil's authority by beating him at the justice game, not the power game, so that men too might imitate Christ by seeking to beat the devil at the justice game, not the power game. Not that power is to be shunned as something bad, but that the right order might be preserved which puts justice first [2].

According to Augustine, both justice and power are God-given goods. Power becomes corrupt when it becomes an end in itself rather than being referred to the higher good of justice [3]. In reflecting on the devil, Augustine notes that his fundamental mistake was placing love of power over love of justice. He desired to play the power game rather than the justice game. Jesus Christ did just the opposite, using his power to prioritize justice. In so doing, he beat the devil at the justice game and freed humanity from the devil's power. In following Jesus, humans are called to imitate Christ by loving justice more than power, by using their God-given power in Christ to play the justice game rather than the power game.

How might a person acquire this love of justice? Here is the potential catch, one that I have been pondering since writing upon these themes in my first book, an exploration of Augustine and contemporary political theory [4]. Within Augustine's framework, love of justice can be acquired *only* in and through the redemptive work of God in Jesus Christ. In his theoretical writings, Augustine maintains that the only society that can be described as just is the one that recognizes Christ as its King, namely the Heavenly City, because outside of Christ citizens' loves are so disordered that they are not able to place justice over power. On their own, apart from grace, they cannot resist the ensnarement of the lust for domination and love of self that mark sinful humanity, which means they are not able to love rightly or act justly. Does this mean that there is no hope for justice in the earthly city? Does this mean that my three undergraduates who want to move to Africa for the sake of justice need a shocking shower of Augustinian realism to wash away their theologically-naive desire to make a difference here and now?

Let us begin to answer these questions by diving more deeply into the theological convictions that lead Augustine to the dramatic conclusion that no justice is to be found in the earthly city and its citizens. In *De Trinitate,* Augustine describes redemption in terms of humility, justice, and power. By divine justice, God allowed humans to be handed over to the power of the devil for the sin of the first humans. God would in due course overcome the devil not by God's power but by God's justice. This was not because God lacks power but because God prefers justice to power. Jesus Christ chose to shed his innocent blood for the sake of those who were guilty; he chose the "justice of humility" even though, through the "power of divinity", he could have avoided this humiliation. In his innocent death, we see justice, and in his resurrection and ascension, we see power [5]. This justice and this power are offered to humanity through Christ, for "by the death of one so powerful we powerless mortals have justice set before us and power promised us" ([5], XIII, 18).

This understanding of justice and power in relation to Christ's redemptive work is intricately connected to Augustine's understanding of order. God's original divine order was one of perfect justice. In this "right order", higher goods are to be preferred to lower goods and all goods are to be enjoyed for the sake of God. But what happens when goods are used for the wrong ends? What is the result when goods are unfaithfully prioritized? Injustice. If any lower good is placed over a higher good, if power, for example, is placed over peace, or love of self over love of God, then the divine order is disrupted and justice is not upheld ([6], XIX, 13). Because Augustine's definition of justice is so deeply tied to right order, true justice is not possible outside of Jesus Christ who reordered all that had become disordered after the fall of humanity. When humans initially chose a lower good to the greatest, unchanging good of God, their loves became so disordered that they needed a fundamental re-ordering. This is what necessitated the justification offered in and through Jesus Christ, for it is only in and through Christ that a fallen people's disordered loves and priorities can be re-ordered. In Augustine's theological framework, only through the transforming power of Jesus' reconciling love can humanity's lust for power be subsumed under a love of justice.

For Augustine, this theological understanding of justice impacts not only individual pursuit of justice but also our collective pursuit of justice in the earthly city. As Augustine writes, "if a soul does not serve God it cannot with any kind of justice command the body, nor can a man's reason control the vicious elements in the soul. And if there is no justice in such a man, there can be no sort of doubt that there is no justice in a gathering which consists of such men" ([6], XIX, 21). This means justice can only be found in a "gathering" whose citizens have had their disordered loves transformed so that by the grace of God in Christ they are united in their rightly ordered love of God and neighbor [7].

To put this differently, only the City of God is capable of true justice [8]. Robert Dodaro explores this when he writes, "Augustine maintains that justice cannot be known except in Christ, and that, as founder (*conditor*) and ruler (*rector*), Christ forms the just society in himself. United with Christ, members of his body constitute the whole, just Christ (*Christus totus iustus*), which is the city of God, the true commonwealth, and the locus for the revelation of justice" [9]. This, in turn, is what leads Augustine to famously critique Cicero's definition of a commonwealth as "the weal of the people" in which the people are "an association of men united by a common sense of right". How can there be a common sense of right when people's loves are wrongly ordered? How can the disordered loves of fallen people lead to a political society that is marked by anything but disorder and injustice? Augustine argues that, "where there is no justice there is no commonwealth" ([6], XIX, 21).

Augustine explores similar themes in *De Trinitate*, using there the language of good will with an extended play on the word "power". Justice, he writes, is a property of good will, and people can only have good will if they are cleansed of their faults. Otherwise they will be overpowered by their faults, and they will "will" badly. Augustine, seemingly wryly, notes that people "hardly ever want to be powerful in order to overpower" their own faults or their bad will; instead they seek power in order to overpower others. In a surprise twist, Augustine encourages people to seek power—but only if their desire is to seek power from Jesus Christ to overpower their faults, so that they might have good will. Once they have this good will restored through Christ, they will be able to be entrusted with power that serves justice rather than power that overpowers justice ([5], XIII, 17–18).

After his critique of Cicero's definition of a commonwealth, Augustine provides an alternative definition of a people as those united by "a common agreement about the objects of its love" ([6], XIX, 24). Although they lack justice, they do not lack love, for even disordered people have things they love and can come to some collective agreement about those loves. Augustine offers love of peace as a love that can be found within every city, even in those cities that are at war. Those who go to war ultimately long for victory and peace, so although it might be a twisted notion of peace, it can be considered a common object of love ([6], XIX, 11). Interestingly, the enjoyment of earthly peace can even be understood as a gift from God to be enjoyed as a God-given good [10].

I write "interestingly" here because I find this to be the site of a fascinating component of Augustine's thought. Augustine has a category for "earthly peace" that he does not have for justice. When it comes to justice, if we are to be consistent with his stated theological framework, true justice lies in the city that has Jesus as its ruler and nowhere else. With peace, he makes a different move. He differentiates true peace from earthly peace, but nevertheless has a place for both of them, and in fact an important place. When Augustine thinks about true peace, he believes that it would be marked by justice and equality under God's rule. When the power game leads fallen humanity to prioritize the peace of pride, the aim is no longer justice and equality but the assertion of will and dominion over others ([6], XIX, 12). This means that earthly cities can only possibly attain earthly peace, a limited peace, a compromise between competing human wills. True peace, heavenly peace, like justice, arises from "the perfectly ordered and harmonious fellowship in the enjoyment of God, and of each other in God" ([6], XIX, 17). Augustine writes that the peace of the earthly city does not compare to that of the Heavenly City, "which is so truly peaceful that it should be regarded as the only peace deserving the name" ([6], XIX, 17).

With lines like these, you think he might be leading you down the "no earthly peace like there is no earthly justice" route—but he stops short of that. On the contrary, he acknowledges the importance of the role of peace in the earthly city. He views it as a good that ought to be pursued by pilgrim and earthly citizen alike. Not so for justice. He does not distinguish between heavenly justice and earthly justice and then offer the pursuit of justice in this earthly city as a good. His convictions about the need for our loves to be reordered for justice to be realized seem to prevent him from making this move. Yet he has acknowledged that peace is the Supreme Good of the Heavenly City; he writes that justice is to be related to the ultimate good of peace; he submits that justice is to be maintained so that peace can be attained. Overall, Augustine argues that the Supreme Good of peace has a counterpart in this earthly city but not the slightly lower good of justice. What does this mean for our pursuits and our hopes for this earthly city? What does this mean for our students who want to give their lives to seeking justice?

Despite his rhetoric here related to justice, I have never seen anyone in writing suggest that Augustine does not care about justice even in the earthly city—although some, like Peter Kaufman, are skeptical of how much can be realized. Even those who strongly put forward the argument that in Augustine's thought only Christ establishes the just society (Robert Dodaro), and only the Heavenly

City is truly public and truly just (Rowan Williams), do not go on to suggest that Augustine gave up any and all hope for justice here and now [11]. In the estimation of Dodaro and Williams, the ideal just society sets the standard for the earthly city and can therefore provide a heuristic device for assessing the earthly city. The ideal may be unreachable, but it allows for the possibility of hope and critique in the earthly city today. Importantly, then, in this understanding, the ideal Heavenly City is held up not to condemn what is happening in the earthly city but to enable critique of the *status quo*. The picture it offers of justice provides the aspiration, the longing for more justice in this earthly city. It is an eschatological hope that impacts one's hopes for and action in the present.

As I read him, while offering a lens for critique and a vision for the present, Augustine's understanding of the eschatological realization of justice and peace tempers Augustine's convictions about our ability to change the world ([12], p. 102). The Heavenly City and its justice and peace cannot be realized in the *saeculum*, despite our best efforts. Our loves are too disordered. Our desire to play the power game rather than the justice game is too strong. It cannot be fully checked by human will or even the intentional creation of structures of checks and balances. In Augustine's estimation, political structures do have an important God-given role to play within a fallen, power-hungry world. But as we engage the world, Augustine reminds us not to place false hopes in what can be accomplished. This represents one of Augustine's significant contributions in his day, as it allowed him to have some critical distance from the political powers and empires [13]. It prevented him from naively believing that an ideal society can be created by human hands or from dangerously acting as if the city of God can be ushered in by human effort. At the same time, his vision of true justice and peace within the Heavenly City gave him a lens through which he could critique present realities.

When it comes to peace, Augustine is more explicit about the role it plays: citizens of the Heavenly City, while here on earth in the *saeculum*, instead of trying to force the eschatological peace of the Heavenly City, can and should enjoy the earthly peace of the earthly city as a good from God, they should view it as a good suitable to the temporal life and a good they seek to foster, even as they recognize that it is not the highest good for which they hope. When it comes to justice, he does not provide such explicit guidance in *City of God*, as the close connections between justice, the right, and properly ordered loves prevent him from using the term "justice" for what can be sought in the political realm. That being said, when we look at his non-theoretical writings, his correspondence with ecclesial authorities, political authorities, friends, and others reveals more of Augustine's "everyday political thinking" and action ([11], p. xi).

A look at Augustine's life "on the ground" as revealed in his letters can be considered an exploration of Augustine as "an inspired subverter of his own idealizations", as James Wetzel puts it [14]. Wetzel views Augustine as both an idealizer and a subverter of those very idealizations he has named, so that we can find in his writings the "ideal type" and places where he pushes beyond the scope or the potential limitations of that ideal. So in Augustine, we see a heavenly city where justice reigns and, as Wetzel puts it, "an earthly city that is divisiveness itself. This is all idealization" ([14], p. 12). Wetzel pushes this idealization by exploring Augustine the subverter, calling this "the more gratifying, and also the more vexing, labor" ([14], p. 10).

When it comes to the topic at hand, Wetzel is concerned that eschatology, while essential to Christian theology, is a "form of idealization" and that at times we see in Augustine "an overheated eschatology" ([14], pp. 21–22). Wetzel in turn worries about those who put too much weight on Augustine's eschatology. So, of Robert Dodaro, who places considerable emphasis on Augustine's eschatology in his exploration of the just society, Wetzel writes, in characteristic style, "Bob is the sanest eschatologist I know. But…" ([14], p. 21). For Wetzel, the "but" has to do with the concern that Augustine's eschatology, taken on its own, overlooks "material difference" and that other areas of Augustine's thought honor more fully the material context in which we live.

A brief look at two of Augustine's letters will help us explore how his eschatological and theological convictions framed and shaped his hopes and actions in the material earthly city in which he lived. By holding "Augustine the idealizer" together with "Augustine the subverter", we get a more complete picture of Augustine's theology in relation to justice (I would suggest that whenever teaching Augustine, it is exceptionally fruitful for students to read a letter or sermon alongside his more theoretical writings to get a more nuanced picture of who Augustine is).

3. Augustine the Subverter

So having looked at Augustine the idealizer through his theoretical writings on justice and the City of God, let us now look at Augustine the subverter through his letters. Reading even just two of Augustine's letters, "Augustine to Alypius" and "Augustine to Macedonius", suggests the extent of his public engagement; he certainly lives as someone who believes his involvement can make a difference in what we from the outside would call just outcomes. To take the example of slavery, all the valid concerns about Augustine's acceptance of slavery as an inescapable institution in this fallen world notwithstanding, from his correspondence with his dear friend and fellow bishop Alypius we see a man horrified by the injustices associated with the actual practice of slavery in his day [15]. We see a bishop motivated by his sense of right to take action against this corruption in his town of Hippo and to write this letter to encourage action against this corruption in other areas along the coast of northern Africa. We see his church regularly involved in freeing slaves, crying over the stories of abduction and kidnapping that led to their enslavement, caring for those who were rescued, and having a reputation for these acts of mercy. We see Augustine appealing to a law written under a previous emperor to check the corruption of the slave trade as a useful help and possible remedy, sending this law to Alypius for his use, clearly having both experienced its effectiveness and having hopes for it to have an impact on limiting injustice. At the same time, we see Augustine reluctant to use and share this law because of how harshly it calls for the merchants of slaves to be punished, noting that they are using the law only to free slaves and not to punish those guilty of wrongfully enslaving them. This is characteristic of Augustine's counsel to those with authority to judge and punish, as he consistently encourages Christians with that power to be as merciful and forgiving as they can be, remembering how much mercy and forgiveness they have received in Christ.

Noticeably, in describing his efforts in relation to slavery and appealing to his Christian brother to take up the same level of advocacy, Augustine never uses the word justice. In another letter, one that is part of his correspondence with Macedonius, the vicar of Africa who had responsibility for the legal administration of the civil diocese then known as Africa, we do find him using language of justice in relation to the earthly city. The need for the letter arose when Macedonius questioned the practice of Augustine and other ecclesial authorities at that time to intercede on behalf of guilty criminals. The practice was to appeal to political authorities to prevent criminals, even those known to be guilty, from receiving severe punishment or in some cases from receiving any punishment [16]. Augustine looks to Jesus' intercession on behalf of the woman caught in adultery, in which she is spared the punishment of stoning, as the basis for this priestly duty.

Towards the end of the letter, Augustine begins to address what to do if corruption and bribery swayed a legal decision. Here he draws on language of justice to describe what ought to be done: "If we are honestly to serve justice, we will say to the advocate: 'Return what you have received when you appeared against the truth and on the side of injustice. You deceived the judge, you opposed the just cause, you won your case through lies'." ([16], section 25). This is one of the rare instances in which Augustine uses language of justice without qualification to refer to the earthly city, implying that it is possible for some kind of justice to be served in that realm.

Very shortly after this, however, he returns to his eschatological perspective on justice. He goes on to write that holding possessions lawfully implies holding them justly, and holding them justly implies holding them well, and almost no one in our earthly city holds possessions well because this would mean despising their own property and their money—"the less they love it, the more rightly they possess it"—which is not possible outside of the reordering we need in Christ. He casts an eschatological vision in which only the just are gathered, in which the citizens of the Heavenly City rightly own all that has been given to them. Importantly, though, between now and the final fulfillment of the Heavenly City, Augustine acknowledges an important place for civil laws to guide the use of possessions. While technically, in Augustine's understanding, all of those whose loves have not been reordered hold their possessions wrongly and therefore unjustly, this injustice is tolerated in the earthly city. Legally this takes shape in civil laws that are intended not "to make them use possessions rightly, but rather to make them less oppressive in misusing them" ([16], section 26). Here is an instance in which we can see very clearly the dynamic role that an eschatological vision of justice can play in the earthly city. Augustine initially seems to offer this reflection on "possessing rightly" as a way of pushing back on the possibility of full justice in this earthly city. What happens ultimately, however, is that his understanding of what will happen in the Heavenly City—when all will use what they have been given rightly (rather than selfishly and oppressively)—informs his sense of what the civil law ought to and can accomplish in this age—namely being less oppressive. In short, his vision of justice in the Heavenly City shapes his hopes for justice in the earthly city.

Of course one could raise the question, as many have, why Augustine's vision for justice is not more ambitious, more wide-ranging, more structural. While lots of ink has been spilled to address this question, particularly in relation to slavery, it is important to remember one other component of Augustine's thought in relation to justice in this earthly city. Augustine was, perhaps surprisingly, hopeful about what Christian rulers would be able to accomplish in the earthly city, at least in his idealizing side. Because Christian rulers would have had their loves reordered in Christ, they alone had the capacity to place justice over power, to place love for God over lust for domination, to remember that even "the loftiest summit of power ... is nothing but a passing mist" [17]. A Christian ruler could, in short and in theory, rule with justice [18]. This conviction is more significant than it might seem to our contemporary ears for, as Dodaro suggests, Augustine follows Cicero in "focusing the concept of the just society on the role of its leaders in establishing justice" [19]. If it is true that Augustine follows Cicero in believing that justice in a society comes through just rulers, then we can understand the consistency of his argument related to the importance of Christian rulers and even interpret it as a sign of hopefulness. A form of justice could be possible in this earthly city. The ideal statesman found in Christ, the just King of the Heavenly City, could inspire and enlarge the imaginations of rulers for justice in the earthly city [20].

What Augustine's theological vision could mean for the earthly city today lies somewhere in between the two extremes of completely abandoning the earthly city and looking to the earthly city to achieve utopian-like harmony, justice, and peace. Augustine is clear that citizens of the Heavenly City share in the goods of the earthly city, making use of its earthly peace and helping to defend and sustain the limited harmony that is possible in the earthly city, "a kind of compromise between human wills about things relevant to mortal life" ([7], XIX, 17). Augustine's understanding of justice, in particular, as an eschatological reality does not prevent him from working towards a form of what we would call justice in this earthly city, nor from finding in the tension between what he hopes for in the age to come and what he sees in the here and now, aspirations for just outcomes. The earthly city can, then, achieve limited goods, limited justice, even if not the greatest goods or the full justice for which humankind was created and which it will experience in full in the City of God.

4. Conclusions

To bring this back to our three students who are motivated by a desire to seek justice, how does this exploration of Augustine the idealizer and Augustine the subverter help them? As a starting place, my hope would be that the idealizing side of Augustine on justice would push them to do some considerable grappling with why injustice exists in the first place. I hope it might help them to articulate their own convictions about what justice, wholeness, and flourishing look like—for each person and for a society, and to consider what it takes to get from present reality to that vision. I likewise hope that they will consider how they are complicit in the existence of injustice, rather than viewing it as a problem "over there", outside of themselves, outside of their own practices and culture.

Augustine the idealizer could also help bring to light for these students the significant role of structures and institutions in any effort to seek justice, as they brush up against the seamlessness with which Augustine moves between individual disordered loves and the societies made up of such individuals. As James Davison Hunter has recently argued so powerfully in his book *To Change the World*, loving the hearts, minds, and (I would add) bodies of individuals is the default approach that many take today, but we have to also acknowledge the collective societies in which these individuals live and the structural realities that either promote or inhibit the flourishing of those hearts, minds, and bodies [21]. Further, I hope that Augustine's sense that things are much more disordered and unjust in the earthly city than we might think combined with his conviction that it is not up to humanity to overcome that disorder and injustice will lift the weight off their shoulders that comes from thinking they have to change the world—and prevent the burn-out that almost inevitably comes down the road when they realize they can't change the world despite their best efforts and initial passions (preventing this kind of burn-out is one of the motivations behind my forthcoming book on justice [22]).

At the same time I hope that this realization will not squash all of their desire to be responsible with what they have been given. May Augustine the subverter motivate them to look for ways to engage people, institutions, and structures right where they are, to recognize, as George Eliot shows us in a very different way through her novel *Middlemarch*, that we do not all have to be celebrated saints like Teresa of Avila to love others and impact our communities right where God has placed us [23]. May Augustine prompt them to seek the grace of God in Christ that in all that they do they might prioritize the justice game over the power game, that they would be faithful, responsible, and as Peter Kaufman reminds us so eloquently in his contribution, humble with the power that has been entrusted to them—not avoiding power as inherently evil but using it for the greater good of justice.

Acknowledgments

With gratitude to Scott McGinnis for organizing the stimulating "Teaching The Christian Intellectual Tradition" conference and inviting me to participate, and to Peter Kaufman for his ongoing belief in both my teaching and my scholarship, our differing interpretations of Augustine notwithstanding.

Conflicts of Interest

The author declares no conflict of interest.

References and Notes

1. Frederick Buechner. *Wishful Thinking: A Seeker's ABC*. New York: HarperOne, 1993, p. 119.
2. Augustine. *The Trinity*. Translated by Edmund Hill, O.P. and John E. Rotelle, O.S.A. Brooklyn: New City Press, 1991, XIII, 17.
3. So Augustine can write of the "power of humility" in *Concerning the City of God against the Pagans*. Translated by Henry Bettenson. Harmondsworth: Penguin Books, 1972, I, Preface.
4. Kristen Deede Johnson. *Theology, Political Theory, and Pluralism*. Cambridge: Cambridge University Press, 2007.
5. For "what could be a greater show of power than to rise from the dead and ascend into heaven with the very flesh in which he had been killed? So he overcame the devil with justice first and power second, with justice because *he had no sin* (2 Cor 5:21; 1 Pt 2:22) and was most unjustly killed by him; with power because dead he came back to life never to die thereafter." Augustine. *The Trinity*, XIII, 18; emphasis in original.
6. Augustine. *City of God* XIX, 13.
7. "It follows that justice is found where God, the one supreme God, rules an obedient City according to His grace, forbidding sacrifice to any being save himself alone; and where in consequence the soul rules the body in all men who belong to this City and obey God, and the reason faithfully rules the vices in a lawful system of subordination; so that just as the individual righteous man lives on the basis of faith which is active in love, so the association, or people, of righteous men lives on the same basis of faith, active in love, the love with which a man loves God as God ought to be loved, and loves his neighbour as himself." Augustine. *City of God* XIX, 23.
8. Augustine. *City of God* II, 21.

9. Robert Dodaro. *Christ and the Just Society in the Thought of Augustine*. Cambridge: Cambridge University Press, 2004, p. 72.
10. Augustine. *City of God* XV, 4.
11. For example, in the introduction to *Augustine: Political Writings* the editors write, "Augustine does not deny the value of civic virtues for purely earthly purposes: Christians and pagans alike benefit from just, peaceful, and orderly societies". E.M. Atkins, and R.J. Dodaro, eds. In *Augustine: Political Writings*. Cambridge: Cambridge University Press, 2001, pp. xvi–xvii.
12. Eugene TeSelle. "Towards an Augustinian Politics." *The Journal of Religious Ethics* 16 (1988): 87–108.
13. Charles Norris Cochrane. *Christianity and Classical Culture: A Study of Thought and Action from Augustus to Augustine*. Oxford: Clarendon Press, 1940, p. 509.
14. James Wetzel. "A Tangle of Two Cities." Unpublished manuscript. Microsoft Word File, p. 10.
15. Augustine. "Letter 10: Augustine to Alypius." In *Augustine: Political Writings*. Edited by E.M. Atkins and R.J. Dodaro. Cambridge: Cambridge University Press, 2001.
16. Augustine. "Letter 153: Augustine to Macedonius." In *Augustine: Political Writings*. Edited by E.M. Atkins and R.J. Dodaro. Cambridge: Cambridge University Press, 2001, para. 10.
17. Augustine. *City of God* V, 26 (drawing on James 4:14).
18. Augustine. *City of God* V, 24.
19. Dodaro raises this point to help explain why Augustine contrasts Cicero's ideal statesman with Christ as the truly ideal statesman who alone can establish the truly just society. See ([9], p. 2).
20. This does not mean that historically they usually do or did—but merely that it is possible!
21. James Davison Hunter. *To Change the World: The Irony, Tragedy, and Possibility of Christianity in the Late Modern World.* New York: Oxford University Press, 2010.
22. Bethany Hanke Hoang, and Kristen Deede Johnson. *The Justice Calling: Where Passion Meets Perseverance.* Grand Rapids: Brazos Press, 2016, forthcoming.
23. George Eliot. *Middlemarch.* London: Penguin Classics, 2003.

Section II.
Pedagogical Contexts

Naming the Mystery: An Augustinian Ideal

Allan Fitzgerald

Abstract: This article, by noticing Augustine's constant questioning, shows that he often talks about not knowing and about his need for God's help to know more. It is therefore better to see how he identifies the mystery than to focus on his answers, because he too recognizes his limits. His intellectual prowess can be seen more clearly when he "names the mystery" than by thinking that he has solved it.

> Reprinted from *Religions*. Cite as: Fitzgerald, A. Naming the Mystery: An Augustinian Ideal. *Religions* **2015**, *6*, 204–210.

1. Introduction

It is not unusual to hear people talk about how important Augustine is today. Some are pleased about that; others are less so. Some see his willingness to be flexible in the interpretation of Scripture and his deeply human understanding of the Christian journey as liberation from the neo-scholastic trends of recent times. Others focus on his influence on ideas like original sin, predestination, infant baptism, and *filioque* as charges to be held against him. Teaching a course—or a part of a course—on Augustine can leave one feeling a bit "hamstrung" by the felt need to take sides, to have to live with a sense of the unresolved tension that these opinions represent. It has become a challenge to appreciate who Augustine really is.

To teach Augustine, therefore, I think that it is important to present him, not primarily in terms of this or that doctrine or view, but as someone with whom people can identify, humanly speaking. The last time that I taught a course on Augustine—a graduate course on his life and thought—I had not found a good way to do that. Some of the same old "issues" came up for discussion more than once: his doctrine of predestination, his presumed condemnation of unbaptized infants, and his heavy, polemical style in the debate with Julian of Eclanum. This talk is about how I have re-visited the teaching of that course, about how to begin the course in a different key by talking about Augustine's personal attitude toward the limits of his understanding. Therefore, this paper is not about a specific classroom experience but a proposal for teaching Augustine, presenting him as fully human before discussing the issues that are often seen in controversial terms.

2. Reaching for Something More

One way to present a balanced—and attractive—view of the man is to identify and talk about the ways that he acknowledged the limitations he felt in own understanding of his life and faith. Or, to put it more strikingly, to talk about what Augustine said that he did not know.

If I have understood one of the mainstays of the thought of Paul Ricœur, the study of another age requires that there be a "passing over" and then a "passing back", that is, a process of leaving the comfort of one's own way of seeing and thinking for a time, and in that way to pay full attention to that which is different or foreign. Applying such an approach to the study of Augustine is to begin to notice an insistent attention to the limits of his words. Why, then, was so important for Augustine to name limits of his thinking—both by asking for God's assistance and the prayers of this people when he is preaching and by noting explicitly some things that he does not know or understand. This is, in other words, not a way of proposing a new methodology for the study of Augustine. It is simply an invitation to notice a facet of his writings that is rather consistently ignored [1]. See, for example, what he says about his understanding about those who do not persevere:

> "If at this point I am asked why God who gave them the love by which they lived as Christians did not give them perseverance, I reply that I do not know. Not with arrogance, but recognizing my limits…" [2].

> "Are you expecting me to tell you why he has mercy on whom he will, and whose will he hardens? Are you expecting it from me, a man? If you're a human being and I'm a human being, then both of us have heard: *who are you to answer back to God* (Rom 9:20)? So trusting ignorance is better than rash knowledge. God says to me, Christ speaks through the apostle, O man, who are you to answer back to God? And I get indignant, do I, because I don't understand God's justice? If I am a man, I shouldn't be indignant. Let me go beyond being a man, if I can, and reach the source. But even if I do reach it, I may not tell about it to a human being. Let him go beyond himself also, and reach it with me." [3].

In addition, Augustine often asked for the assistance of God when he preaches on difficult topics. Why does this matter? Did he experience, as has been claimed [4], an uncharacteristic failure in intellectual rigor when he invoked God's hidden justice instead of trying to address the relationship of human freedom to divine grace? Is this a kind of false humility?

3. Naming the Mystery for the Common Good

In the case of Augustine, it is all-too-easy to let the focus shift from the study of his thought—set within its own cultural context—to taking a stance on the answers that we think he gives. It is almost as if his texts are often analysed—exhaustively—in relation to the way we think in our time and culture. By highlighting the place that Augustine gives to what he does not know or does not yet understand, there is a greater chance of giving appropriate attention his intention, to the interior dimension of his thinking. Rather than a failure in intellectual courage or a kind of false humility, Augustine is doing something quite positive and useful. He *names the mystery* in a way that does not put an end to his searching but acknowledges a simple reality: there is always going to be more to know about any real mystery. To name something as a mystery, therefore, is not a way of closing the discussion but of accepting present limits and of making the searching a truly Christian moment where the human effort and divine grace are both necessary. Hence, the focus is not on Augustine's ignorance. It is an acceptance of that which is—and will remain—open-ended—a point that is clearly affirmed in a fascinating article by Charles Mathewes [5].

Augustine never claimed to have all the answers; he had no desire to be an *"auctoritas"*. Neither skeptic nor dogmatist, he was nonetheless able to give positive value to his humanity by invoking the assistance of God and by recognizing the inscrutability of God. I chose to entitle this paper "naming the mystery" because I think that it is important to pay attention to the way that Augustine was constantly trying to do more than talk about some truth [6]. His searching was always set within the context of his faith-seeking-understanding and was a part of his spiritual life and prayer as well. He is, practically speaking, acknowledging the importance of continuing to seek, ask and find (cf. Mt. 7:7), not in order to *end* with an answer but to affirm his ongoing relationship with the one who is Truth.

Again and again he asks for divine assistance, requests correction if his readers/listeners notice that he has erred, confesses his own sins, and respects differences of opinion where the truth is not compromised. Another way to say this can be found in a book by Paul van Geest on Augustine's negative theology:

> "The reading of Augustine's works acquires a new brilliance when they are viewed in the light of ... [his] reticence and uncertainty. It is true to say that for him, *apophasis* [=unknowing] formed the heart of his "theology". Whenever the fact is forgotten that his treatment of the great theological themes ... was accompanied by caveats about the relativity of such discourse, its essential tenor is obscured." [7].

Paul van Geest wrote persuasively about Augustine's awareness of the incomprehensibility of God. Again and again he insists that we cannot know God. But Augustine's interest is not a pessimistic theology or a cop-out. Let me again quote van Geest:

> "[Augustine's] familiarity with Scripture and tradition imbued him with the idea that humans are part of a "reality", of a whole, which they cannot possibly comprehend, but upon which they depend." Even intelligent fish can't say much about the sea in which they swim! Paul van Geest continues: "Therefore they cannot analyse things merely as spectators. Human beings are encompassed by a Mystery of which they themselves form a part, and which, moreover, determines their hightest "I". For Augustine the mystagogue, the fact that this recognition causes a salutary uncertainty is an intended purpose rather than a chance result." [8].

It was already important for Augustine to name the mystery. That applies to his concerns about the salvation of the unbaptized, to his life-long quandary about the origin of the soul [9], and to his efforts to identify analogies for the Trinity. Even more important, however, was his ability to see that he was part of that mystery and not a spectator, thus providing a model that was a way of working for the good of all without setting oneself apart. In other words, to recognize his ignorance was to affirm a larger picture: seeking in a way that did not make him the teacher, but "said" that only one is Teacher.

How does that understanding become an integral part of teaching others about Augustine's life and thought? Examples can be found in the way he frequently prayerfully asks for divine assistance along with the community to whom he spoke, and asserts the unknowability of the mind of God when it comes to the application of justice and mercy.

4. Divine Assistance in Preaching

Augustine often says that his preaching needs the help of God and the prayers of the community. Thus does he that he is not reading from a script but that he is developing his message as it unfolds; he improvises as he speaks [10]. Here are a couple of examples from his sermons on John's Gospel:

> "I put off until today the task of opening up, with his help, what is mysteriously contained in the sacraments [11] that are in the event described in the gospel reading." [12].

> I have had that reading read to you again, so that in Christ's name and with the help of your prayers I may finish what there was not time to deal with then [13].

> Whatever I cannot manage will be supplied for you by the same one by who helps me do what I can [14].

It could be easy to think that Augustine is just trying to arouse the people's sympathy or using a rhetorical commonplace to engage or co-opt his people. Such phrases are rarely given much attention by commentators. But he is being fully faithful to his faith in the Word of God: any helpful understanding of that Word requires God's help—both for him to explain it accurately and for it to be well received.

But there is more to this example than may at first be obvious. Not only is he making his limitation quite plain [15], but, by asking his listeners to pray, he is proclaiming that the process of discovery, of understanding the Word is a communal process. His listeners are fellow-learners (*condiscipuli*); their teacher is Jesus Christ, the interior master. In this way, Augustine also refuses to be the *auctoritas*. It's as if his time as imperial rhetor showed him the danger of setting oneself us as an oracle on whose expressions and doctrines the others may sit in judgment. His preaching, however, is not just giving his listeners a sound hermeneutical understanding; it is part of his lifelong truth-seeking and that cannot happen if he allows himself to be, as it were isolated from the love of God and the love of neighbor. That may be a difficult reality to introduce into a college classroom, but it does help to see that prayer is more than a religious practice; it is also an act that is integral to the community of learning and to the truth that is being sought.

5. Doctrinal Limitations

More complicated—and perhaps more interesting—is the frequency and the consistency with which he cites Romans 11:33 in relation to the justice and mercy of God. That biblical passage reads: "Oh, the depth of the riches and wisdom and knowledge of God! How inscrutable are his judgments and how unsearchable his ways!" It is invoked when he is touching upon a difficult theological issue: God's justice.

Several scholars have criticized Augustine's appeal to God's inscrutable mystery, suggesting as I have already said that it represents a failure in intellectual rigor, suggesting that such failure is unusual for Augustine [16]. Paul Rigby prefers to see Augustine's use of that verse in a positive light, addressing the value of Augustine's appeal to ignorance in topics as fundamental as predestination, original sin and unbaptized infants. By failing to look for Augustine's positive motivation, scholars have pointed out a lack of coherence in what he does say, but without offering any way to avoid a dilemma. Is it even possible that a human being will know the mind of God or know how to speak about God's application of his salvific will? Of course not. Augustine, therefore, is not suffering from a failure of nerve; he is proposing a significant Scriptural truth: God's justice is a mystery. He names the mystery without abandoning the search.

In the case of unbaptized infants, for example, Augustine cites Romans 11:33, acknowledging his ignorance. Augustine repeats the criticism that has been brought against him: "if, as you would have it, it's only a small pain, a small punishment; even a small one is great, if there is no fault. Defend God's justice here; why should even a small punishment be inflicted on the innocent, in whom absolutely no sin at all is to be found?"

Augustine responds:

> "I am myself keenly aware of how profoundly problematic this question is, and I recognize that my powers are not sufficient to get to the bottom of it. Here too I like to exclaim with Paul, *Oh the depths of the riches!* (Rom 11:33). Unbaptized babies go to damnation; they are the apostle's words, after all: From one to condemnation (Rom 5:16). I cannot find a satisfactory and worthy explanation—because I can't find one, not because there isn't one. So where I cannot find bottom in the depths, *I must take account of human weakness, not condemn divine authority*. I certainly exclaim, and I'm not in the least ashamed of it, *Oh the depths of the riches of the wisdom and knowledge of God! How inscrutable are his judgments, and untraceable his ways*! ... For my part, I fortify my weakness with these words." [17].

Has Augustine, once again, shown nothing but his lack of intellectual rigor and proclaimed his weakness? He says elsewhere:

> "It is indeed, to be wondered at, and greatly to be wondered at that [baptized Christians lapse and the wicked are converted and that the children of Christian's die unbaptized and the children of pagan parents die baptized] ... who would not wonder at this? Who would not be exceedingly astonished at this! Certainly, in this case the judgments of God, because they are righteous and deep, may neither be blamed nor penetrated." [18].

In other words, there are no options at all. Rather than trust his own logic and reasoning, he prefers to accept the Word of God. Wisdom demands acknowledgment of our small measure. It forces us to confess that God's mercy and justice are far beyond ours. He is not callous but knows the limit of human knowing.

Has the dilemma that Augustine and his contemporaries faced ever been answered? Limbo was no better an answer. Baptism is, in fact, required. By re-defining baptism as baptism of desire and not using that as a way to deny the existence or interest of original sin, we did what Augustine wanted to do: neither deny our need for Christ nor our human condition in the process of trying to understand God's plan. But the mystery remains as an invitation to further searching.

6. Humility

Augustine is not satisfied with naming the mystery as insoluble. That would be too simple. By turning exchanges away from information-sharing, something more lasting can develop. While the cultural context helps to move beyond this or that fact or this or that idea, what is really needed is a way to address Augustine's attitude: what emotion was part of his thinking? What was at the heart of his thinking? It seems to me that a course on Augustine needs to *begin* with some significant presentation on how Augustine saw himself, shifting the tonality beyond "answers" toward ideas with a "feel" to them. It turns out to be important to those beginning to know Augustine that they be able to relate to him and not just to some idea of his or some ideas about his culture. That happens when the limits to what he knows are noticed. That would mean that a course on Augustine would begin by noticing how impossible it was for him to stop himself from asking questions [19], because questioning is a way of making progress rather than an effort to end reflection with a firm answer.

Augustine does not just seek to foster humility—in the face of mystery—but to engage in the kind of reflection that places everyone at the level of discovery rather than placing the focus on a detached, as it were, objective reading of the ideas of others. This reflection from within the human community is capable of integrating prayer, thought, exchange and awareness of meaning without "sitting in judgment" on the theological or philosophical adequacy of this or that expression or doctrine. Instead of systematic presuppositions, this process avoids mere intellectual speculation and is therefore forced (from within) to emphasize historical context. Is that a denial of systematic theology? No it is an historical statement.

7. Concluding Remarks

This paper has suggested that Augustine's awareness of his own limits often led him to identify those questions and issues that he did not understand and which he still tried to penetrate. By thus naming the mystery, he made it clear that he was not a kind of dogmatist nor a skeptic. Rather, he wanted others to know the value of searching—even when there would be no conclusion to that effort.

Conflicts of Interest

The author declares no conflict of interest.

References

1. Paul Rigby. "The Role of God's 'Inscrutable Judgments' in Augustine's Doctrine of Predestination." *Augustinian Studies* 33 (2002): 213–22.
2. Augustine. *On Rebuke and Grace (de correptione et gratia)* 8, 17.
3. Augustine. *Sermon 27*, 4.
4. John M. Rist. "Augustine on Free Will and Predestination." *Journal of Theological Studies* 20 (1969): 439–40. In Rist's exclusively ethical interpretation, the doctrine of original sin reveals a "puppet-like status of fallen man".

5. Charles T. Mathewes. "The Liberation of Questioning in Augustine's *Confessions*." *Journal of the American Academy of Religion* 70 (2002): 539–60.
6. Paul Rigby. "Augustine's Use of Narrative Universals in the Debate over Predestination." *Augustinian Studies* 31 (2000): 181–94.
7. Paul van Geest. *The Incomprehensibility of God. Augustine as a Negative Theologian*. Leuven: Peeters, 2011, p. 227.
8. Paul van Geest. *op. cit.*, p. 218.
9. See the lucid article by Michael Mendelson. "'The Business of Those Absent': The Origin of the Soul in Augustine's De Genesi Ad Litteram 10.6–26." *Augustinian Studies* 28 (1998): 25–81.
10. See J. William Harmless, S.J. "A Love Supreme: Augustine's 'Jazz' of Theology." *Augustinian Studies* 43 (2012): 145–73.
11. *In sacramentis*, *i.e.*, in the sacred signs that are part of this gospel narrative.
12. Augustine. *Commentary on the Gospel of John* 9, 1.
13. Augustine. *Commentary on the Gospel of John* 12, 1.
14. Augustine. *Commentary on the Gospel of John* 17, 1.
15. He asks for the help of the Holy Spirit: "*Sanctus Spiritus Adiuvat Infirmitatem Nostrum*"; *cf. Ep.* 130, 28: *Docta Ignorantia*.
16. Susanah Ticciati. "Reading Augustine Through Job: A Reparative Reading of Augustine's Doctrine of Predestination." *Modern Theology* 27 (2011): 414–41.
17. Augustine. *Sermon* 294, 7.
18. Augustine. *On Rebuke and Grace* (*de correptione et gratia*) 8, 18.
19. This practical emphasis is linked to Augustine's statement that there is no better way to learn than by questioning and answering (*Soliloquies* II, 7, 14).

Teaching Socrates, Aristotle, and Augustine on *Akrasia*[1]

J. Caleb Clanton

Abstract: A long-standing debate among moral philosophers centers on the question of whether ignorance is always at the root of moral wrongdoing, or whether, in certain cases, wrongdoing stems from something else—namely *akrasia*. This paper is a discussion of how undergraduate core curriculum teachers can incorporate Augustine's work into this debate. I begin by briefly reconstructing Socrates' and Aristotle's accounts of wrongdoing, and then I sketch an Augustinian approach to the issue. Socrates contends that ignorance is the fundamental source of all wrongdoing; hence, *akrasia* is illusory. Though Aristotle's view can seem more roundabout than Socrates', it, too, is plausibly interpreted as entailing that robust, open-eyed *akrasia* is impossible. For Augustine, prior to receiving the illumination that comes with God's grace, an individual's sinfulness can be characterized as being the result of ignorance concerning the proper focus of one's love. However, after receiving this illuminating grace, sinful action can be characterized as an instance of *akrasia*.

Reprinted from *Religions*. Cite as: Clanton, C.J. Teaching Socrates, Aristotle, and Augustine on *Akrasia*. *Religions* **2015**, *6*, 419–433.

1. Introduction

The great twentieth century theologian Reinhold Niebuhr is often quoted as having said that "original sin is the only empirically verifiable doctrine of the Christian faith" ([1], p. 24). To be sure, there are any number of ways one might wish to challenge Niebuhr's claim. An ambitious apologist, for instance, might try her hand at showing that there are other Christian doctrines beyond original sin that are empirically verifiable. Alternatively, one might simply reject the notion that sinfulness or moral culpability is in any way original to the human condition or otherwise inherited from one's ancestors. At any rate, virtually all such quibbling ends if we interpret Niebuhr's claim as asserting merely that every individual—if given enough time, at least—will at some point find herself guilty of moral wrongdoing. To err is human, after all.

Nonetheless, supposing we have all erred and fallen short of moral perfection, it is less obvious as to why. What, broadly speaking, leads us to act wrongly? Why do we sometimes do precisely what we ought not do? Why do we sometimes fail to do those things we should have done? As gloomy as these questions can seem, it is easy enough to see why we should seek the answers: if we can better pinpoint the fundamental source of our moral failings, we should be better able to tackle the challenges associated with moral education, punishment and rehabilitation, and personal discipline.

A long-standing debate among moral philosophers centers on the question of whether an agent's ignorance *vis-à-vis* what is best is really at the root of every instance of moral wrongdoing, or whether, in some cases at least, wrongdoing stems from *akrasia*, or what commonly gets described as

---

[1] This is a revised version of a paper presented at the "Teaching the Christian Intellectual Tradition" Conference on Augustine, Samford University, Birmingham, AL, USA, 2–4 October 2014.

weakness of will or incontinence. To reframe the question just a bit: Is an intellectual failure of some sort—say, a failure to obtain knowledge or correct belief with respect to the good or the right—always the main driving force behind an agent's moral wrongdoing? Or, are there cases where an agent's wrongdoing is the result of an affective or volitional failure? Is it possible for a person to be fully aware of what she should do, but nonetheless fail to do it? Or is one's failure to act as she should a clear indication that she simply lacked the relevant moral knowledge in the first place?

Socrates and Aristotle are, of course, *loci classici* for discussion of questions like those, and it is fitting for teachers to turn to their work in undergraduate core curriculum courses. But their views can sometimes leave students—particularly religious believers—with the impression that something important has been left out of the discussion. Fortunately, Augustine can supplement this discussion in a way that addresses at least some of the concerns students may have when considering the Socratic and Aristotelian accounts. The point of this essay is to outline in very rough form how teachers might incorporate Augustine's work into discussions about the source of moral wrongdoing. In what follows, I briefly sketch a way of positioning Augustine as a counterpoint to Socrates' and Aristotle's well-known analyses of wrongdoing. This should not be taken to imply that Augustine saw his treatment of wrongdoing as a response to Socrates and Aristotle; but there is certainly pedagogical value in viewing it in that light. To be perfectly clear, my objective here is not to engage in the penetrating analysis and painstaking scholarship most characteristic of the literature in classical philosophy; nor do I mean to be advocating for Augustine's account of wrongdoing over those of Socrates and Aristotle. Rather, my aim is simply to outline how core curriculum teachers might turn to Augustine, as one of the chief representatives of the Christian intellectual tradition, to inform an important debate in the broader Western intellectual tradition.

To set the stage, it might be helpful to say a little something about the word *akrasia*. As mentioned above, *akrasia* sometimes gets translated as "weakness of will" and sometimes as "incontinence". While these translations are helpful for moving us in the right direction, unfortunately, they are imperfect. On the one hand, translating *akrasia* as "weakness of will" is probably somewhat anachronistic when talking about Socrates and Aristotle, in part because they probably did not have a robust conception of will in the way we do today. On the other hand, translating *akrasia* as "incontinence" can present unnecessary distractions, given that word's association with difficulties related to the bathroom. For these reasons, it makes sense to leave the term *akrasia* as it is and, instead, simply offer a working definition of it.

Scholars define *akrasia* in various ways, but for our purposes we can capture the common gist of these definitions in the following manner:

> AKRASIA: The condition in which you know (or otherwise correctly believe) that you should Φ, but—against your own better judgment—you do not Φ.

I turn now to Socrates's analysis of wrongdoing in Plato's *Protagoras*.

2. Socrates on *Akrasia*

Socrates asks his interlocutor, Protagoras, whether knowledge is like "a slave, pushed around by all the other affections" such as passions, pleasure, pain, love, or fear ([2], 352c). Now, the million-dollar question Socrates is posing here is whether knowledge—particularly knowledge of the good or the right—is fully capable of ruling a person such that, if she truly knows what is best, she will act on that knowledge. If a person can have knowledge but not act on it, then clearly knowledge can be overruled by such things as emotions, passions, appetites, and like. Protagoras responds to Socrates by asserting that wisdom and knowledge are "the most powerful elements in human life" and, of course, Socrates quickly agrees ([2], 352d). However, Socrates conjectures that most people do not agree with them on this matter. The masses, he says, believe that people sometimes "recognize the best, but are unwilling to act on it" ([2], 352d–e). In other words, popular opinion holds that an individual can suffer from *akrasia*: a person can have knowledge of the best course of action but still be overcome by some affection, whereupon she ultimately fails to act in accordance with her own better judgment. Consequently, if the masses are correct, knowledge does, or at least can, get pushed around like a slave.

For Socrates, though, the masses are simply mistaken, because what seems like *akrasia* is really just an illusion. Admittedly, it can sometimes seem to us that an agent correctly discerns what is best but nonetheless fails to do it (such that the agent is akratic). However, in Socrates' view, the agent who does not do what is best actually just fails to grasp correctly what the best course of action is.

Suppose that some action R is, objectively speaking, the best course of action and that W is not. And suppose further that someone reports to us that she recognizes that R is the best course of action but that—due to the pull of some passion or fit of emotion—she chooses to do W instead of R. Although we might be tempted to think that she is suffering from *akrasia* in the moment, in Socrates' view, what is really going on here is that this person is choosing W over R because, in that moment at least, she simply judges W to be the best course of action to take. Accordingly, the problem is not that she lacks command over herself; the problem is that she fails to believe correctly: she is ignorant about the best course of action. If she had really believed that she should choose R over W, then she would have done R. Socrates claims, for example, that

> no one *willingly* goes to meet evil or what he thinks to be evil. To make for what one believes to be evil, instead of making for the good, is not, it seems, in human nature, and when faced with the choice of two evils no one will choose the greater when he might choose the less ([2], 358c–d).

If Socrates is right that we always act in accordance with what we ourselves judge to be good, then, when it comes to wrongdoing, what might appear to be *akrasia* is really just the output of the agent's misjudgment concerning the various goods and evils or pleasures and pains at stake. This misjudgment results in her believing incorrectly concerning the proper course of action, which, in turn, results in her wrongdoing. So the failure at play is a failure to grasp correctly what is best.

Fittingly, Socrates's solution is to advocate for better all-things-considered judgment, or what he thinks of (in his conversation with Protagoras, at least) as the art of good measurement. He says, for example, that we should

> ... like an expert in weighing, put the pleasures and the pains together, set both the near and distant in the balance, and say which is the greater quantity. In weighing pleasures against pleasures, one must always choose the greater and the more; in weighing pains

against pains, the smaller and the less; whereas in weighing pleasures against pains, if the pleasures exceed the pains, whether the distant, the near, or vice versa, one must take the course which brings those pleasures; but if the pains outweigh the pleasures, avoid it ([2], 356b–c).

Presumably, if we practice this sort of measurement properly in every situation, we will better arrive at correct beliefs concerning what is best, which should ultimately prevent wrongdoing. Of course, at the heart of Socrates's account here is the assumption that we always desire what we *take* to be good [3]. If it is true that we always desire what we believe to be good, then when a person chooses one course of action over another, she simply chooses what she judges to be best. Hence, wrongdoing comes about only as a result of the agent's miscalculation. To know the good is to do the good. Accordingly, Socrates concludes in his conversation with Protagoras that when a wrong action is done, it is done out of ignorance ([2], 357d). He reiterates the general point in Plato's *Gorgias* when he declares: "As for me, if I act wrongly at all in the conduct of my life, you may be assured that my error is not voluntary but *due to my ignorance*" ([4], 488a; emphasis added).

Clearly, then, Socrates denies the possibility of *akrasia*. This is because, in his view, wrongdoing always stems from a misjudgment, and that as opposed to a lack of self-control or a weakness in the face of one's impulses or emotions. Wrongdoing, then, stems most fundamentally from an intellectual failure. After all, a person's desires are always directed toward what she takes to be good; but whether she really has knowledge of the good at the time of action is a different story.

3. Aristotle on *Akrasia*

Aristotle responds to Socrates' account of wrongdoing in Book VII of the *Nicomachean Ethics*. There, he contends that Socrates' view, "contradicts things that appear manifestly" ([5], 1145b28). In other words, Socratic intellectualism conflicts with what we seem to experience in our workaday lives—namely, knowing that you should do something, but not doing it (or, alternatively, knowing that you should not do something, but doing it anyway). For Aristotle, a different methodological approach is called for:

> The proper procedure will be the one we have followed in our treatment of other subjects: we must present phenomena, <that is, the observed facts of moral life and the current beliefs about them, > and, after first stating the problems inherent in these, we must, if possible, demonstrate the validity of all the beliefs about these matters, and, if not, the validity of most of them or of the most authoritative. For if the difficulties are resolved and current beliefs are left intact, we shall have proved their validity sufficiently ([6], 1145b5).

The idea here is that the proper way of proceeding is to start with the datum of our experience—in this case, the appearance of akratic behavior—and try, if possible, to validate our ordinary beliefs about it—the belief, say, that *akrasia* is a real enough phenomenon. Put differently, we should start with an assessment of our everyday experience and work our way up to a philosophical theory, as opposed to the other way around.

So how might we explain what appear to be akratic behavior? A noteworthy feature of Aristotle's multifaceted treatment of this issue comes to the surface in his discussion of practical syllogisms. We can think of a practical syllogism as the line of thinking that links an agent's moral deliberations with her practice. Accordingly, the premises of a practical syllogism, if true, recommend a certain course of behavior. Now, as Aristotle sees things, practical syllogisms contain at least two premises, namely the universal premise and the particular premise. We can most easily elucidate the distinction between the universal and particular premise by means of Aristotle's own example. A universal premise would be something akin to the claim that "everything sweet must be tasted". A particular premise would be something akin to the claim that "this thing here is sweet". Thus, the practical syllogism Aristotle has in mind here would look like this:

UNIVERSAL PREMISE ⟶	1. Everything sweet must be tasted.
PARTICULAR PREMISE ⟶	2. This thing here is sweet.
PRACTICAL CONCLUSION ⟶	3. ∴ [The free & rational agent tastes the sweet thing in question]

If a person works through this sort of syllogism properly, then she will inevitably eat the sweet thing in question because, as Aristotle writes, "it is necessary for someone who is able and unhindered also to act on this at the same time" ([5], 1147a30).

The problem, though, is that a person may very well be hindered with respect to grasping the particular premises, precisely because "perception controls them" ([5], 1147a27). In other words, sense perception in some way influences a person's evaluation of the particular premise in a practical syllogism. And because sense perception is involved in the evaluation of a particular premise, a person may very well be affected by an onslaught of passion or emotion in her assessment of that particular premise. Accordingly, it is possible for a person to have knowledge about the universal premise—she could know, for example, that everything sweet must be tasted—but nonetheless fail to taste the particular sweet thing in front of her, precisely because some sort of pathos impaired her sense perception in assessing the particular premise. Hence, the person's wrongdoing in this case is seemingly akratic: she knows that she should Φ, but—against her own judgment on some level—she does not Φ. More precisely, she has deliberated properly at the level of the universal premise (thus she correctly grasped on some level what is best), but she has failed to reach the proper practical conclusion of that deliberation because some pathos affected her assessment of the particular premise.

Ultimately, then, for Aristotle, the apparently akratic person can be characterized as having some sort of knowledge of the good (*viz.*, knowledge of the *universal* premise). But this knowledge is clearly not enough to prevent wrongdoing. Because the apparently akratic person has only propositional knowledge of the universal premise, she does not act on it due to some sort of weakness. In this sense, as Aristotle sees it, the apparently akratic person is "like a city that votes for all the right decrees and has excellent laws, but does not apply them" ([5], 1152a20).

We are right, however, to wonder whether the apparently akratic person in Aristotle's account really and truly has knowledge of what is best. In turn, we are right to wonder whether Aristotle's apparently akratic person is genuinely and robustly akratic on final analysis. He admits, for example, that the sort of knowledge he attributes to the apparently akratic person "is not the sort that seems to be *fully* knowledge" ([5], 1147b16–17; emphasis added). Thus, if we take Aristotle at his word here, it seems that there is at least some component of full knowledge that the apparently akratic person lacks. Accordingly, in some important sense, the agent in question is still ignorant of what is best, so the agent's wrongdoing seems to stem fundamentally from an intellectual failure after all.

For Aristotle, a more robust conception of knowledge—full knowledge of the good in this case—seems to be what he refers to as prudence or practical wisdom. Knowledge *qua* practical wisdom is where one both correctly grasps how she should behave and also acts in accordance with that awareness ([5], 1152a8–9). As such, Aristotelian practical wisdom seems roughly similar to what Socrates takes knowledge of the Forms, in general, to be. For Socrates, genuine knowledge of the Forms amounts to a sort of conversion experience, such that if one really has knowledge of the Forms, she is so drawn to the good that she is compelled to act accordingly ([7], 518d–19a). Along similar lines, Julia Annas contends that the

> ... Forms are ... more than theoretical entities in a theory that explains the phenomena; a knowledge of them is part of the *good* person's understanding. Plato sometimes (though not in the *Republic*) talks of one's ascent to the Forms as being one of love and desire, as though the Forms had an attractive force. But this should not be misunderstood: the Forms are not equally attractive to the philosopher and to the clever ruthless exploiter. Rather, Plato thinks that no amount of intelligence will grasp the Forms if it is directed to self-interested and narrow ends ([8], p. 237).

Following Annas, we might say that, for Socrates, if one "knows" the Forms in merely some truncated sense—in what amounts to nothing more than a cognitive grasp of correct propositions—then that person does not really have knowledge of the Forms in any robust sense. And Aristotle's conception of knowledge *qua* practical wisdom seems to align with this robust Socratic conception of knowledge of the Forms.

So perhaps, then, we should read Aristotle as agreeing with Socrates' conception of knowledge on final analysis—that is, if we take knowledge *qua* practical wisdom to be what Aristotle means by full or complete knowledge. Robert Solomon contends, for example, that Aristotle indeed adopts the Socratic conception of knowledge at 1152a8–9. So if it is true that Aristotle adopts this Socratic conception of knowledge, then Aristotle's account of wrongdoing, like Socrates', would imply that full-blown *akrasia* is impossible. Solomon writes:

> Aristotle's use of "knowledge"…is such that no room is left for *akrasia*, for if one acts wrongly, he is, by definition, not practically wise, and thus Aristotle is, in fact, denying *akrasia* in the same manner as Socrates, viz., both claim that the phenomenon of *akrasia* is illusory, for by definition, one cannot act wrongly if he has the appropriate knowledge ([9], p. 15).

Ultimately, then, the question of whether Aristotle's account of wrongdoing allows for the possibility of full-blown *akrasia* seems to turn on the relevant conception of knowledge attributable to him. If Solomon is right, Aristotle adopts the Socratic conception. And if that is correct, then Socrates and Aristotle ultimately agree that robust, open-eyed *akrasia* is impossible. To Solomon's credit, Aristotle himself hints at this interpretation of his view when he admits that, insofar as having knowledge of the universal premise alone would not entail having knowledge to the fullest extent, "even the result Socrates was looking for would seem to come about" ([5], 1147b15). Thus, it seems that Socrates and Aristotle agree that, in every instance of wrongdoing, some form of ignorance is the fundamental source of wrongdoing and, hence, that full-blown, open-eyed *akrasia* is impossible.

4. Augustine on *Akrasia*

Undergraduates sometimes want to resist the Socratic and Aristotelian accounts of wrongdoing, in part because they find the conclusions of those accounts counterintuitive. Their perplexity is enough to reproduce: How can it be that the fundamental root of every wrongdoing is intellectual in nature? Is it not the case that at least some instances of wrongdoing are attributable to problems of the heart, so to speak, and not just problems of the head? In any case, it is unclear that Socrates and Aristotle settle the score on this issue, even if it can be difficult to spot where they go wrong. Fortunately, Augustine offers a sufficiently different approach to the matter, one that may help teachers broaden the discussion.

Now, unlike Socrates, Augustine seems assume that *akrasia* is possible precisely because he thinks it is actual. Consider, for example, his famous depiction of what can seem to be wantonly akratic behavior from his own teenage years:

> There was a pear tree near our vineyard, heavy with fruit, but fruit that was not particularly tempting either to look at or to taste. A group of young blackguards, and I among them, went out to knock down the pears and carry them off late one night, for it was our bad habit to carry on our games in the streets till very late. We carried off an immense load of pears, not to eat—for we barely tasted them before throwing them to the hogs. Our only pleasure in doing it was that it was forbidden. Such was my heart, O God, such was my heart: yet in the depth of the abyss You had pity on it. Let the heart now tell You what it sought when I was thus evil for no object, having no cause for wrongdoing save my wrongness. The malice of the act was base and I loved it—that is to say I loved my own undoing, I loved the evil in me—not the thing for which I did the evil, simply the evil: my soul was depraved, and hurled itself down from security in You into utter destruction, seeking no profit from wickedness but only to be wicked ([10], II.iv.9).

Would this theft constitute an instance of genuine, open-eyed *akrasia*? To address this question, we should pause to consider the reasons the young Augustine may have had for stealing the pears ([11], p. 189).

Augustine labors throughout much of Book 2 of his *Confessions* to identify the underlying motive for his behavior. Did he steal the pears out of need, or perhaps out of a desire to improve his personal holdings? No. Was it for the pleasure of tasting the pears or for the beauty of the stolen fruit? No—after all, he barely even tasted them and, besides, he had even better pears of his own. Was his theft aimed at winning the approval of his blackguard companions, or perhaps to elicit a good laugh? Again, no and no. Admittedly, Augustine insists that he would not have committed the crime had he been alone at the time. And even though he surmises that his "friendship unfriendly" somehow contributed to his desire to commit the crime, he is not convinced that he stole the pears for the sake of the crowd ([10], II.viii.16).

Is there simply no remaining explanation for why the young Augustine stole the pears? Was he simply akratic?

Maybe not. After all, Augustine hypothesizes that perhaps his motive was simply "the *thrill* of acting against Your [God's] law—at least in appearance, since I had no power to do so in fact, the delight a prisoner might have in making some small gesture of liberty—getting a deceptive sense of omnipotence from doing something forbidden without immediate punishment" ([10], II.vi.14; emphasis added). Now, suppose we extend Augustine's hypothesis here. Perhaps the young Augustine thought that the excitement of defying God—together with the exhilaration of vainly trying to place himself above God's authority—was just so titillating that he judged in the moment that stealing the pears was, all things considered, the best course of action. If the young Augustine had reasoned in this way, then the fundamental source of his wrongdoing would not have been *akrasia*, but simply an erroneous judgment about what was best (*viz.*, the mistaken belief that the thrill of defying God trumps obedience to God's law).

Of course, there is a rather big if afloat here because Augustine does not actually indicate that he reasoned through the matter in the way imagined. Instead, he tells us that he stole the pears simply because doing so was forbidden and evil—and not for the thing for which the evil was done. What distresses him about this fact is that it seems to Augustine that evil itself could not be the end for which he acted: "Could you find pleasure only in what was forbidden, and only because it was forbidden?" ([10], II.vi.14). Presumably not. As T. D. J. Chappell notes, "such a motive [doing Φ *because it is forbidden*] seems to him [Augustine] hardly an adequate reason for doing anything!" ([11], p. 189). This is because, as Chappell contends, Augustine affirms the directedness thesis according to which "all voluntary action is rational in the sense of being necessarily directed towards some good or other" ([11], p. 189). The implication, then, is that Augustine's theft was simply inexplicable; to explain it would require a description of the good at which it was aimed, and Augustine has come up short. It appears, then, that the only thing left to say is that the young Augustine suffered from a bad will. Thus, the specter of *akrasia* looms large.

Leave the pear tree episode to the side. At this juncture, it will be helpful to take a step back and appreciate the teleological eudaimonism of Augustine's moral philosophy. For Augustine, the chief end of all human endeavors is to attain happiness—we all desire to live happily, he says ([12], p. 153). Of course, whether a person obtains happiness is ultimately contingent on her various pursuits in life. Augustine characterizes these pursuits as being indicative of what a person really loves: he says, for example, "*Pondus meum amor meus*"—or "my weight is my love" ([13], p. 134). Hence, as Étienne Gilson notes, the basic moral problem for Augustine, "is not *whether* one should love, but *what* one should love" ([14], p. 135).

The object of a person's love is crucial for Augustine because, depending on its worth and the corresponding manner in which one loves and pursues it, one's will is rendered either good or bad accordingly. If one loves what is supremely good—and if one loves it properly and to the appropriate degree—then she has a good will. Alternatively, if one loves inferior things improperly or disproportionately, then her will is bad to that extent. In turn, the moral quality of a person's behavior is driven by the moral quality of her will.

Ultimately, for Augustine, true happiness can be found only in the proper love and pursuit of God, the highest good. Accordingly, we might characterize sin in his view as the misdirected and inordinate love of non-divine things—things inferior to the God who created them—whereby the will is turned away from God in the process. In effect, then, the sinful will does not appropriately love, and thus does not properly pursue, that which is supremely worthy of its affection. In other words, sin is *perversio* from God, where one turns toward and inordinately loves God-inferior things as though they were actually worthy of the love that is appropriate only for what is supremely good. Augustine explains, for example, that while such God-inferior things as human friendship are indeed good and admirable:

> Yet in the enjoyment of all such things, we commit sin if through immoderate inclination to them—for though they are good, they are of the lowest order of good—things higher and better are forgotten, even You, O Lord our God, and Your Truth and Your Law. These lower things have their delights but no such as my God has, for He made them all: *and in Him doth the righteous delight, and He is the joy of the upright of heart.* ([10], II.v.10; emphases in original).

Along similar lines, he writes:

> [W]hen I now asked what is iniquity, I realised that it was not a substance but a *swerving of the will* which is turned towards lower things and away from You, O God, who are the supreme substance: so that it casts away what is most inward to it and swells greedily for outward things ([10], VII.xvi.22; emphasis added).

This is a key passage because it shows that, for Augustine, sin is not a substance created by God. After all, God is omnibenevolent and, thus, cannot be the efficient cause of sin or evil. Rather, sin is a privation of good that occurs when the will turns away from God. Along similar lines, Augustine explains in *City of God* that "the bad will is the cause of bad action" and that nothing beyond the will itself accounts for the badness of the will in question ([12], p. 159). In short, the will becomes bad by "wickedly and inordinately desiring an inferior thing" ([12], p. 160). This is not to say that the perverse will is the efficient cause of evil; rather, the point here is that the inordinate love and pursuit of God-inferior things is simply a description of the evil will.

One of Augustine's most significant contributions to the history of philosophy is his very robust notion of the will; but, of course, his take on it is complex. In his view, a person cannot simply freely will to pursue God without God's help. This is because, prior to receiving God's grace, even though the will may be free in some mundane sense, it is inclined toward, and hence encumbered, by sin. Consider, for example, what Augustine says in his *Enchiridion*:

> For what good work can a lost man perform, except so far as he has been delivered from perdition? Can they do anything by the free determination of their own will? Again, I say, God forbid. For it was by the evil use of his free will that man destroyed both it and himself. For, as a man who kills himself must, of course, be alive when he kills himself, but after he has killed himself ceases to live and cannot restore himself to

life; so, when man by his own free will sinned, then sin being victorious over him, the freedom of his will was lost...Accordingly, he who is the servant of sin is free to sin. And, hence *he will not be free to do right*, until being freed from sin [by grace], he shall begin to be the servant of righteousness ([12], p. 181; emphasis added).

Prior to receiving God's grace, the will is confined to being turned away from God. As such, an agent is capable of loving and pursuing only those things that are inferior to God; yet the agent loves those things as though they were worthy of the inordinate love that she has for them.

The fundamental problem, so it seems, is that the agent in question is mistaken—that is, she mistakenly assumes that God-inferior things are worthy of her utmost love (the love she should reserve solely for the supreme good, God). Consequently, prior to receiving the illumination that comes with God's grace, an agent's sinfulness can be plausibly characterized as being the result of her ignorance of the fact that God's alone is worthy of her utmost love (and, hence, as a result of her ignorance *vis-à-vis* the worth of God-inferior things). Construed in this way, pre-illumination sinfulness for Augustine seems to run parallel to the Socratic view that ignorance of what is best is at the root of moral wrongdoing. In other words, the fundamental source of wrongdoing here is intellectual in nature, and not *akrasia*.

Admittedly, it might be tempting to think that this Augustinian account of pre-illumination sinfulness differs from Socratic intellectualism in an important way that is relevant to the *akrasia* issue. For Socrates, when a person acts wrongly, she is acting in this way because of her of ignorance. The obvious implication is that, had she not been mistaken in her judgment, she would not have erred. For Augustine, though, pre-illumination agents act wrongly (so one might say) not because they hold incorrect beliefs about what is best, but simply because they love improperly. Prior to receiving God's illuminating grace, agents love, say, sexual pleasure or power or even family in the place of loving God with all their hearts. Thus, so the thought goes, while pre-illumination wrongdoers act perhaps *in ignorance*, they do not act wrongly *because of their ignorance*, but because of their inordinate love of God-inferior things.

Note, though, that this sort of move simply shifts the role of ignorance up a level. Why would a person love God-inferior things as though she assumed they were worthy of the love she should reserve for the supreme good? The answer, so it seems, is that she believes that those God-inferior things are worthy of the love they receive (when in fact they are not). Thus, while it is true that pre-illumination wrongdoers are guilty of misdirected and inordinate love, there appears to be a deeper explanation as to why: ignorance concerning what is and is not worthy of one's utmost love seems to be at the root. Accordingly, we might say that pre-illumination wrongdoers act both *in* and *because of* their ignorance concerning what is truly worthy of their highest love.

At any rate, this ignorance can be overcome by the divine illumination that comes with God's grace. For Augustine, divine grace involves both a cognitive and a volitional dimension [15]. He writes:

The grace of God through Jesus Christ our Lord must be understood as that by which alone men are delivered from evil, and without which they do absolutely no good thing, whether in thought, or will or affection, or in deed; not only *in order that they may know* by the manifestation of the same what should be done, but moreover *in order that by its enabling they may do with love* what they know ([12], p. 176; emphases added).

The relevant point here is that, through the special and unmerited acts of divine grace, the individual is made aware that God is the highest good (and hence supremely worthy of her deepest affection); moreover, the individual is given the volitional wherewithal to love and pursue God. Augustine hints at this dual nature of grace in even more dramatic, first-personal terms in his *Confessions*:

> Thou [God] didst call and cry to me and break open my *deafness*: and Thou didst send forth Thy beams and shine upon me and chase away my *blindness*: Though didst breathe fragrance upon me, and I drew in my breath and do now pant for Thee: I tasted Thee, and now *hunger and thirst* for Thee: Thou didst touch me, and I have *burned* for Thy peace ([10], X.xxvii.38; emphases added).

In receiving God's illuminating grace, a person is no longer blind to the fact that God is worthy of one's deepest love nor to the fact that one's inordinate love for God-inferior things should be recalibrated in light of God's supreme worth. Furthermore, the will is emancipated to pursue God, whereas, prior to grace, the will was constrained to pursuing God-inferior things. Augustine refers to this post-grace freedom of the will as "true liberty" ([12], p. 181). The will can now "begin to be the servant of righteousness", take pleasure in righteous pursuits, and freely submit to a "holy bondage" whereby one freely obeys God's will ([12], pp. 181–82).

Nonetheless, despite the fact that divine grace has both a cognitive and a volitional effect on a person, those two effects do not (necessarily) come about simultaneously. In fact, Augustine depicts himself as having been fully aware that God is worthy of his highest love well before he turned his will to love and pursue God with all his strength: "whereas You [God] showed me by every evidence that Your words were true, there was simply nothing I could answer save only laggard and lazy words: 'Soon', 'Quite soon', 'Give me just a little while'." ([10], VIII.v.12). The period between the cognitive effects of divine illumination and the full volitional transformation brought on by God's grace proves significant with respect to the possibility of *akrasia* in Augustine's view. Insofar as divine grace illuminates the true and supremely worthy object of one's love, the individual is now no longer unable to grasp what she ought to turn toward and pursue. Hence, Augustine writes: "I no longer had the excuse which I used to think I had for not forsaking the world and serving You [God], the excuse namely that I had no certain knowledge of the truth" ([10], VIII.v.11). Nonetheless, even she who correctly grasps the highest good can still fail to love and pursue it with all her strength—and thus she can fail to live as she should. The wrongdoer in this case appears to be robustly akratic: she correctly grasps that she should love and pursue God, but she fails to do it anyway.

But how could a person grasp what is best, but nonetheless fail to do it? Augustine's answer is to emphasize the residual effects of pre-grace *perversio* on the will ([16], pp. 93–100). When a person inordinately loves God-inferior things in the place of loving God fully, those perverse desires give way to the cultivation of evil habits, and those habits calcify in such a way that she becomes imprisoned by her old ways of loving God-inferior things. We might say, then, that she becomes encumbered by her old delicious burdens (to twist a line from Walt Whitman). Augustine explains in his own case, for example, that

> I longed for the same chance [the chance to devote himself to God], but I was bound not with the iron of another's chains, but by my own iron will. The enemy held my will; and of it he made a chain and bound me. Because my will was perverse it changed to lust, and lust yielded to become habit, and habit not resisted became necessity. These were like links hanging one on another—which is why I have called it a chain—and their hard bondage held me bound hand and foot. The new will which I now began to have, by which I willed to worship You freely and to enjoy You, O God, the only certain Joy, was not yet strong enough to overcome that earlier will rooted deep through the years. My two wills, one old, one new, one carnal, one spiritual, were in conflict and in their conflict wasted my soul ([10], VIII.v.10).

Here, Augustine seems to locate the source of his wrongdoing not in the intellect, but in the divided and, hence, weakened will. The individual in Augustine's situation grasps what is best (*viz.*, loving and pursuing God), but her will is compromised at this juncture because it is conflicted. On the one hand, through the volitional gifts of divine grace, the individual is now beginning to will to love and pursue God. On the other hand, the will is haunted by the lingering habits of its pre-grace *perversio*, and so it still yearns on some level for God-inferior things.

How can the agent overcome this predicament? For Socrates, since the root of wrongdoing is an intellectual failure, the solution is to improve our intellectual position. We might be tempted to think that, by analogy, since intellectual problems have intellectual solutions, perhaps volitional problems would have volitional solutions for Augustine. That is, we might be tempted to think that the solution here is for the agent to will herself out of the situation.

Robert Pasnau explains why this cannot work. He depicts the will in Augustine's work as being "whatever power within us has [the] final conscious responsibility for triggering action" ([16], p. 97). An agent's will, then, is effectively what issues commands to the agent in question. Unfortunately, though, the will may or may not listen to reason in making its commands. For example, the will might command the agent to turn toward and pursue something that clashes with what the agent grasps as best. It may seem, then, that the only recourse that the agent would have in cases where her will is divided (e.g., in case where she wills to love God, but, due to her old habits, she also wills to love God-inferior things inordinately) is simply to rely on another command of her will. Suppose, then, that the agent issues to herself what Pasnau labels a "metacommand"—say, the metacommand to overcome the will's dividedness and to pursue God full tilt. This would avail nothing because, as Pasnau explains

> The metacommand [to overcome the conflict in the will] can have no more force than the initial command [to love God full tilt], because the metacommand in effect reiterates the initial command…There is nothing beyond will and reason that can take charge and alleviate the agent's predicament. If one's will is weak, there is no higher executive power on hand to provide further motivation. At that point, all one can do is wait for help to arrive ([16], p. 100).

For Augustine, the only solution to the problem of a compromised will is, again, God's grace. Grace, so it seems, is needed both for the initiation of the volitional wherewithal to love and pursue

God in the first place and for the strengthening in that pursuit so that the agent in question can eventually overcome the residual effects of her old ways of loving.

5. Concluding Remarks

Whereas for Augustine an agent's pre-illumination *perversio* can be plausibly characterized as being the result of ignorance, post-grace *perversio* would apparently constitute an instance of genuine, full-blown *akrasia*. Accordingly, in contrast to Socrates and Aristotle, Augustine's account of wrongdoing allows for the possibility that something other than an intellectual failure can be at the fundamental root of an agent's wrongdoing—namely, a compromised will.

Questions remain, though. Is this post-grace *perversio* an instance of robust, open-eyed *akrasia* on final analysis? Or should we say that it is actually the result of some deeper sort of ignorance or misjudgment concerning what is best?

One might be tempted to think that, for Augustine, even post-grace wrongdoers as described above are not robustly akratic precisely because they do not (and cannot) have full and complete knowledge of the supreme good (God) in this life. Full knowledge of God would come only in the beatific vision. Thus, the problem of wrongdoing is still a problem of ignorance on some level, or so it may seem.

Still, though, even if an individual could not obtain complete knowledge of God in this life, it does not follow that she could not come to grasp, by means of God's illuminating grace, that God is supremely good and alone worthy of her utmost love and pursuit. And it seems that only the latter—and not the former—would be needed for *akrasia* to be possible.

So suppose we set that concern to the side. We might still wonder whether post-grace wrongdoers are robustly and genuinely akratic *all the way down*. In other words, we might wonder whether an intellectual failure, as opposed to a volitional failure, is at the very bottom of Augustine's analysis of wrongdoing. Why is this? Post-grace wrongdoing in his view seems to stem from the lingering effects of the will's pre-illumination *perversio* from God—the will is divided and compromised because of entrenched habits formed prior to receiving God's illuminating grace. And it is plausible enough to think that at least some of these habits were formed in and because of the individual's pre-illumination ignorance. Accordingly, the most fundamental source of wrongdoing in these cases would seem to be intellectual in nature, even though this intellectual failure does its damage indirectly by means of compromising the will.

If so, then perhaps we are left with questions about whether Augustine's account of wrongdoing moves somewhat more in the direction of Socratic intellectualism than it may initially seem. In any case, I leave these questions for others with the hope that the foregoing sets the stage for a fruitful conversation to come—one that is helpful for core curriculum teachers who are interested in exploring Augustine's work as a way of supplementing discussions of moral wrongdoing.

Acknowledgments

For helpful comments on previous drafts of this paper, the author thanks the anonymous reviewers of this journal and the attendees of his paper session at "Teaching the Christian Intellectual Tradition" Conference on Augustine (Samford University, Birmingham, AL, USA, 2–4 October 2014).

Conflicts of Interest

The author declares no conflicts of interest.

References and Notes

1. Reinhold Niebuhr. *Man's Nature and His Communities*. New York: Charles Scribner's Sons, 1965. Niebuhr here, it should be noted, is quoting from the *London Times Literary Supplement*.
2. Plato. *Protagoras*. Translated by W.K.C. Guthrie. In *The Collected Dialogues of Plato*. Edited by Edith Hamilton and Huntington Cairns. Princeton: Princeton University Press, 1989, pp. 308–52.
3. Socrates' assumption (that we all desire the good) is articulated in a number of places throughout Plato's dialogues. For example, Socrates expresses this assumption rather explicitly in conversation with Clinias in Plato's *Euthydemus* (278e and following). And, in Plato's *Apology*, Socrates conveys a similar point when he gets Meletus to admit that there is no one who prefers to be harmed (25d–26a).
4. Plato. *Gorgias*. Translated by W.D. Woodhead. In *The Collected Dialogues of Plato*. Edited by Edith Hamilton and Huntington Cairns. Princeton: Princeton University Press, 1989, pp. 229–307.
5. Aristotle. *Nicomachean Ethics*. Translated by Terrence Irwin, 2nd ed. Indianapolis: Hackett Publishing Co., 1985.
6. Aristotle. *Nicomachean Ethics*. Translated by Martin Ostwald. Upper Saddle River: Prentice Hall, 1990.
7. Plato. *Republic*. Translated by Paul Shorey. In *The Collected Dialogues of Plato*. Edited by Edith Hamilton and Huntington Cairns. Princeton: Princeton University Press, 1989, pp. 575–844.
8. Julia Annas. *An Introduction to Plato's Republic*. Oxford: Clarendon Press, 1981.
9. Robert C. Solomon. "Aristotle, the Socratic Principle, and the Problem of *Akrasia*." *Modern Schoolman* 49 (1971): 13–21.
10. Augustine. *Confessions*. Translated by F.J. Sheed, 2nd ed. Indianapolis: Hackett Publishing Co., 2006.
11. T.D.J. Chappell. *Aristotle and Augustine on Freedom: Two Theories of Freedom, Voluntary Action and Akrasia*. New York: St. Martin's Press, 1995.
12. Augustine. *The Essential Augustine*. Edited by Vernon J. Bourke. Indianapolis: Hackett Publishing Co., 1974.
13. Augustine's words quoted in Étienne Gilson. *The Christian Philosophy of Saint Augustine*. Translated by L.E.M. Lynch. London: Victor Gollancz, Ltd., 1961.
14. Étienne Gilson. *The Christian Philosophy of Saint Augustine*. Translated by L.E.M. Lynch. London: Victor Gollancz, Ltd., 1961.

15. We might think that we should separate out divine illumination from the volitional aspect of divine acts of grace and reserve the label of grace exclusively for the latter. For example, Robert Pasnau characterizes divine illumination as being *analogous* to the volitional effects of divine grace, though he does not straightaway depict them as dual features of divine grace. See Robert Pasnau. "Divine Illumination." *The Stanford Encyclopedia of Philosophy*, 2011 Edition. Edited by Edward N. Zalta. Available online: http://plato.stanford.edu/archives/sum2011/entries/illumination/ (accessed on 23 March 2015).
16. Robert Pasnau. "Plotting Augustine's *Confessions*." *Logos: A Journal of Catholic Thought and Culture* 3 (2000): 77–106.

Seeking the Place of Conscience in Higher Education: An Augustinian View[1]

Ian Clausen

Abstract: This article explores the place of conscience in higher education. It begins by reconstructing the place of conscience in Augustine's thought, drawing on Augustine's reading of Genesis 3, the Psalms, and his own spiritual journey. Its basic aim is to clarify Augustine's account of conscience as self-judgment, identifying the conditions under which self-judgment occurs. After identifying these conditions it addresses the question: does conscience still have a place in modern higher education? It acknowledges the real limitations and obstacles to moral education when pursued in the context of the modern research university. However, it also argues that moral education proceeds in stages, and that educators can anticipate and clear a way for the place of conscience—though not, of course, without reliance on the movement of grace.

> Reprinted from *Religions*. Cite as: Clausen, I. Seeking the Place of Conscience in Higher Education: An Augustinian View. *Religions* **2015**, *6*, 286–298.

1. Introduction

Does conscience have a place in liberal arts higher education? What kind of "place" does it refer to or designate, and why does it matter?

While several books denounce the decrepit moral state of modern higher education [1], few suggest that the road to recovery lies on the path to conscience—why? Perhaps because, as Thomas F. Green suggests, conscience continues to bear a negative connotation ([2], p. 21). Its association with religious indoctrination does not endear us to its function ([3], p. 24), while confusion constantly surrounds it as a concept in moral psychology. To this list, one might add that "moral pluralism" in the Academy tends to undermine any robust appeal to the role and significance of conscience, as teachers reasonably assume that conscience ought to remain a private endeavor.

It need not be so. Properly defined, conscience still has the potential to illuminate, helping to mark the ends and also the limits of higher education. This article is one attempt to mark those boundaries by discussing the "place" of conscience in the thought of St. Augustine. Augustine's account of the place of conscience in moral-intellectual development spurs reflection on the moral purposes higher education serves, and demonstrates the obligations educators bear to reality, or "the way things are" (*ordo rerum*), requires clearing up a space for the individual conscience to operate.

In particular, Augustine's account can shed light on the process by which human beings *become* agents in the morally relevant sense. It shows us that to teach with a view to the act of conscience requires teaching with an openness (or receptivity) to reality itself. This requires not only patience on the part of the teacher, but also acknowledgment that education is neither something we

---

[1] This article is a revised version of a paper presented at the "Teaching the Intellectual Tradition" Conference at Samford University, Birmingham, AL, USA, 2–4 October 2014.

achieve—lest we undermine the agent's participation in his or her own development—nor something we *control* by way of strategic engineering. In Augustine's terms, education dances to the rhythms of grace. It can only be anticipated not achieved or controlled for—and that for the simple reason that it involves the work of conscience. What does this work entail, require, and point to?

To answer these questions we proceed from a brief history of conscience (Section 2) to Augustine's account of conscience in theological and biblical terms (Sections 3–5). To conclude, this article draws together Augustine's insights on conscience to discuss the place of conscience in higher education, locating it within the structure of humanistic education. It then raises, but does not answer, the far more ambitious (two-fold) question as to whether and to what extent conscience operates in the Academy, and what are the conditions for its retrieval and flourishing.

2. Putting Conscience in Its Place

Why speak of the *place* of conscience instead of just conscience? The answer lies in the confusion conjured up by the term conscience. For example, it is sometimes thought that conscience circumvents moral judgment. Conscience operates on this view independent of reason and judgment, foreclosing on the moral agent's responsibility to reality. Such a view invests the conscience with an unmediated moral authority; it permits only obedience in response to its dictates. This abolishes the intermediary function conscience serves in the moral life, collapsing the moral life into brute moral intuition.

For the history behind this (later) development on the operations of conscience, we turn to Oliver O'Donovan [4,5]. O'Donovan beings by tracing conscience to its Greco-Roman context in which the term tended to denote simply *moral self-consciousness*: "especially that uneasy awareness that one has of oneself when one knows one has done something wrong" ([4], p. 114). Such awareness finds acute expression in the thinking of St. Paul, who, though refraining from elaborating its full operation, bequeaths to subsequent Christians a view of conscience as universal ([6], pp. 134–35). It is only when Christian thinkers begin developing Paul's thoughts—in combination with earlier thoughts in Greco-Roman culture—that conscience attains a wider function than simply moral self-consciousness. It begins to take on a discursive role in the moral reasoning process, establishing a new sphere for human responsibility and judgment. O'Donovan explains:

> "[c]onscience in the Christian tradition has been a consistently *discursive* self-consciousness, a roomy mental space for reflection and deliberation, where every kind of information was at home, and above all information about the redemptive goodness of God. Conscience was memory in responsibility, the workshop of practical reason, a formal rather than an efficient or final cause. Insofar as it laid claim to authority, it was simply the believer's authority to reach decisions reflectively rather than accept decisions made for him by others—an authority conceived dialectically in response to that of the church to give moral counsel" ([5], p. 302).

Here, conscience funds the wider operations of human agency and judgment. It is the act by which human beings become reflective and responsible agents, locating their "moral placement" in a network of moral relations ([7], pp. 13–15). This view implies that agency is a process not a presupposition. Conscience is not a power we simply "have" as human beings—as in a faculty psychology—but is a process we must undergo to recover our freedom ([8], pp. 6–17; [9]). It further implies a prior alienation and ignorance of the moral life, in which the road to recovery lies on the abandoned path of conscience. Thus, it also intimates that the moral life is a journey. It is a journey on which each of us plays a role in determining our course, yet not without bearing obligations to reality as we encounter it.

In sum, conscience represents a beginning-point not an end-point. Better still, it is an *entryway* to the life we are called to live: the life of moral agency, accountability, and judgment, all of which implies responsibility to the reality of "the way things are" (*ordo rerum*).

In contrast to this "ancient" view of the intermediate place of conscience, O'Donovan argues that the modern view tends to displace judgment altogether. In fact it threatens to displace the moral agent as well, since it tends to overtake the agent's responsibility to deliberate towards action. The modern view of conscience as unmediated moral authority is typified, according to O'Donovan, by Bishop Butler's famous characterization. "'[Conscience is that] superior principle…which distinguishes between the internal principles of (the) heart…which without being consulted, without being advised with, magisterially exerts itself…and which, if not forcibly stopped, naturally and always of course goes on to anticipate a higher and more effectual sentence'" ([4], p. 118). By arguing that conscience dictates what ought (not) to be done, Butler depicts it as an "arbitrary tyrant" rather than helpmate to moral reasoning ([4], p. 118). Its authority no longer derives from the order of moral reality, that to which our agency is called to respond, but asserts its own authority to which the agent has no access—that access being impeded by the usurpation of judgment ([5], pp. 302–03).

By speaking of the *place* of conscience—to return to our original query—we underscore the role of conscience in pursuit of self-possession. To occupy the place of conscience is to re-possess moral self-consciousness: that is, the state preliminary to the act of judgment, action, and—for Augustine at least—confession to God. As such, conscience rings synonymous with agency, responsibility, basically anything that lifts humanity into the realm of the moral life. Perhaps the better metaphor to use is that of *illumination*, exposing an agent's responsibility to the reality of "the way things are". In any event, the crucial insight to take forward in this discussion is that *agency implies a process*—though not an automatic process. Instead it is more than possible and indeed, unfortunately, more than likely, that agents fail to "heed the call" that animates the moral life.

More on that anon. However, before we attend to an agent's failure to heed the call, let us first attend to the nature of the call itself. To do so we turn attention to the thought of St. Augustine, particularly his account of the fall of humanity in Genesis. By uncovering for us the foundation on which the place of conscience rests, Augustine reveals the fundamental *question* at the center of the moral life—and by extension the fundamental question at the center of education.

3. The Place of Conscience in Genesis 3: Augustine's Reading of the Fall

In Augustine's account of humanity's Fall in Genesis 3, conscience emerges as a (moral) place of divine encounter and self-judgment. Adam and Eve, through sin, have abandoned that place, opting to "hide" the truth (and hide *from* the truth) of their compromised position. The story, as Augustine reads it, reveals the evasion of moral self-consciousness by recounting humanity's refusal to assume responsibility for its agency. By preferring to pass blame rather than step forward to confess, Adam and Eve lay the foundation for the habit of self-deception. And yet—a very important yet—despite laying such a foundation, Adam and Eve do not manage to displace conscience altogether. It continues to be "held in place", though not by the ones who abandoned it, but by the God who deigns to address them—and humanity through them—with a simple, startling question.

On this question hangs a great deal, or at least we plan to argue. Augustine, it is true, does not seem to take much interest in it; but what he says lends support to our account of the place of conscience. The relevant details of the Genesis 3 story may be summed up as follows: Adam and Eve are tempted by the serpent to disobey God, and do in fact disobey God to their exposure and loss of innocence. Upon hearing God walking *in the cool of the day* (Genesis 3:8, RSV), Adam and Eve hide in fear of God and (perhaps) fear of punishment, and God responds to their apparent absence by speaking out loud a question: *Where are you?* (Genesis 3:9).

In commenting on this part, and in view of Manichean literalism, Augustine clarifies what God's question does *not* in fact betray. It does not betray divine ignorance or anything of the sort. To insist on this reading is not only blasphemous to God; it also repeats the very error that God's question seeks to highlight. By interpreting God's question in a flat-footed way, perhaps attempting to heap ridicule on the bumbling God of the Old Testament, the reader merely showcases his own ignorance and blindness to sin, failing to perceive that God's question is not intended for God's benefit *but for ours*. It extends to us, that is an invitation to confess—in other words, to step forward and re-occupy the place of conscience. "Adam is now questioned by God", Augustine writes, "not because God doesn't know where he is, but in order to oblige him to confess his sin" ([10], 2.16.24).

Further on, Augustine diagnoses Adam and Eve as suffering the sin of pride. It is pride not only in their outright disobedience, but pride in trying to cover up that disobedience with excuses. Despite God's invitation to confess their disobedience, Adam and Eve fail to "own up" to their complicity in sin, and end up abandoning the meeting-place of God and humanity. "What else is pride, after all, but leaving the inner sanctum of conscience [*deserto secretario conscientiae*] and wishing to be seen outwardly as what in fact one is not?" ([10], 2.5.6). The scene that perfectly captures this abandonment in Genesis is not the outright disobedience of Adam and Eve, but their subsequent denial of any blame in the matter even to the point of accusing God for sin.

> Next, as is the way with pride, [Adam] doesn't plead guilty to being the woman's accomplice, but instead puts all the blame for his own fault on the woman; and in this way, with a subtlety seeming to spring from the cunning the poor wretch had conceived, he wanted to lay his sinning at the door of God himself. He didn't just say, you see, "The woman gave it to me", but more fully: *The woman whom you gave to me* (Gen. 3:12; [10], 2.17.25).

For Augustine, Adam's response amounts to more than evasion of blame, but constitutes a subtle effort to displace God as judge. It represents the failure of self-judgment and abandonment of conscience, which works to obscure humanity's place beneath the judgment-seat of God.

Had Adam and Eve been successful in seizing God's place, the possibility of returning to truth would no longer remain. Responsibility *to* truth would cease to exist, effecting the displacement of conscience as a witness. Thus, Adam and Eve would ever remain in their deception and (willful) ignorance, having recourse to no authority outside their own volition. Of course, Augustine thinks that no such scheme can be successful. It is one thing to abandon conscience as an act of defiant will, another to abolish conscience whose witness depends on truth. Truth, or rather God, upholds the place of conscience, as God refuses to allow the self-destruction of his creation. Such is the implication of God's question *Where are you?* that humanity remains haunted by its ceaseless wandering state, yet in that haunting retains a trace of a prior invitation.

This suggests that to re-occupy the abandoned place of conscience, one must re-hear without delusion the question *Where are you?* It posits a kind of origin-tale of the human intellectual endeavor: that in inheriting a displacement in the manner of their own existence, humans face questions about their origin, nature and destiny that continually elude their investigations into the truth of the world. Driven to ask questions about the world they inhabit, they forget that it is a world that *they* inhabit, and inhabit uneasily, leaving them devoid of self-knowledge and openness to truth ([11], 4.1). However, the claim to which the Genesis story alludes, and Augustine captures, is that God has not abandoned his creation without question. The hope remains that God's question, and myriad questions leading up to it, can entice humanity to re-enter the place we call conscience.

That at least is one way to interpret Genesis 3. As an overarching or implicit framework for conceiving the human quest, it reveals that such a quest has been generated by a question—and not a question that we have raised or imposed on ourselves, but a question that confronts us from outside our own existence. In re-entering the sphere of conscience in response to this question, we enter upon the beginnings of our creaturely confession.

4. Augustine's Innovations on Conscience

It is unlucky that in the otherwise comprehensive encyclopedia *Augustine through the Ages* (Eerdmans: 1999), the editors opted not to include an entry for the term *conscientia*. It is unlucky not least because, on the witness of not a few scholars, Augustine writes a formative chapter in the history of conscience [12,13]. We already observed this at work in his account of Genesis 3. There, conscience corresponds to the act of self-judgment (or its failure), thus explaining the poor judgment Adam and Eve exercise in God's presence. It also shows that God's judgment ultimately prevails over this misjudgment, thus preserving the possibility of future repentance by not allowing human sin to have the final word.

God's question *Where are you?* holds the conscience in place. It is a question we might interpret as suspended over humanity, haunting its every enquiry, animating its every step, and enticing it ever further into the open air of truth. As Abraham Heschel comments in his aptly titled book, *God in Search of Man*: "It is a call that goes out again and again. It is a small voice, not uttered in words, not conveyed in categories of the mind, but ineffable and mysterious, as ineffable and mysterious as the glory that fills the whole world. It is wrapped in silence; concealed and subdued, yet it is as if all things were the frozen echo of the question: *Where art thou?*" ([14], p. 137).

For Augustine, conscience constitutes that inward self-awareness through which the soul is called and challenged by the authority of truth. Having set out the place of conscience in the (post-lapsarian) human condition, we turn to its larger significance within Augustine's intellectual framework, and in particular its operations in relation to God and truth.

In his exposition of Psalm 5, Augustine integrates the work of conscience into the journey of the soul's desire for truth, wisdom, and happiness. We ought to trust no one on our journey to truth but God, he argues, for God alone "sees" us and guides us to himself. Hence, "for that reason we must take flight within, to our conscience, the place where God sees" ([15], 5.11). In taking flight within we are turning to the heart; this is the inner chamber in which we call out to God, and where God is able to hear us "by the majesty of his presence" ([15], 5.2). His idea is that conscience is not a faculty we possess, but a place we must *run to* in recollecting the self. The process of re-collecting the moral self before God, moreover, includes re-inhabiting the place of conscience so that God can enter us—so that God may speak to us *in and through* conscience.

Thus, Augustine holds that "[i]t is in turning to reflect upon the mind's *conscientia* that we meet with God so as to share with God a true judgment about ourselves" ([12], p. 195). Conscience provides a "home" not just for us but for God, and serves as a primary medium through God communicates with us ([15], 30(4).8). At this point, it should be clarified that God's presence within conscience does not preclude the act of human judgment, but rather reinforces it. As Manfred Svensson rightly argues in his account of the Augustinian conscience, Augustine's integration of conscience into his account of illumination does not entail an ontologist theory of divinely imparted knowledge. "[H]is insistence on conscience as *vox Dei*…by no means excludes the idea that conscience is a part of the process of moral reasoning… Augustine's conception of conscience is not a form of inner illumination that confers moral certainty apart from reason, sense and emotion, but rather an act of judgment integrates these faculties and activities in the search for a good life" ([13], p. 51).

Even so, Augustine further innovates on the meaning of conscience when he suggests that *who we meet in conscience* is none other than Christ himself ([12], pp. 195–98). This arises from his attempt to combine Platonic and Christian elements—in what manner and to what effect is widely disputed—to fund his theory of human knowledge as "divine illumination" [16]. Here is not the place to weigh in on this theory's claims, except to note that at its core lies an emphasis on creaturely dependence, and concurrently on the movement or "intervention" of divine grace to secure true self-knowledge apart from deception. In short, illumination involves turning the soul "inside out" so that it stands before the light of truth naked and unfurled. The authority that summons forward the soul through conscience is the same authority that summoned creatures into existence *ex nihilo*, and that continued to summon creatures even after their disobedience: in short, the Word of God and true Teacher of all, Jesus Christ (John 1:1; Matthew 23:9–10). For Augustine this is more than pious sentiment or religious ornament, but addresses the intimate penetration of human darkness by divine light. God communicates to us not simply through a question. Supremely, we might say, he became the question *for us* in Christ.

Correspondingly, it must be acknowledged how dark the darkness is: how difficult it is to re-occupy the obscured place of conscience. In a passage probing the power and extent of self-deception (*Confessions*, 10), a diagnosis that could double as a commentary on Genesis 3, Augustine highlights the conflicting motives of the soul in relation to truth, singling out its unwillingness to stand corrected by the truth. It may be read to address the difficulties any educator faces in attempting to bring students into contact with the human condition. Augustine asks:

> But why is it that "truth engenders hatred"? Why does your man who preaches what is true become to them an enemy (Galatians 4:16) when they love the happy life which is simply joy grounded in truth? The answer must be this: their love for truth takes the form that they love something else and want this object of their love to be the truth; and because they do not wish to be deceived, they do not wish to be persuaded that they are mistaken. And so they hate the truth for the sake of the object which they love instead of the truth. They love truth for the light it sheds, and hate it when it shows them up as being wrong (John 3:20; 5:35)…Yes indeed: the human mind, so blind and languid, shamefully and dishonourably wishes to hide, and yet does not wish anything to be concealed from itself. But it is repaid on the principle that while the human mind lies open to the truth, truth remains hidden from it. ([17], 10.22.34).

Human beings on this account face a problem indeed: they are a "bundle" of conflicting loves which resist true judgments ([18], p. 256). Here love of truth rubs up against love of happiness, and both of these are deflected and deformed by yet another love—the wish not to be deceived. The desire not to be deceived or persuaded one is wrong—as Adam and Eve in the Garden—distils a common obstacle to educational formation. It is the result of several factors that hardens the heart, but for Augustine, it can be reduced to one desire in particular: inordinate self-love, pride.

On this view, individuals not willing to occupy the place of conscience, hiding from "the question" at the center of existence (or at least "fallen" existence), have instead elected themselves as the arbiters of truth, rejecting the very condition for the possibility of judgment. In evacuating the place of conscience they adopt a different posture, one that screens out unsettling facts and questions about themselves, but which in turn impairs their judgment by inflating their vantage point—and from so lofty a position they are unable to perceive the truth. Their problem has less to do with their capacity to reason, and more with the desires that mal-form their perceptions.

All this being admitted, and the place of conscience remains. God has not withheld from us the question *Where are you?* Therein lies our hope for the renewal of conscience, not only in religious but in educational terms as well—though of course, such a distinction would be lost on Augustine (see below). As long as we are wandering, and no matter where we are heading, there is "'still a little light'. May they walk, may they indeed walk, 'so that the darkness does not capture them' (John 12:35)" ([17], 10.22.33).

5. Augustine's Journey to Conscience

It has been shown that Augustine locates the activity of conscience at the center of the divine-human encounter in Genesis. In re-occupying the place of conscience humanity "opens up" to truth, becoming receptive of and susceptible to the question of existence. It is not for the sake of conscience that one re-occupies conscience. Such is the result of some contact with truth—an illumination made possible by the activity of grace—yet which also requires something *from us* as well, namely a desire or willingness desire to know. Dialectic is one mode by which this process unfolds. But dialectic alone cannot generate self-awareness, nor can it engineer or control its development. It can only invite human beings into the place of conscience, putting to them some question that captures their interest. Those questions extend invitations to embark on a quest, to submit to the end that one dimly perceives and wants (if they do). In contrast, by avoiding God's invitation to communicate, Adam and Eve followed pride to an ultimate displacement. They no longer "hear the question" as a summons and a commandment, but instead became too proud to place themselves within it.

It should be noted that Augustine's dichotomy between "pride" and "humility"—the evasion or embrace of conscience, as we interpreted it above—should be taken as two extremes demarcating the boundaries of the moral life. It is not, for this reason, strictly applicable to individual people, even Adam and Eve, as one is never *either* full of pride *or* full of humility (at least in this life), but a bundle of conflicting loves gives ground to each one. Pride and humility have a foot in each of us.

Moreover, this mixture can make for occasionally contradictory responses. Humility may prevail in response to *this* object, yet fail to transfer over to another (perhaps more worthy) object, all in a seamless sequence from one object to the other. The problem has little to do with a failure to "employ" humility—as if humility, and the virtues in general, could be selected willy-nilly. Neither does it stem from some prior failure to "teach values"—a phrase Green condemns as the modern educator's "grand delusion". In the first case, it is incorrect to treat virtues as shelf items from which students can simply draw whenever opportunity demands. Humility is not the product of individual making. It is begotten *within us* through encounter with truth (or beauty, wisdom, *etc.*). In the second case, it is incorrect and misleading to advocate that educators "teach values" as part of their curriculum. Such moralizing discourse reinforces the assumption that values are items that we choose to possess. Lost from view in this assumption that *individuals* have values, however, is that *things* have value independent of our estimation. Encountering those "valuables" (or "goods", in traditional terms) constitutes the real agenda of moral education. "The transformation in our vocabulary of value", Green writes, "is not simply a different way of talking. It represents a different way of seeing things, a different way of being. It creates an entirely different kind of world" ([2], p. 125). As pointed out decades ago by philosopher George Grant (channeling Nietzsche and Heidegger), our modern emphasis on "values" betrays a technological culture that cannot countenance, let alone contemplate, the truth of "the way things are" ([19], pp. 40–43). If reality is "of God" as creation and gift, to receive it as such requires acknowledging its source. That implies humility, an openness to receive *what is*.

In short, Augustinian humility requires *attention to reality*. One is humbled not by exerting a will to be humble, but by allowing reality to penetrate to the soul's inmost depths: that is, to conscience. This is part and parcel of the Christian Platonist tradition. It sets the stage for understanding the educational endeavor as something we neither will nor control in any immediate sense, but which we nevertheless can contribute to as communicators of the question.

Simone Weil, another Christian Platonist, brilliantly captures this point in distinguishing between the exercise of attention and will: "We have to try to cure our faults by attention and not by will…What could be more stupid than to tighten up our muscles and set our jaws about virtue, or poetry, or the solution of a problem. Attention is something quite different" ([20], pp. 116–17). Indeed, the former corresponds to the sin of pride and lack of grace, whereas the latter "presupposes faith and love" and is even a form of prayer. Such a distinction further clarifies two episodes in Augustine's journey that usefully highlight the place of conscience in humanity's intellectual development.

The first episode marks the beginning of Augustine's journey to God. In the midst of a tumultuous period full of conflicting desires and emotions, Augustine recalls his powerful encounter with a specific author and book: Cicero's *Hortensius*. Praising Cicero in *De beata vita* (386) and over a decade later in *Confessiones* (397–401), Augustine confesses he was ignorant at what actually was taking place, yet recalls the indisputable presence of a desire to seek wisdom. In *De beata vita*, that desire is combined with a suggestive phrase, *factus erectior*, to indicate what precisely his awakening consisted in: "And after I had been made more upright [*factus erectior*], I scattered that fog and was convinced that I should yield to those who teach rather than who command obedience" ([21], 1.4).

R. J. O'Connell convincingly argues that the phrase *factus erectior* is best taken in a positive sense as relating back to Cicero [22]. In setting Cicero forth as a catalyst to re-formation, the passage suggests that Cicero's impact on Augustine at the time led our author to *take responsibility for the act of rational judgment*. *Erectior* derives from *erigere*, which can be taken in two senses: negatively, as an arrogation of lofty self-esteem, and positively, as an occupation with loftier thoughts. The latter better accords with Cicero's positive influence, and the emphasis Augustine places on seeking out "those who teach". The phrase in fact corresponds with Augustine's later account of Genesis 2, where God is said to have made Adam "upright" [*erectus*] to the image of God ([10], 1.27.28). That alone is highly suggestive given Cicero is a pagan, implying Augustine was truly open to discovering wisdom "wherever found". The greater point is that Augustine did not work for this experience, did not expect it to happen, and did ecognition—as is his aim throughout *Confessiones*, admittedly—that "education" unfolds in circumstances not wholly under our control. There is nothing we can do to engineer a meaningful outcome. Conscience, if it takes place, takes place without our will.

The second episode immediately follows the account of the first episode, and does so for a reason. Effective as Cicero is in evoking desire, Cicero does not resolve Augustine's condition overnight. Cicero positions him to find out he *has* a condition, and one in need of addressing; but this judgment does not arrive right away for Augustine, but is worked out in dialectical tension with his longing for wisdom. In discovering his love *for* wisdom, though, Augustine does begin to step out from hiding. He enters upon the journey he was always already on, returning step by step to the abandoned place of conscience. In doing so he lets light shine on his desires and attachments: both the objects he should desire and the ones he should not, intensifying his self-judgment in response to the truth. The difference this makes can be seen by way of contrast with his subsequent attempt to "find wisdom" in the pages of Holy Scripture.

This episode starkly contrasts with the Cicero-encounter by emphasizing the lingering effects of pride on Augustine. It is partly because Cicero's book did not mention "the name of Christ" ([17], 3.4.8) that Augustine seeks wisdom in the pages of Scripture. What he finds in those pages fails to impress him. Nothing very sophisticated rhetorically or philosophically, and certainly no match for Cicero's flowing prose. Promptly Augustine turns away from it disappointed and offended. The Bible, he feels, is simply beneath him, the irony of which he comes to recognize and develop in the passage. The Bible defies pretentiousness through its consistently humble idiom. Therein lies its power and wisdom and strength—access to which is barred to those lofty-minded *philosophes*, such as Augustine thought he was, but which appeals to those seekers who are humble, receptive, and patient with the disclosure of whatever God intends. "I was not in any state to be able to enter into that", writes Augustine, "or to bow my head to climb its steps…My inflated conceit shunned the Bible's restraint, and my gaze never penetrated to its inwardness…I disdained to be a little beginner. Puffed up with pride, I considered myself a mature adult" ([17], 3.5.9).

And to the extent he regarded himself as above the divine revelation, Augustine could not entertain the questions it communicated. Of course, not every "failure" to encounter the question boils down to a failure to submit oneself to illumination. It may be that a certain work fails to capture a student (or certain students), or suffers under mitigating circumstances that render its question silent. Insofar as history confirms the value of a book—or in case of religious belief, its divine inspiration—the struggle to comprehend and to contemplate its contents cannot always be qualified by appeal to circumstance. In the end, truth demanded full acknowledgment of those motivations, desires, ambitions, *et cetera*, which ultimately prevented Augustine from inhabiting the place of conscience. Thus, it is in the case of higher education, we might say, where the curriculum is an invitation to take up and (re-)read.

6. Conclusions

Augustine offers us an account of conscience as the act of self-judgment. Lured into the open by a question of some kind, the soul begins to "stand up" to take responsibility for its judgment. The Latin root for education according to Green is *educo*: a "leading forth" into knowledge, as opposed to merely transmitting it. The Romans described the process a few different ways, sometimes using verbs such as *instruere* ("insert") or *instituere* ("to place in order to remain upright") ([2], p. 43). Education on this view is not detached but self-involving. It requires something from us as active participants—for we are the ones summoned (invited even) to respond to the question.

If that is so, what is the place of conscience in higher education? How does Augustine help us think about its role and limitations? We bear in mind Augustine's ignorance of the institution called "the modern research university". Widespread distribution of the good of education was not thinkable in his age, even as it is difficult to achieve in ours; and that is to leave aside the larger question of God, or religious consciousness, so crucial to his philosophy and so contested in ours.

That said, the Augustinian conscience helps to clarify certain goals. One goal that defines (or ought to define) modern education is the act of self-judgment in pursuit of the truth. Not that education seeks self-judgment as an object itself, but self-judgment *follows as a consequence* of seeking (or waiting on) truth. To make room for conscience is to make room for self-judgment; and self-judgment is only possible where truth is acknowledged. Education, therefore, which is committed to the pursuit of truth, likewise can be said to have a place for the activity of conscience.

There is more to say. Self-judgment is self-*judgment*, implying there is something to judge (*i.e.*, reality, truth). Self-judgment is also *self*-judgment, implying a form of freedom. Not the "freedom" that assumes no responsibility to "the way things are", but the freedom *to make* judgments based on a given reality. Personal experience plays a role here as an entryway to discussion, helping us to uncover the question(s) we need to ask. Experience does not contain everything we want to say or have to say, but neither can it be discounted as a "way in" to conscience. In short, Augustine holds that to educate with a view to conscience, one must teach with a view to students as *agents in the world*, as individuals summoned on the journey of the moral life.

One must teach with a view to the *human condition*, therefore, the truth of which unfolds on the journey of the moral life. Higher education has a role to play on this journey to truth; but educators should neither seek to control its development, nor assume that *only* higher education (or liberal arts) can draw out the truth. As Gilbert Meilaender points out in a recent essay on higher education:

> The liberal arts should help us to understand the truth about our lives—which means, in part, the truth of our contingency and neediness, and, ultimately, our dependence on the divine. An openness to what transcends us is what the "leisure" that is study of the liberal arts should, at its best, cultivate. It seeks not power but wisdom, not to change the world but to know it in truth. And to know the world truly is to know it as creation, as a gift that invites our gratitude more than our mastery ([24], pp. 107–08).

Meilaender proceeds by questioning the assumption that a liberal arts education is the only or even the best way to form moral agents. At its best, it may do this for some but not others; and should we not be grateful that it is not the *only* means?

Perhaps we should. For as has long been argued the "modern research university", as a reflection of the "modern age" of which it partakes (and, of course, contributes to), is increasingly inhospitable to the place of individual conscience. In elevating knowledge *production* over knowledge *transmission* (or virtuous formation), the university has ceased to entertain the question of existence, eroding the foundational element of the humanistic disciplines.

Twenty years ago, Mark Schwehn in *Exiles from Eden* raised precisely this worry with modern higher education. Schwehn pointed out that modern educators, in their very use of terms "production" and "transmission" ([25], p. 14), betray commitment to a technocratic culture bent on *making* truth not *knowing* it—and certainly not *acknowledging* or *contemplating* its giftedness. Implicit to this shift in how we think about knowledge, Schwehn argued, lurks an intellectual perspective drawn from the legacy of Max Weber ([25], pp. 3–21). The resultant "Weberian ethos" conditions administrators and educators to view knowledge as "mastering" a subject of increasing specialization.

This "Weberian ethos" also has its corresponding virtues, some of which stand in direct contrast to the Augustinian tradition. "[O]n Weber's account, the process of knowledge formation, if conducted rationally, really does favor and cultivate the emergence of a particular personality type. And this personality does exhibit virtues—clarity, but not charity; honesty, but not friendliness; devotion to the calling, but not loyalty to particular and local communities of learning" ([25], p. 18). According to Schwehn, this observation ought to undercut the illusion (still present in much talk of "secularism") that education not only can but *must* remain "morally neutral". If that were possible the university would be a very different place (or *no*-place). Any ethos implies its own set of privileged norms and virtues, and honest reflection on the habits educators endorse and promote—the "ideal" academic, say—reveals moral judgments they have made or allowed others to make for them.

If our argument about the place of conscience in education proves persuasive, then it follows that to "make room" for conscience in higher education, educators must remain open to the possibility of illumination. Or to put this in the idiom of the Genesis 3, educators must strain to hear the "question of existence" neither by forcing an encounter with its total obligation, nor by stifling the possibility of such an encounter in the long run (or short). Instead, as part of their resistance to the corrosive effects of Weberian rationalism, they must keep alive the questions that call forth our humanity, and that allow for the possibility of (re-)receiving our humanity afresh.

The educator who teaches with a view to conscience, then, has at least a haunting sense that there is something to be found. They believe that there is something that has already been found, perhaps, and that nothing we produce can suffice to contain it, nor prevent it from calling out to us through the authority of conscience. "You, Lord, are my judge…you, Lord, know everything about the human person; for you made humanity" ([17], 10.5.7).

Acknowledgments

The author gratefully acknowledges the contributions to this paper made by audience members at the "Teaching the Intellectual Conference" held at Samford University, Birmingham, AL, USA, on the weekend of 2–4 October 2014. The author also bears a debt to two anonymous reviewers whose comments improved this paper from its original version.

Conflicts of Interest

The author declares no conflict of interest.

References and Notes

1. Many examples could be cited, e.g., William Deresiewicz. *Excellent Sheep: The Miseducation of the American Elite and the Way to a Meaningful Life*. New York: Free Press, 2014.
2. Thomas F. Green. *Voices: The Educational Formation of Conscience*. Notre Dame: University of Notre Dame Press, 1999.
3. Beryl W. Holtam. *Let's Call It What It Is: A Matter of Conscience: A New Vocabulary for Moral Education*. Rotterdam: Sense Publishers, 2012.
4. Oliver O'Donovan. *Resurrection and Moral Order: An Outline for Evangelical Ethics*, 2nd ed. Grand Rapids: Eerdmans, 1994.
5. Oliver O'Donovan. *The Ways of Judgment*. Grand Rapids: Eerdmans, 2005.
6. Ernest Fortin. "The Political Implications of St. Augustine's Theory of Conscience." *Augustinian Studies* 1 (1970): 133–52.
7. Oliver O'Donovan. *Common Objects of Love: Moral Reflection and the Shaping of Community*. Grand Rapids: Eerdmans, 2002.
8. Oliver O'Donovan. *Self, World, and Time: Ethics as Theology, an Induction*. Grand Rapids: Eerdmans, 2012, vol. 1.
9. For further reflection on social dimension of free agency and responsibility, framed with a view to advances in neuroscience, see Michael Gazzaniga. *Who's in Charge?: Free Will and the Science of the Brain*. New York: HarperCollins, 2012.
10. Augustine. "On Genesis: A Refutation of the Manichees." In *On Genesis*. Translated by Edmund Hill. New York: New City Press, 2002, pp. 39–102.

11. Augustine. *The Trinity*. Translated by Edmund Hill. New York: New City Press, 1991, pp. 152–53.
12. Ryan N.S. Topping. *Happiness and Wisdom: Augustine's Early Theology of Education*. Washington: The Catholic University of America Press, 2012.
13. Manfred Svensson. "Augustine on Moral Conscience." *The Heythrop Journal* 54 (2013): 42–54.
14. Abraham Heschel. *God in Search of Man: A Philosophy of Judaism*. London: Souvenir Press, 2009.
15. Augustine. *Expositions of the Psalm, 1–32*. New York: New City Press, 2000, vol. 1.
16. Lydia Schumacher. *Divine Illumination: The History and Future of Augustine's Theory of Knowledge*. West Sussex: Wiley-Blackwell, 2011, pp. 1–24.
17. Augustine. *Confessions*. Translated by Henry Chadwick. Oxford: Oxford University Press, 1998.
18. For the phrase "bundle of loves" see Eric Gregory. *Politics and the Order of Love: An Augustinian Ethic of Democratic Citizenship*. Chicago: Chicago University Press, 2008.
19. George Grant. *Technology and Empire*. Ontario: Anansi, 1986.
20. Simone Weil. "Attention and Will." In *Gravity and Grace*. Translated by Emma Crawford and Mario von der Ruhr. London: Routledge, 2002, pp. 116–22.
21. Augustine. "The Happy Life." In *Trilogy on Faith and Happiness: Augustine of Hippo*. Edited by Boniface Ramsey. Translated by Roland Teske. New York: New City Press, 2010, pp. 9–54.
22. R.J. O'Connell. "On Augustine's First Conversion: Factus Erectior (De Beata Vita 4)." *Augustinian Studies* 17 (1986): 15–29.
23. John Hammond Taylor. "St. Augustine and the 'Hortensius' of Cicero." *Studies in Philology* 60 (1963): 487–98.
24. Gilbert Meilaender. "Who Needs a Liberal Education?" *The New Atlantis* 41 (2014): 101–08.
25. Mark R. Schwehn. *Exiles from Eden: Religion and the Academic Vocation in America*. Oxford: Oxford University Press, 1993.

Modern Restlessness, from Hobbes to Augustine

Peter Busch

Abstract: Only with difficulty do modern readers grasp the full import of Augustine's confession, "Restless is our heart, until it rests in you", or seriously consider that it might be true. An unexpected remedy is to be found in reading Thomas Hobbes, who introduces and defends the view of happiness that is now commonly accepted without argument. According to Hobbes, human beings find their happiness not in a single, supreme good but in many objects, the securing of which requires a lifelong quest for power. But this teaching, influential and revealing though it is, fails to satisfy. Meditating on that dissatisfaction is a first step towards more serious engagement with Augustine.

Reprinted from *Religions*. Cite as: Busch, P. Modern Restlessness, from Hobbes to Augustine. *Religions* **2015**, *6*, 626–637.

1. Introduction

Why read Augustine "across the curriculum"[1]—in courses that do not settle in any particular specialty, but sojourn among them all? One answer would note the many discoveries to be made in a variety of disciplines. When students encounter a mind as incisive and fertile as Augustine's, they are bound to learn something, not only in theology but likewise in philosophy, psychology, political science, history, and literature. True as that reply may be[2], however, I see an even more important reason for including Augustine in certain interdisciplinary courses. When students study Augustine alongside the seminal thinkers of modernity, they can begin to question the assumptions and preoccupations that prejudice most modern readers against him, and they can turn, or return, to Augustine with the urgency and care needed for understanding his writings and the truth found in or through them.

This thesis is based on more than ten years' experience as a teacher of beginners and as a beginner myself. My discussion here will draw on that experience and will often be anecdotal or personal in its argument. If that approach is unusual among scholars, it is likely to be helpful for teachers whose students are finding their way to the *Confessions*.

2. Struggling to Read Augustine

Villanova is a Roman Catholic institution founded by the Order of Saint Augustine. The importance of Augustine for undergraduate education at our university is clear in the "Augustine and Culture Seminar", a two-semester course required of every student. In the first semester, "Ancients", students read books of Greek and Roman antiquity alongside the Bible, and they see how

---

[1] This essay began as a paper presented at the conference "Augustine across the Curriculum", Samford University, Birmingham, AL, USA, 2–4 October 2014.

[2] For numerous examples of how Augustine fruitfully intersects with many different disciplines and themes in the academy, consider the series *Augustine in Conversation: Tradition and Innovation* [1].

these influences came to intersect in Augustine and the medieval tradition after him. The spring semester, "Moderns", begins with a play of Shakespeare and ends with a book of recent memory. By year's end, students have not only thought about Augustine's critical reflections in his own time, they have the opportunity to proceed with his work: examining key texts of modern times with an abiding concern for justice and truth, and in relation to a Catholic intellectual tradition that still, in many ways, hearkens back to Augustine.

One might expect students reading *Confessions* in this context to praise Augustine as a model of faith, and that is indeed what they often do. They also notice, however, that Augustine's self-assessment is far more critical. Saving his praise for the God who made him and everything good in his life, he claims for himself only the sins that he committed from the day he was born. "Why is he being so hard on himself?" my students always ask, although they are themselves rather shocked to learn of his extracurricular activities in Carthage. Shocked, but also curious, for they would rather talk about the sin that surprises them than the faith that they expected all along.

In neither case, however, does the conversation go far on its own. Many are the motives that can persuade bright first-year students to read a few pages of Augustine, but careful reading at length requires a different kind of concern. Augustine's narrative in the *Confessions* describes his youth as a time spent running away from his own happiness, and this perversity remains in many ways a mystery to him. In prayer he asks God literally hundreds of questions, longing to understand his wretchedness and the conversion that he failed to accomplish on his own. That Augustine should take a keen interest in this intensely complicated dialogue is unsurprising, but why should others care as he does? Nothing is more tedious than to hear a man go on about his personal problems.

I have learned to expect this resistance and offer the following explanation: Augustine's quest and questions are more than merely personal. In confessing to God, "Restless is our heart, until it rests in you"[3], Augustine speaks not only for himself but for "us"—that is, for all humanity. This observation by no means ends students' misgivings, however; it only exposes the stumbling block underlying them all. How could Augustine presume that his readers find their happiness only in God—"my God", as he often says? Is it not obvious that people seek many things and have every right to do so? Even those who believe in Augustine's God have no choice but to juggle many priorities while struggling to live a happy, successful life, do they not? These objections point to a conclusion that most students are too polite to say, even if they should happen to think it. Augustine's book reveals a great deal about him—his own preoccupation with God, his view of people as wretched sinners—but little that applies to us, whatever Augustine himself may think.

Now, anyone who holds that opinion might read *Confessions* as a requirement for graduation, which in turn is needed for a secure future—but not as something to be taken seriously, wrestled with, remembered long afterwards, returned to, and learned from. Reading Augustine truly begins, therefore, when students no longer ask the above questions rhetorically, but do so with heart and mind open to the possibility that he is right about happiness. There are, in fact, many ways of inviting them to read Augustine in that spirit. So ingrained is the presumption against him, however, that much time and effort can still be lost in that first reading.

---

[3] I have supplied my own, more literal translation of this crucial line from the *Confessions* (1.1.1); otherwise, all quotations in this paper are from the Boulding translation [2].

The problem does not appear to have escaped the notice of Augustine, who was once a resistant reader himself. In *Confessions*, Augustine tells the story of reading the Bible for the first time and finding it unworthy compared with the refined and urbane writing of Cicero ([2], 3.5.9). As for his own readers, Augustine touches more than once on the subject. In Book II, he says that he is telling his story to "my own kin, the human race, however few of them may chance to read these writings of mine" ([2], 2.3.5). In a later passage, however, Augustine expresses hope for not just any reader, but for those who will read his book with love and "a brotherly mind" ([2], 10.3.3–10.4.5); his confession is made "in the ears of believing men and women, the companions of my joy and sharers of my mortality, my fellow citizens still on pilgrimage with me" ([2], 10.4.6). However these statements are to be read in relation to one another, their apparent tension highlights the challenge of teaching the *Confessions* to modern students, many of whom do not share Augustine's faith or see themselves joining him on pilgrimage.

For this reason, I have found it helpful to pursue a longer road in the spring semester, when our seminar turns to modern texts. My syllabus has always included *Leviathan*, by Thomas Hobbes, a book that strikes modern readers as immediately plausible in the very respect that the *Confessions* seems alien. In particular, it is Hobbes who teaches us to seek happiness in many objects of desire rather than in one greatest good.

One might expect that such a book would only stiffen the resistance, but that is not what I have found with my own students, at least. It is true that they recognize much of themselves in Hobbes, but the reflection leaves many of them puzzled and uneasy about what they see. In what follows, I would like to describe their encounter with Hobbes, identify what I think their dissatisfaction is, and suggest how it encourages a new openness to Augustine.

3. Our Hobbesian View of Happiness

No one needs to read Hobbes in order to believe that people seek happiness in different ways and have every right to do so. The conviction comes from everywhere, so to speak: it belongs to the popular culture of modern democracy. That culture can be traced to Hobbes by way of philosophic successors like John Locke and then to philosophically educated statesmen like Thomas Jefferson and Benjamin Franklin. What matters most for students' education, however, is that Hobbes makes the original *argument* for opinions generally held even without argument.

Hobbes's best-known teaching on happiness is found in chapter 11 of *Leviathan* [3]. Oddly enough, however, Hobbes declines to use the word "happiness" in this context; he speaks instead of "felicity"[4]. Felicity had previously been defined in chapter 6 as "continual success in obtaining those things which a man from time to time desireth, that is to say continual prospering". But as Hobbes immediately adds, he means "the felicity of this life", not the next life. "What kind of felicity God hath ordained to them that devoutly honour Him, a man shall no sooner know than enjoy, being joys

---

[4] I suggest that this is because Hobbes recognizes "how necessary it is for any man that aspires to true knowledge, to examine the definitions of former authors, and either to correct them where they are negligently set down, or to make them himself" ([3], 4.13). In this case, the very word must be upgraded. "Happiness" does appear in the *Leviathan*, but only six times, and always in the context of discussions of religion. See ([3], 12.24, 31.9, 36.19, 38.4, 38.15, 44.4).

that are now as incomprehensible as the word of school-men *beatifical vision* is unintelligible" ([3], 6.58). That is the particular negligence to be avoided: allowing unknowable, religious-metaphysical visions of happiness to confuse an otherwise rigorous account of the "continual prospering" available here on earth.

Now since we are talking about the felicity of *this* life, one thing follows, according to Hobbes. Felicity means success in getting the things that we desire, and those things are many and diverse. Hobbes denies that there is any one good that can satisfy all human beings in common, or even any individual for an entire life. Such a good simply does not exist. "For there is no such *Finis ultimus* (utmost aim) nor *Summum bonum* (greatest good) as is spoken of in the books of the old moral philosophers" ([3], 11.1).

But why should one think that life has no ultimate purpose? Hobbes's initial explanation is this: if we wanted one thing in life, attaining that object would complete all change, all movement, all desire. In that case, however, all life would cease as well. "Nor can a man any more live, whose desire is at an end, than he whose senses and imaginations are at a stand." Felicity of this life must be defined in accordance with this insight, as "a continual progress of the desire, from one object to another, the attaining of the former being still but the way to the latter" ([3], 11.1; see also 6.58).

The argument quickly succeeds in persuading many students, especially when they reflect on the fact that what they want now, as 18- or 19-year-olds, is different from what they wanted at 6 or 12, and it is also different from what they are likely to want at 30, 42, or 90. A youth may be nostalgic for days wholly devoted to Legos, but he is unlikely to find them endlessly satisfying now. A young woman who would be terrified to hear that she is pregnant today might move mountains for a baby when she is 40. A middle-aged man might spend a sleepless night brooding about the promotion he missed or the cough that never seems to go away: such are not the anxieties of the typical 18-year-old.

On further examination, however, the argument is less convincing. Life may be impossible without motion of *some* sort, but that motion need not come from changes in what is desired most. It is possible that human beings make mistakes about what truly satisfies, and when this occurs, they have no choice but to keep searching for it. Even when they do not make mistakes, the greatest good may be difficult or impossible to attain completely. Or again, even if they do attain it, their happiness might be an *ongoing activity* rather than a goal to be accomplished only once. That is to say, human existence may culminate in a certain *way of life* that, when discerned correctly and practiced well, satisfies our deepest desire as completely as possible, for as long as it lasts. These ideas essentially comprise the view of happiness offered by Aristotle, one of the "Old Moral Philosophers" dismissed in this passage (see *Nicomachean Ethics* [4], 1097a15–1098b19). Perhaps those codgers still have some kick in them?

Nevertheless, Hobbes, who certainly knew his Aristotle, does deny that there is a greatest good. Since this claim is not *necessarily* true, it requires further explanation, which Hobbes does in fact provide. In a second argument, he explains why felicity consists in "continual progress" of the desire from one object to another:

> The cause whereof is that the object of man's desire is not to enjoy once only, and for one instant of time, but to assure forever the way of his future desire. And therefore the

voluntary actions and inclinations of all men tend, not only to the procuring, but also to the assuring of a contented life, and differ only in the way; which ariseth partly from the diversity of passions in divers men, and partly from the difference of the knowledge or opinion each one has of the causes which produce the effects desired. ([3], 11.1).

Why does each of us go through life wanting different things, different not only from what *other* people want, but from what *we ourselves* want, in times past and future? The reason—"*the cause*"—is that we expect the future to be precarious and know we must work make it secure.

The connection needs to be spelled out, and doing so brings a flash of self-recognition. At 18, my students are already looking ahead to life after college. Immediately they will need to pay rent; soon afterwards, some will want to buy a house. Many will have very large student loans that need to be paid off. Some will start a family. Falling sick, they will all need doctors, which requires health insurance. Retirement is of course a long way off, but even that must be provided for. None of these things will take care of themselves; all of them require forethought and preparation if they are to happen well.

What then does it mean to live always preparing for the future? As students know well, it means *wanting a host of things that they otherwise would not have wanted.* Last year, instead of indulging their childhood fascination with mummies, playing in a rock band, or dancing in musical shows, they found themselves caring about the SAT exam and getting into a highly rated college. Now that they are here, however, the SAT means nothing; instead they are double majoring, interning, and otherwise credentializing themselves with their eyes on graduate school. When they are 30, the internships, entrance exams and GPAs will mean nothing. Lawyers had better be with a good firm and moving up in the ranks; academics must be done with their Ph. D. and pumping out three articles a year. Securing the future is a lifelong project for us all.

The crucial point for Hobbes is psychological. Moving from one activity to another shapes our very desires; what we no longer seek, we *stop wanting*. If I put off my pleasure reading because of my busy schedule, I will miss it at first, but not for long; my desire moves on to different objects. Indeed, even before my desire moves on, it is already limited by my awareness that I will soon need to seek other things. Whatever I happen to want now is less important to me than the assurance that I will keep getting what I want in the future. As Hobbes says, "not to enjoy once only, and for one instant of time, but to assure forever the way of his future desire" is "*the object* of man's desire" ([3], 11.1, emphasis added). To be thus is nothing; but to be safely thus!

Human desire does have a single object, then, but only in this sense: the capacity to get what we desire, *whatever* it might be, is always desirable. It follows that what we always seek, more than any single satisfaction, is power.

> So that in the first place, I put for a general inclination of all mankind, a perpetual and restless desire of power after power, that ceaseth only in death. And the cause of this is not always that man hopes for a more intensive delight than that he has already attained to, or that he cannot be content with a moderate power, but because he cannot assure the power and means to live well, which he hath presently, without the acquisition of more ([3], 11.2).

Let us be clear on what this pursuit of power is and what it is not. All mankind seeks power, in Hobbes's view, but *not* because everyone delights in lording it over other people. There is such a delight, of course—Hobbes calls it "glory"—but that passion motivates some more than others, and as a leading cause of quarrel it ought to be suppressed by a healthy dose of fear (see especially [3], 13.14, 17.1–2). But the pursuit of power *as such* can never be suppressed, for it is a reasonable response to the insecurity that humans face all their lives. Instead, Hobbes wants to *enlighten* the pursuit of power by teaching his readers, first, to admit that power is indeed the object of their desire, and second, to seek power more effectively by maintaining peace and unity with others, so far as it is possible to do so.

Thus, for Hobbes, the need for power keeps us always in motion. Unattached to any single thing, we seek first one object, then another, and another. Power is the one object that we do desire all our lives, but there can never be enough of power. We seek it in new quantities, new places, new forms, reinventing our very selves to gain a bit more assurance that we will have what we desire in years to come.

4. Restlessness, Reconsidered

It remains to be seen, however, whether this account of happiness gets to the heart of the matter, for as Hobbes himself insists, what people say and appear to be doing is often misleading: "The characters of man's heart, blotted and confounded as they are, with dissembling, lying, counterfeiting, and erroneous doctrines, are legible onely to him that searcheth hearts" ([3], intro. 3). Anyone who does not have the power to search hearts must limit himself to examining his *own* thoughts and passions, but in such a manner as to read in them "not this or that particular man, but mankind". That is just what Hobbes claims to have done, and now that he has set down his reading, "the pains left another, will be onely to consider, if he also find not the same in himself. For this kind of Doctrine, admitteth no other Demonstration" ([3], intro. 4).

To read the *Leviathan*, therefore, is to join in an experiment that began with the book's first publication in 1651. My own students have been participating for several years now, and at first glance, their march to professional success could seem to be just as Hobbes describes. Few of them appear to be Genghis Khans or Lady Macbeths, but by their own testimony they do feel obliged *to gain control over a precarious future*. One cannot understand the "professionalization of the university" today apart from Hobbesian anxiety.

Nevertheless, it is doubtful whether Hobbes has accomplished the demonstration that he hopes for. Even as Hobbes presents, with startling clarity, the reasons that effectually govern their life-choices, students say that they are uncomfortable with his account of human happiness, and that discomfort seems to me to be genuine.

To illustrate, I would now share a story that I always relate while teaching *Leviathan*. It is designed to show, as faithfully as possible, what is entailed in Hobbes's teaching.

> Imagine a young couple who fall in love and get married. It's a beautiful wedding and lovely honeymoon, but afterwards it is time to worry about the future. They know they will want to pay off their loans, buy a house, and start a family, which of course will take a lot of money. This being the case, they agree that both of them need to work long hours and climb the ladder in their respective professions. So that is what they do. They work for weeks, months, years, making good progress, though of course they are

sorry to spend so much time away from home. A few more years, and they notice that they are spending more time with their co-workers than with each other—but for some reason, it doesn't really bother them all that much. It isn't long before they realize that they just don't love each other as much as they once did. So they agree on a divorce. They make their arrangements in a calm and reasonable manner, split up, and then—life goes on. Each of them pursues new goals, new objects, making new friends and allies, moving on once again, always working, never resting, until their striving ends, as it must, in death.

After telling the story of my imaginary couple, I offer a Hobbesian interpretation of it. For Hobbes, it is the story of two happy people. Their decision to work long hours is entirely reasonable, in his view. Granted that it was hard on their marriage, but would it have been any easier for them to endure poverty, illness, and failure? Then, when the passion of love has ceased and no other advantage requires them to stay, the marriage is no longer good for either of them. Each one has every reason to get on with maximizing his or her ability to gain the objects of desire, for that is what it means to be happy—and in that endeavor they are both successful.

But even though I present my Hobbesian reading as eloquently as I can, students receive the story rather differently. They do agree that working long hours would help provide financial security, and they also admit that it can have the consequences that I describe; most are reluctant, however, to concede that a life lived as I have described should be considered happy. Shuttling from one object to another, competing for position, moving ahead but never reaching any destination except the grave, seems to them "pointless" and "depressing". The latter word is revealing, for it implies that they are imagining the unhappiness as their own.

As we have seen, Hobbes questions whether one can know that this is what my students feel in their hearts. It is possible that, despite their testimony to the contrary, they embrace a life spent enjoying the objects of particular, temporary desires and struggling to avoid—or eventually, to medicate—the terror and pain of death. What seems more likely, however, is that they do feel dissatisfied with the all-too-Hobbesian life that stretches before them, even if they are also reluctant to give up its advantages or to face the dangers of abandoning it.

Like all humans, my students want to be happy, not miserable, and any sign of coming distress is bound to make them restless, just as Hobbes says. That is not to say, however, that a life spent acting on that restlessness deserves the name of happiness. It is worth highlighting three areas of dissatisfaction.

1. *Love and friendship.* Although students do seek power, the empowerment they seek is not always their own. Indeed, they immediately care about the couple in my story because they suppose them to be working and even sacrificing for one another, as a family. And while my students agree that desire can move to new objects, they are uncertain how to judge that change in the case of friends, lovers, or spouses. Hobbes does not ignore the phenomena of love and friendship, but he reduces the former to one desire among many ([3], 6.33) and the latter to an "instrumental power" ([3], x.1). These formulations seem to describe incomplete, broken, or perverse relationships, not love and friendship as they ought to be.
2. *The promise of beauty.* Love and friendship also inspire hope. When students find my illustration of Hobbes to "depressing", they imply that they were *expecting* an alternate

ending, and finding it otherwise is a disappointment—including, somehow, for themselves. How is that expectation understood by Hobbes? Hobbes defines hope as an appetite "with opinion of attaining" the object desired ([3], 6.14). What then is the opinion, and where does it come from, where love and friendship are concerned? A passage that deserves most attention is his definition of *pulchrum*, a Latin word that means "beautiful" (whether in appearance or in manners or morals). For Hobbes, *pulchrum* is "that which by some apparent signs promiseth good" ([3], 6.8). Beauty, therefore, is what promises that love, friendship, and other things will prove to be good in some way, beyond their evident pleasure and utility at this time. But while this thought is revealing and deserves further consideration, it is hard to consider it further with the help of Hobbes, who seems intent on cutting the phenomenon of beauty down to size or avoiding it altogether.

3. *Longing for eternity.* As we have seen, Hobbes observes that human beings desire to enjoy more than once and for an instant of time. Once again, students do not reject Hobbes's claim simply, but they do wonder whether it should be interpreted, with Hobbes, as a desire to be gratified through the accumulation of power in this life. The problem comes to a head in Hobbes's formulation that "the object of man's desire" is "to assure *forever* the way of his future desire" ([3], 11.1). For if, as Hobbes apparently assumes, desire hits a dead end when earthly existence concludes, its path cannot possibly be assured forever, not even by the greatest of visible powers. "Forever" is the one thing that Hobbes can never promise. It *is* promised by the things that move us profoundly by their beauty.

One should not even assume that Hobbes has nothing further to say about the restlessness provoked by his account of felicity. After all, in the very next chapter of *Leviathan*, he compares anxiety for future time with the suffering of Prometheus, who every day had to endure it when an eagle pecked away as much of his liver as had grown back in the night; this anxiety, in Hobbes's view, is a natural seed of religion ([3], 12.5 and context). In sum, reconsidering the "perpetual and restless desire of power after power that endeth only in death" provokes another kind of restlessness, one that continues despite attempts to obscure, distract, entice, mock, scare, argue, or define it out of existence.

5. Restless Hearts

As I now hope to show, the peculiar unease that one feels in reading Hobbes helps prepare students for more serious reading of the *Confessions*.

Beset by deepening doubts about their own quest for empowerment, students can follow Augustine with interest as he grows weary of a career that by worldly standards was wildly successful. They can understand why he would confide to his friends that a drunken beggar whom they happened upon was happier than they were, for while the beggar was joyful and carefree, they were anxious and preoccupied with all the labors demanded by their overweening ambition ([2], 6.6.9–10). And having identified with Augustine at that time, they will also understand why his conversion would lead very soon to his abandoning the career that had grown so burdensome to him ([2], 9.2.2–4).

With a sharpened awareness that they do *not* view friends merely as props of their power (see [3], 6.43, 10.2), students recognize themselves in Augustine as he delights in the company of friends, especially in the passage on how they spent their time reading books and conversing together ([2], 4.8.13). They also notice how power distorted his passionate but dysfunctional relationship with an unnamed friend, and their own dissatisfaction with temporary goods can help them see why Augustine would see death *everywhere* when his friend has gone ([2], 4.4.9). All of this prepares them to ponder Augustine's confession that friendship is true "only when you bind fast together people who cleave to you through the charity poured abroad in our hearts by the Holy Spirit who is given to us" ([2], 4.4.7).

Those who suspect that Hobbes somehow reduces away the phenomenon of beauty are likely to sympathize with Augustine in his wanderings, which spring from a similar dissatisfaction. Love affairs in Carthage are fascinating for Augustine, as they are for his readers—but only temporarily so. Augustine tires of the beauty that only promises to gratify some particular desire, because the beauty, the desire, and the gratification, being tied to bodies, all rise and fall, live and die with them. His true longing, he discovers, is for that which neither comes into being nor passes away, but *is* eternally.

For some time Augustine seeks that *summum bonum* through the writings of the "Platonists", which describe an intellectual ascent that bears a family resemblance to the ladder of love in Plato's *Symposium*[5]. But these efforts, even when they are drawn onwards by divine beauty, give Augustine no more than a glimpse of "that which is", for they too are hobbled by "carnal habit"—the habit of clinging to mortal, created things instead of moving among and beyond them to eternal being ([2], 7.23). The restlessness of the human heart—the restlessness that one feels in response to Hobbes's explicit teaching—cannot be satisfied through human philosophy. Augustine's teaching is that happiness exists in this life only in hope, the great blessing enjoyed by citizens of the City of God during their sojourning on earth (see *City of God* [6], 19.20). What is missing from the writings of the Platonists—to say nothing of Plato himself—is Christ, "the mediator" who connects mortal humanity with God, because he is not only a man born of a woman, but God as well ([2], 7.18.24).

One sees the difference made by Augustine's conversion and baptism in Book IX. When staying in the port city of Ostia, Augustine attempts another ascent to *that which is*, but now he makes it with his mother just days before she is to fall sick and die. Together Augustine and Monica try to discern how God is experienced eternally by the saints in heaven. Instead of summarizing their progress from a distance, as he had done when speaking of his solitary efforts in Book VII, Augustine here relates some approximation of the thoughts expressed in their conversation ([2], 9.10.23–26). In a passage that opens with "Then we said…" ([2], 9.10.25), he drops any distinction between what he said with his own lips and what Monica said with hers. Does he imply that they spoke in unison? However that may be, this moment more than anywhere else offers readers a glimpse of what it means to be bound fast by the Holy Spirit.

Ostia is, of course, the very model of the "beatifical vision" that Hobbes excludes from his definition of happiness, complaining of its unintelligibility. One can hardly expect to render it intelligible, when Augustine himself laments how little they were to express what they saw in "the

---

[5] Diotima asserts in Plato's *Symposium* that everyone wants the good things for themselves, not for a time but always, and erotic lovers seek out beauty as the occasion for finding that "always" by giving birth to offspring beyond their mortal selves ([5], 206a–c). Above all, immortality is promised by the investigation of "beauty itself", the contemplation of which allows production of examples of true virtue (210e–212c).

noise of articulate speech" ([2], 9.10.24). Nevertheless, the experience stands as a peak of the *Confessions*. Would Hobbes be hasty to deny that it could possibly be the *summum bonum*?

6. An End and a Beginning

That is how I would sketch the beginning of a more searching encounter with Augustine, made possible by students' reading of Hobbes. It is necessary, however, to say something more about how that encounter actually happens for my students. We do not, of course, read *Confessions* all over again in the spring semester. There is simply no time, nor would it be advisable in a course devoted to modern thought.

My general approach while we study Hobbes is to consider from time to time how our current reading compares with *Confessions* in the previous semester. Several opportunities for making that comparison come in chapter 6 of *Leviathan*. For example, someone usually directs our attention to Hobbes's definition of religion as "*fear* of power invisible, feigned by the mind, or imagined from tales publically allowed"; as for superstition, it is the same thing, but when the tales are "not allowed" ([3], 6.36). It takes a few minutes to tease out what this statement asserts about religion—that its defining passion is fear, that it has no necessary connection to reality, and that religion in one place will be superstition in another. Then I ask how Hobbes's definition compares with religion as Augustine seems to practice it in *Confessions*. Other occasions for comparison in the chapter include his definitions of the beautiful as "good in the promise" ([3], 6.8), of love as an appetite, the object of which happens to be present ([3], 6.3), and of felicity as "continual prospering" ([3], 6.58).

A more sustained comparison comes after our line-by-line examination of the account of felicity in chapter 11 (see Sections 3 and 4, above). If an insightful student has not already raised the issue, I first invite them to consider whether what Hobbes says about the "the books of the old moral philosophers" ([3], 11.1) applies to Augustine as well. Students usually notice that when Augustine confesses, "Restless is our heart until it rests in you" ([2], 1.1.1), he is asserting that God is, indeed, the *summum bonum*. The question to ask, therefore, is whether Hobbes's argument actually refutes Augustine. Simply by returning to the beginning of *Confessions*, students can make a number of important observations, the most important of which is that *praising* God is, for Augustine, an activity that continues to be good for us humans for as long as we walk the earth. "You arouse us so that praising you may bring us joy", Augustine declares ([2], 1.1.1).

After we finish Hobbes, my classes read a recent author who illustrates how the Catholic intellectual tradition and its fellow-travelers have continued Augustinian thought in the midst of modern culture. This spring, for example, we are reading T. S. Eliot's *Four Quartets*. Eliot resonates deeply with Augustine in the restlessness that he expresses and induces in his poetry. By showing us our "strained time-ridden faces", Eliot forces us to reconsider our struggle to provide for the future without truly living in the present ([7], 1.100), and he draws us into serious consideration of how our finitude may be baptized in "a further union, a deeper communion" ([7], 2.206).

Still, *Four Quartets* is not the *Confessions*, and I do want students to have a last look at Augustine as the spring semester concludes. I am asking them to compare the last poem in *Four Quartets* with a passage from much later in the *Confessions*, a prayer-poem that further illustrates what the *summum bonum* means for Augustine. It shows an Augustine who is not preoccupied with future threats and promises, but immersed in a relationship that is utterly present yet fully active with the highest pitch of longing.

> Late have I loved you, Beauty so ancient and so new,
> Late have I loved you!
> Lo, you were within,
> but I outside, seeking there for you,
> and upon the shapely things you have made I rushed headlong,
> I, misshapen.
> You were with me, but I was not with you.
> They held me back far from you,
> those things which would have no being
> were they not in you.
> You called, shouted, broke through my deafness;
> you flared, blazed, banished my blindness;
> you lavished your fragrance, I gasped, and now I pant for you;
> I tasted you, and I hunger and thirst;
> you touched me, and I burned for your peace.

7. Concluding Remarks

What I have sought to do in this essay is to show how Hobbes, despite his own intentions, can induce students to question their habitual assumptions about happiness and thus to entertain the possibility that Augustine truly understood our restless humanity. Students may gradually discover that they long for the same divine truth that Augustine seeks in *Confessions*, and in seeking it they may also find it. If Hobbes does not himself teach the lesson, he can still offer a surprising introduction to a book written "so that whoever reads [these writings] may reflect with me on the depths from which we must cry unto you" ([2], 2.3.5).

Acknowledgments

I wish to thank the participants of the "Augustine across the Curriculum" conference for their comments on the original version of this paper; students and colleagues in the Augustine and Culture Seminar, who constantly help me notice new ways of improving my teaching; and the anonymous reviewers, who urged me to bring out certain pedagogical points more fully.

Conflicts of Interest

The author declares no conflict of interest.

References

1. John Doody, and Kim Paffenroth, eds. *Augustine in Conversation: Tradition and Innovation.* Lanham: Lexington Books, 2005–2015, 10 vols.
2. Augustine. *The Confessions.* Translated by Maria Boulding. New York: New City Press, 1997.
3. Thomas Hobbes. *Leviathan: With Selected Variants from the Latin Edition of 1668.* Edited by Edwin Curley. Indianapolis: Hackett, 1994.
4. Aristotle. *Aristotle's Nicomachean Ethics.* Translated by Robert C. Bartlett and Susan D. Collins. Chicago: University of Chicago Press, 2011.
5. Plato. *Plato's Symposium.* Translated by Seth Benardete. Chicago: University of Chicago Press, 2001.
6. Augustine. *The City of God against the Pagans.* Translated by R.W. Dyson. Cambridge: Cambridge University Press, 1998.
7. T.S. Eliot. *Four Quartets.* New York: Houghton Mifflin Harcourt Publishing Company, 1971.

Section III.
Rarely Read Augustine

Augustine's Introduction to Political Philosophy: Teaching *De Libero Arbitrio*, Book I

Daniel E. Burns

Abstract: Book I of Augustine's work *On Free Choice* (*De Libero Arbitrio*) offers a helpful introduction to some of the most important themes of political philosophy. The paper makes a case for teaching this text in introductory courses on political thought, theology of social life, and similar topics, alongside or even in place of the more usually assigned excerpts from *City of God*. The text is written as a dialogue in which Augustine seeks to introduce a student of his to reflection on the ways in which our moral outlook is profoundly shaped by our political citizenship. It invites all of us, whether Christian or non-Christian citizens, to enter into the dialogue ourselves as Augustine's students and so to reflect on the moral significance of our own citizenship.

Reprinted from *Religions*. Cite as: Burns, D.E. Augustine's Introduction to Political Philosophy: Teaching *De Libero Arbitrio*, Book I. *Religions* **2015**, *6*, 82–91.

1. The Pedagogical Value of the Text

When Augustine gets taught in survey courses of the history of political thought, he usually appears as something of an outlier. I know that many of my fellow political scientists who teach those courses conceive of him along the lines of a misanthropic uncle sitting silently in the corner at the family Christmas party: it is hard to question his right to be there or our concomitant obligation to tolerate his presence, but it is equally hard not to be slightly embarrassed whenever one has to glance in his direction. Some even seem to think that having Augustine on a syllabus about political thought is comparable to having him on a syllabus about visions of human sexuality. We show our open-mindedness by including in our readings this strange author who seems to have contempt for the whole subject of the course, who sees it as at best an ugly necessity, and who probably would say we should not be teaching courses like this at all. For one week in the semester, we wonder about a radical alternative to all the other authors we teach: maybe everything else we say in this course is a waste of time, because maybe all that really matters is God, and maybe the subject of this course ought then to lose a lot of its previous interest for us—for although it may indeed be important insofar as it can impede our journey towards God when it is conducted badly, as in fact it nearly always is, still we ought for that very reason to avoid dealings with it as much as possible, and to the extent that we (sinful beings that we are) cannot avoid such dealings, we should at least somehow feel sad about that. After opening our minds to such difficult thoughts for one week, we return for the rest of the semester to authors who manage to write about the same subject with much less distaste, and who finally confirm our own inclination to think that its human importance cannot be dismissed so easily as the old bishop of Hippo would have us believe.

Now, the view of Augustine's attitude toward politics that I have just sketched is not one that I share, and I think that courses in which he is taught this way are doing students a real disservice.

They prevent those students from confronting aspects of Augustine's thought that could pose a more genuine challenge to their own understanding of the relation between morality and politics. And those aspects are most clearly on display in a text of Augustine's that makes for a wonderfully compact introduction not only to his political thought but even to political philosophy as a discipline: Book 1 of his dialogue *On Free Choice* (*De Libero Arbitrio*). I would therefore like to make a case for teaching this text in classes on political thought, intellectual history, theology of social life, and similar areas of study—for teaching it, possibly even in place of the more usual excerpts from *City of God*, but in any case at least alongside them.

My impression on the basis of very limited anecdotal evidence is that many students, especially at secular schools but even at religious ones, do not exactly warm to the political teaching they find in *City of God*. Some of them find it too didactic or dogmatic. Others are bothered when they think they see Augustine using his Christian faith to dismiss the political attachments that were felt very strongly by his Roman contemporaries and in a way are still felt by many of our students today, attachments to which they are inclined to give serious moral weight. Is it really the case that Christians must be, not true citizens (of the United States for example), but merely foreigners passing through, all carrying green cards as it were ([1], 19.17, 19.26)? Is it really the case that the choice between different forms of government is all but irrelevant in this brief earthly life, as long as our rulers "do not compel [us] to impious and wicked deeds" ([1], 5.17)? Does Augustine really have no sympathy for those who feel themselves to be genuine Christian citizens, "citizens of both cities" [2]? For that matter, what about all the pagan citizens, then or now: can patriotism, this massive fact of common human experience, really be dismissed as at best a noble delusion, and in any case a delusion from which Christ is supposed to have freed us (see, e.g., [1], 14.28)? And finally, again in a related vein, some students are put off by what seem in *City of God* to be Augustine's unacceptably low expectations from politics. If the earthly city is and always will be an aggregation of vicious sinners, a "Babylon" whose most valuable accomplishment is securing a fragile "earthly peace" ([1], 19.17, 19.26), then it seems hard to justify, for example, disobedience to *unjust* laws. Of course the laws are unjust, the Augustinian position would seem to say: we cannot expect any better, but for precisely that reason, as long as they are keeping the peace, we must leave them in place rather than cause any disturbance by trying to change them. The same would be true even for the extreme case of overthrowing a tyrant, as long as that tyrant is not stopping anyone from going to church: if every city without justice is no better than a gang of robbers ([1], 4.4), and true justice is found in no earthly city but only in the Heavenly City ([1], 19.21, 19.24–25, 19.27), then it is hard to see on what grounds one would go to the trouble of replacing the tyrant of one's earthly city with whatever gang of robbers is sure to take his place. Augustine seems then to allow little possibility of holding our country's laws or government to any standard of morality. And this, understandably, rubs many students the wrong way.

Again, in my own view, this is an inadequate reading of even the most famously anti-political passages of the *City of God*. But I would hardly blame any undergraduate who came away with impressions like these after reading just a week's worth of excerpts from that text. And that would be a great shame, because these impressions certainly do not paint an accurate picture of how Augustine himself approached the study of politics. We learn this from Book 1 of *On Free Choice* which, unlike

City of God, explicitly claims to treat certain moral-political questions in the very order in which Augustine himself worked through them on the road toward his own religious conversion (see [3], 1.2.4.10–11).[1] The reflections outlined in this book thus lay the groundwork for the understanding of politics that Augustine would later elaborate in greater detail in *City of God* and elsewhere. For this reason and others, Book 1 of *On Free Choice* is a text uniquely well suited to introducing students to his thoughts on politics, one that in particular does not suffer from some of these pedagogical difficulties that *City of God* may seem to present.

First, Book 1 of *On Free Choice* can hardly be called dogmatic, because its literary form is that of a philosophic dialogue. There are two characters, Augustine and his friend Evodius; the book is based (loosely) on real conversations that these two men actually had [5]. And Augustine's main role in the conversation, like that of any Socratic teacher, is simply to get Evodius to state clearly and coherently his own opinions about a number of moral and political questions. This means that the task of extracting the author's own view from the conversation poses certain interpretive challenges. But what may be frustrating to some scholars can be all the more exciting for undergraduates, and I do find that students enjoy coming to see how the literary form invites them, as indeed it invites all of us as readers, to enter into the conversation themselves: Do you agree with Evodius's answer here? How could he have answered differently? Why didn't he give the answer you would have expected? and so on.

For the same reason, this book is not vulnerable to the charge sometimes leveled by readers of *City of God* that Augustine sets himself on a lofty Christian peak from which all political attachments appear petty and vain, and that he thus unfairly dismisses the moral and political experiences of ordinary Christian citizens or for that matter of pagan citizens. For Evodius, whose opinions (to repeat) are the focus of the dialogue, turns out to be very much a Christian citizen. He does not think politics is petty or meaningless, and his attachment to his political community runs very deep indeed. In fact, the dialogue shows us how much the moral opinions that Evodius holds as a Christian citizen have in common with opinions that would be held by an equally upright pagan citizen. This is one of its most interesting aspects from the point of view of scholarship on Augustine, since it forces us to question the assumption, common to nearly all studies of his political thought, that he thinks Christian attitudes towards politics must be radically different from pagan attitudes toward politics. And it also makes this text particularly relevant to those of us who teach a religiously diverse student body. Since the text shows us Evodius struggling with questions that must be faced by any citizen, Christian or otherwise, it has immediate appeal even for students who do not share Augustine's (and Evodius's) Christian faith. In fact, although Evodius is still struggling with those questions as a believing Christian, Augustine seems to say that he himself worked through them before his own conversion to the Christian faith, and even that he *had* to work through them before he could be free

---

[1] Citations to *De Libero Arbitrio* are given by book number followed by several section numbers. The most faithful translation available [4] offers the same section numbers, as does the best critical edition [3], to whose line numbers I occasionally also refer. Unfortunately, most other translations refer to only some of these section divisions: what appears here as section 1.5.11.33 would elsewhere be section 1.5.11, 1.33, 1.11, or a similar combination. But any translation's section numbers can easily be "keyed" to those given here by a glance at the last section of Book 1, which would be cited here as 1.16.35.118.

of the intellectual obstacles that held him back from that faith (see again [3], 1.2.4.10–11). So when non-Christian students are introduced to those questions by reading this book, they have in one respect more in common with the author himself than do Christian students in the same position.

Finally, when it comes to the accusation that Augustine's unacceptably low expectations from politics seem to leave no place for morality in political life, for legitimate disobedience to unjust laws, or for legitimate resistance to tyranny, Book 1 of *On Free Choice* is perhaps the strongest defense of the author against any such accusations. The character Augustine in this book, in one of the rare contributions he offers in his own name (as opposed to the majority that merely draw out Evodius's views), makes what is perhaps the single statement that has most famously and frequently been quoted by centuries' worth of Christians resisting political injustices: "An unjust law, it seems to me, is no law at all" ([3], 1.5.11.33). This dialogue even includes a short discussion of the principles to which one may legitimately appeal in undertaking a political revolution, along with an example of such a justified revolution that Augustine offers as apparently indisputable ([3], 1.6.14.45–47). So again, this text engages much more closely with our ordinary moral intuitions about politics than the *City of God* at least appears to. And while I believe that a careful study of *City of God* would reveal that even the views presented there are much more nuanced than many attempted summaries of Augustine's political thought would have it (see, e.g., the detailed reading of Burnell on the justifiability of political revolution [6]), such a careful study may not be possible in the short time to which many undergraduate survey courses are forced to limit their treatment of Augustine. There is therefore a case to be made for beginning where Augustine himself begins and following out his own original reflections on politics; in light of these, students interested in pursuing the matter further may in later studies turn to *City of God* with more of the background needed to appreciate its subtleties.

Since this text then has many features that recommend it to our students, and I would say to all of us as well, I would like to walk through a few of the ways in which this very compact and extraordinarily rich dialogue could provoke reflection and stimulate discussion over the course of a week or so in an undergraduate survey course.

2. Highlights of the Text for Classroom Discussion

On Free Choice as a whole is dedicated to the problem of whether God is responsible for the evil in the world, the theological problem that had held Augustine up for so long on his intellectual journey towards the Christian faith. Book 1 treats the preliminary problem of what we mean when we speak of evil, in particular of moral evil: it discusses the question *quid sit malefacere*, "what is wrongdoing?" ([3], 1.3.6.14). Although Book 1 must ultimately must be understood in the context of the investigation of divine providence that governs the whole work, its discussion of political topics does turn out to have value independent of that investigation, as is already suggested by Augustine's presentation of its theme as distinct from that of the rest of the work (see [3], 1.3.6.14 with 1.16.34.115, 1.16.35.118). It is on the way to answering this moral question "what is wrongdoing?" that Augustine and Evodius articulate a distinction between the "temporal law" that governs human political communities and the "eternal law" by which God governs the universe ([3], 1.5.13.41–6.14.42; 1.6.14.48–15.51; 1.14.30.101–15.32.112). (Hence Book 1 of *On Free Choice* is cited frequently, for example, in Aquinas's so-called "Treatise on Law.") The distinction between these two types of law has obviously been a very important one in the history of western thought. It is drawn in this text with a sharpness that I am not aware of in any pre-Christian treatment of natural law, and with a clarity that I have not seen in any pre-Augustinian Christian thinker. But my remarks here will concentrate only on the part of the conversation that leads up to that distinction. Augustine subjects Evodius to a Socratic dialogue on this question "what is wrongdoing": he shoots down some of Evodius's inadequate answers, presses him to give better ones, complains when Evodius evades the question, and so on. In the course of this dialogue, Augustine ends up presenting to Evodius four sets of moral-political dilemmas that are meant to challenge Evodius's understanding of his own political attachments, and again are (I believe) meant also to do the same for us as readers.

The first of these dilemmas is one that could be encountered by any citizen or subject, because it has to do with the question whether to obey the law. Under interrogation from Augustine, Evodius reveals that on the one hand he ordinarily assumes that the law of his political community ought to be obeyed. In particular, he generally takes for granted the distribution of property, the definition of mine and thine, that that law supplies. When he thinks about who is married to whom, for example, he assumes that it is the couples whom his legal system recognizes as married (*cf.* [3], 1.3.6.15–17, lines 23, 26, 27 [*mea, suam, cuius*], with 1.3.7.18, lines 34–35). He is barely even conscious of doing this: he uses terms like "my house" and "your wife" all the time, attaches significant moral weight to these terms, and yet hardly thinks of the fact that their definitions are, at least primarily, supplied to him by his community's legal system. (I like to think about the angry parent exclaiming "not in my house!"—imagine how much of a smart-aleck teenager it would take to respond, "well how do I know it *is* really your house?" We often forget to question these definitions, even when we might have had an interest in doing so.) But on the other hand and at the same time, Evodius does recognize in principle that not all laws are morally binding. He thinks serious moral progress has been made in his own community's laws in the past hundred years—which means that he thinks the older laws were wrong, and therefore not morally binding ([3], 1.3.7.18–19). Augustine reminds him of this fact by referring to the "divine authority" of the Christian Church, which clearly teaches that the old Roman laws outlawing Christian worship were wrong, but in the same breath Augustine says he could also have chosen to refer to "other books" that do not rely on this "divine authority" (ibid.): one does not then have to be a Christian to recognize the insufficiency of human law as a moral standard, or the insufficiency of what we today might call legal positivism. Evodius implicitly holds the law to some higher standard than itself, without often having to think about what that standard really is. A thoughtful citizen, though, wants to know what that standard is, so that he can make sure he is judging rightly as to which laws should and should not be obeyed.

So in the second set of hypothetical dilemmas, Augustine moves Evodius up a level in the scale of political responsibilities. He now puts Evodius in the position of, not a citizen or subject who is asked merely to obey the law, but a judge who is asked to apply that law in particular cases. He asks Evodius in effect to imagine judging the trial of a slave who has murdered his master, but who did so only out of fear that the master was going to hurt him first ([3], 1.4.9.22–10.29). The details of this case are interesting, but I will focus here on just one point. The question of principle that this case raises is whether one can ever kill another human being without being guilty of murder. In discussing it, then, Evodius brings up the fact that he recognizes at least four other types of people who do indeed kill without thereby becoming murderers: first, people involved in accidents with weapons, and then more interestingly, soldiers, judges, and public executioners, with the latter three all defined as blameless on the ground that their actions have positive legal sanction ([3], 1.4.9.25). So we see here again what enormous importance the law has in Evodius's moral life. The law defines the difference between murder and justified killing—a difference that a Christian, at least, sees as having great relevance to the well-being of his soul. The law tells us that certain forms of killing are acceptable while others are not. And in many cases, we tend to take for granted what it tells us. Certainly Evodius does so. As Augustine says, "such persons are not *customarily* called murderers": most of us do not ordinarily think that a soldier is no more than a hit man with tuition benefits (ibid., emphasis added). Yet as Augustine immediately reminds Evodius, a Christian in particular, and really any human being, has no right to assume that something must be right merely because the law commands it (see [3], 1.4.10.26; cf. [3], 1.3.7.18–19). So the question is raised even more sharply: what makes a law justified, or what defines a just law?

This brings them to the third set of dilemmas, in which Augustine now puts Evodius in the place of a politician, especially a legislator, who is tasked with writing the laws that a judge only applies and that a citizen (ordinarily) obeys. Here Augustine zeroes in, as does no other political philosopher whom I have read, on two particular laws that seem to suggest very different answers to the question "what makes a just law." He asks Evodius whether either or both of these laws are just. The first is what we could call the law of self-defense: the law granting to all citizens permission to kill a violent robber or murderer when they are under attack and cannot defend themselves in any other way. The second could be called the law of military service: the law demanding that a soldier (which under a draft could mean almost any citizen) must risk his own life in order to protect his country ([3], 1.5.11.33). The first of these two laws—as John Locke would later make very clear—seems to suggest that the fundamental purpose of law as such is to protect our rights, especially our rights to life and bodily security, so that if the law cannot so to speak get there fast enough to protect those rights for us, we are justified in bypassing the whole legal system and taking the law into our own hands (see [7]). The second law, however—as Aristotle had argued just as forcefully—suggests rather that the purpose of law is to enforce our obligations, including above all our obligation to our country, and that these obligations even trump our individual rights since, in their name, we can rightly be required to give up our own life and bodily security (see [8]). By forcing Evodius to explain how both these laws can be justified, Augustine in effect demands to know which of these two basic moral-political phenomena are truly primary: our rights or our duties.

The dialogue to this point already provides ample material for discussion in the modern classroom. I believe that many students even in our modern liberal democracy, whether Christian or non-Christian, would sympathize with most or all of the positions Evodius has taken up to now, and those who do not would at least find in them a springboard for discussion of these issues with their classmates. At this point in the conversation, though, Evodius's answers may begin to seem somewhat more foreign. For he does not here put forth any view of government as a mere social contract aimed at protecting rights that no duty can ever require us to lay down. But the reason he does not adopt such a view is one with which many of our students would have some sympathy: he refuses to abandon that aspect of his moral experience according to which we have a genuine and compelling duty to fight and die for our country when it asks us to (see [3], 1.5.12.35–37, esp. line 43, *cogit*). This is an experience that centuries of liberal political theory have famously had trouble making sense of, and students would undoubtedly benefit from reflection on whether such experiences, which surely are still common to many Americans today, can be reconciled fully with the Lockean terms in which we are used to discussing questions of political legitimacy.

In any case, Evodius does believe that the protection of his own political community is in principle worth both killing and dying for, and even that he is morally obligated to do as much when that community requires it of him. But to understand this obligation, we would then have to ask what defines his political community. And his statements here turn out again to be taking something for granted, namely what we would call the constitution or regime of that community (see [3], 1.5.12.34–36, esp. lines 40–41). Soldiers die, not just to defend their fellow citizens as individuals, but more fundamentally to defend the "freedom" of their entire political community, and hence especially its legal order or constitution; our own American soldiers take an oath that makes this explicit (see [3], 1.5.11.32, line 6, *libertate*; [3], 1.5.12.35, lines 28–29, with 1.7.16.52, lines 2–3; [9]). What then would make that constitution so worth defending? This is the implicit question that leads at last to Augustine's fourth set of dilemmas. Here he now encourages Evodius to imagine himself raised from the level of a legislator to that of a revolutionary, *i.e.*, a person who effectively tears up an old constitution and writes a new one. On what basis can such a person rightly take such an action? What makes a constitution good or just? To help Evodius with this question, Augustine suggests two examples of apparently just constitutions. The first is written for a morally virtuous and public-spirited populace, and it allows them to rule themselves in a democratic republic. Evodius immediately agrees that this is a just constitution ([3], 1.6.14.45). (This is also interesting from a historical point of view, since republicanism might be thought to have been dead in Rome for over 400 years, but somehow Evodius agrees to this point without hesitation even in A.D. 388.) On the other hand, in the second example, that same populace has undergone dramatic moral degeneration and has corrupted the democratic process to elect criminals who both perpetrate and permit moral atrocities. Is there some point, Augustine asks, at which they lose the right to govern themselves, and at which then a revolution could be justified, where a few people or even one person would seize power out of that populace's hands? (The classic example today would of course be Germany in the 1940s.) This too, Evodius grants with equal readiness, would be just ([3], 1.6.14.46). And if we agree with him, as it seems to me most of us would find ourselves forced to at some point, then we have made a morally important claim. For to accept the justice of this example is to agree that there is some moral standard in the name of which a number of other morally binding political principles that we normally claim to accept—whether government by consent of the governed, respect for existing legal authorities and structures, or even the illegitimacy of extralegal force against one's fellow citizens—can all in certain extreme circumstances be ignored. Augustine calls this moral standard the "eternal law" ([3], 1.6.14.47–15.49). So according to the reasoning sketched in the conversation to this point, which I believe Augustine himself accepts in its essential points, it would seem that all earthly laws are justified only to the extent that they promote the moral common good of their citizens under this eternal law ([3], 1.6.15.50–7.16.52).

Now, this conclusion sounds like a far cry from the assertion that cities are all hardly more than gangs of robbers, and anyone familiar with Augustine's political writings may well wonder how a conclusion like this could have anything to do with his famous so-called pessimism or realism about the limits of earthly politics. But it is in fact only a small step from the one to the other. Evodius himself had admitted, although it is not clear that he ever sees the full significance of this, that he expects even a revolutionary to promote this moral common good only to the extent that this is actually possible for him (see [3], 1.6.14.46, line 31, *si...possit*). And for reasons that come out both in this text (see esp. [3], 1.15.32.108–33.112) and in other writings of his, Augustine's own judgment seems to have been that all the political laws we see around us do at best a very mediocre job of promoting such a common good. Yet precisely because our political communities always have been and always will be so mediocre at performing their highest task, any attempts at radical political reform will fail, in almost all and perhaps even all cases, to bring about real improvement in the lives of those communities' citizens. We are therefore almost always better off, in Augustine's view, when we try to make no more than minor improvements to our earthly cities—as Augustine himself often did as a bishop, and as for example his great student Thomas More would do many centuries later as a politician. Hence Augustine turns out to have arrived at his famously "realistic" view of politics, which he presents in pithy summary form at the end of this dialogue in a manner that strongly anticipates the "two cities" doctrine he would later develop more fully (ibid.), not by contemptuously ignoring ordinary moral-political experience but through sympathetic engagement with that experience: he uncovers the limits of politics when he judges it by precisely the high moral standard which that ordinary experience, upon examination, turns out to presuppose. Whether or not students end up accepting Augustine's "realistic" conclusions, it seems to me in principle preferable than they think through his own reasons for them than that they merely confront them without seeing those reasons, as a superficial acquaintance with excerpts from *City of God* might well encourage them to.

3. Concluding Remarks

One fascinating aspect of this text that I have not discussed here is the way in which Evodius, the character, embodies the difficulty that Augustine sees in convincing Christians to have such a moderate view of the limits of politics as I have just attributed to Augustine himself. Evodius, who is I think a kind of typical Christian citizen, vacillates visibly over the course of the dialogue between tendencies toward an apolitical despair or pacifism on the one hand, and a hyperpolitical moralism or even revolutionarism on the other. Both of these are errors that the author seems to think represent dangerous and typically Christian tendencies, both in different ways are traceable to unrealistically high expectations from politics, and both are tendencies that, by the end of this book, Augustine has successfully combatted in Evodius, as indeed he would go on to try to combat them in millions of his fellow Christians [10]. By the end of the book, Evodius is a better educated Christian citizen. His conversation with Augustine has given him a stronger sense of how far all temporal laws necessarily fall short of the moral standards prescribed by the eternal law, and of why the temporal law nonetheless should not be held in contempt for the limited but important work it can do ([3], 1.15.32.108–112). But I have not dwelt on this aspect of the dialogue here because, although I do think that Augustine intended to have just such an effect on his broader audience as he had had on his friend Evodius, I do not think that what is most valuable in this book is its portrait of Augustine's pedagogical rhetoric, as beautiful as that portrait is. Because to a significant extent, it does remain rhetoric: Evodius is not all that promising as a student, he does not turn out to be interested in thinking through the questions that Augustine has pushed on him, and Augustine ends up having to persuade him of views that approximate his own without ever really taking him through the arguments for those views. And my own experience leads me to think that concentrating on this rhetoric of Augustine's is not the most helpful way to approach this text. When I first began studying it four years ago, I was mainly concerned to show what silly mistakes Evodius made on almost every page of the conversation, and how far he was from grasping what I assumed to be Augustine's own views; this led me to write many pages of interpretation that I now find embarrassing to read. I only really began learning from this book when I stopped trying to show how much Augustine sees that Evodius does not, or for that matter how much I see that Evodius does not, and went to work instead on uncovering what Evodius sees that I had not previously seen. I believe it is a great and rather painful secret of the book that we all have more in common with him than we would like to think. Even Augustine, after all, says that he himself had to struggle for some time (probably years) with the very questions that Evodius here finds so difficult (see again [3], 1.2.4.10–11). And Augustine is able to teach us more when we make that struggle our own rather than look down on Evodius for failing to reach its conclusion—as indeed few if any of us can claim to have done.

The most valuable aspect of this book, then, for ourselves and our students alike, is the introduction that it offers to the difficult questions of moral and political philosophy that Augustine wishes his readers to grapple with. For the book shows that Augustine regarded this grappling—with our own elementary moral experiences as individuals and citizens—as by no means something that Christian faith has freed anyone of the need for. Rather, he saw it as the starting point of his own understanding of politics, and indeed of self-knowledge more generally. And I believe we will offer our students the best possible introduction to Augustine's reflections on politics when we allow him to introduce them to that difficult but ultimately rewarding experience to which he tried, with only limited success, to introduce his friend Evodius.

Acknowledgments

I am grateful to Kimberley Burns, Erik Dempsey, Heather Pangle, and the three anonymous reviewers for their helpful comments on this paper; to the Thomas Jefferson Center for the Study of Core Texts and Ideas at the University of Texas at Austin for supporting me while I wrote it; and to Robert Bartlett, Nasser Behnegar, Christopher Bruell, Robert Faulkner, Christopher Kelly, Joseph MacFarland, Pierre Manent, and Susan Shell for helping me with generous criticisms of my doctoral dissertation, without which help I would have been in no position to write this paper.

Conflicts of Interest

The author declares no conflict of interest.

References

1. Augustine. *De Civitate Dei*. Edited by B. Dombart and A. Kalb. Stuttgart: Teubner, 1993, 2 vols.
2. Vatican II. *Gaudium et Spes*. In *Sacrosanctum Oecumenicum Concilium Vaticanum II: Constitutiones, Decreta, Declarationes*. Vatican: Libreria Editrice Vaticana, 1966, pp. 681–835, section 43.
3. Augustine. *De Libero Arbitrio*. In *Contra Academicos, De Beata Vita, De Ordine, De Magistro, De Libero Arbitrio*. Edited by W.M. Green and Klaus-Detlef Daur. Turnhout: Brepols, 1970, pp. 210–35.
4. Peter King, trans. and ed. *Augustine: On the Free Choice of the Will, On Grace and Free Choice, and Other Writings*. New York: Cambridge University, 2010.
5. Augustine. *Epistulae*. In *Patrologia Latina*. Paris: 1841 vol. 33, Letter 162, section 2.
6. Peter Burnell. "The Problem of Service to Unjust Regimes in Augustine's *City of God*." *Journal of the History of Ideas* 54 (1993): 177–88.
7. John Locke. *Second Treatise of Government*. In *Two Treatises of Government*. Edited by Peter Laslett. Cambridge: Cambridge University Press, 1988, pp. 267–428, sections 18–19.
8. Aristotle. *Politica*. Edited by W.D. Ross. New York: Oxford University, 1957, Book 5, chapter 1.
9. Oath of Enlistment. Available online: http://www.army.mil/values/oath.html (accessed on 31 October 2014).
10. Daniel Burns. "Saint Augustin et les fondaments rhétoriques de la démocratie chrétienne." *Revues Électroniques de l'Université de Nice*, March 2013. Available online: http://revel.unice.fr/symposia/rhetoriquedemocratique/index.html?id=610 (accessed on 12 January 2014).

Teaching Augustine's *On the Teacher*

Robert D. Anderson

Abstract: This paper examines the merits of introducing undergraduates to the philosophical thought of Augustine by means of his short dialogue *On the Teacher*.

> Reprinted from *Religions*. Cite as: Anderson, R.D. Teaching Augustine's *On the Teacher*. *Religions* **2015**, *6*, 404–408.

On the Teacher is an excellent text for undergraduates' initial contact with the philosophical thought of the Christian thinker Saint Augustine. While other texts better introduce Augustine's theological thought or his public life as priest and bishop or his personal life, *On the Teacher* reveals Augustine the philosopher. The text works well in a small Great Books seminar where discussion is the order of the day as well as in a large lecture class in Medieval Philosophy with limited opportunities for Socratic interaction. Moreover, the text works well when supplemented with other philosophical writings by Augustine (such as *Against the Academicians*, especially book three, and *On Free Choice of the Will*), as well as when it is the stand-alone sample of his philosophizing. What is the case for teaching Augustine's *On the Teacher*?

For one, the complete work is short (about fifty pages) and, thus, doable in two classes. Its shortness keeps the work tight and thereby minimizes the Ciceronian meandering that Augustine liked and often imitated but that annoys and confuses modern undergraduates. For another, the work is readily accessible like Plato's *Meno* after which it is modeled. The work is a dialogue between a father (Augustine) and his son (Adeodatus), a son who is talented, beloved, and around eighteen and who died shortly after the work was completed. The work also is interesting, especially to Christian students or students at Christian colleges and universities, because it shows Augustine doing what Christian philosophers typically do. They attempt to integrate their Christian beliefs and philosophical reflections.

With Augustine the efforts at integration take many forms. Sometimes he attempts to prove articles of faith like God's existence. Other times he attempts to articulate Christian doctrine with precision and to manifest that, besides being intelligible, Christian doctrine is noncontradictory and even plausible. Still other times he attempts to harmonize his different sets of beliefs: his Christian faith and his philosophical convictions. This harmonization can consist not only in showing that the two sets are consistent but also in synthesizing the two into a unified set. Such a synthesis is the focus of *On the Teacher*, where Augustine is specifically reflecting on scriptural verses like I Corinthians 3:16, "Do you not know that you are God's temple and that God's Spirit lives in you?" and Matthew 23:9–10, "Nor are you to be called *teacher*, for you have one teacher, the Christ" and attempting to square those verses with how he thinks people come to know.

In a second way, *On the Teacher* is interesting to undergraduates (those with and those without a creed) because its subject is something they have a stake in: education. Most undergraduates already have strong views about teaching and learning. In fact, undergraduates are often passionate (sometimes even articulate) about what has gone wrong and what has gone right in their educations to date. Thus, the subject of the work is well suited to undergraduates.

What then does Augustine say about teaching and learning?

In the first half of the dialogue, Augustine and Adeodatus establish quickly that all communication is teaching because it attempts to inform a person about what is in somebody's mind ([1], pp. 94–95). They also quickly agree that all teaching is carried out either with language that communicates or by examples that exhibit what is to be taught ([1], p. 102). The remainder of the first half of the dialogue is a discussion of various puzzles about human language. The puzzles result from imprecise definitions, the blurring of the distinction between the use of a term versus its mention, ambiguity in terms, and self-referential oddities.

Students themselves are puzzled at this point in the dialogue. In fact, they are usually frustrated with the apparent disconnect between Augustine's linguistic problems and his main topic of teaching. They are not alone in their frustration, however. Augustine senses a similar frustration in Adeodatus, and he addresses it thus:

> With so many detours, it's difficult to say at this point where you and I are trying to get to! Maybe you think we're playing around and diverting the mind from serious matters by little puzzles that seem childish, or that we're pursuing some result that is only small or modest…Well, I'd like you to believe that I haven't set to work on mere trivialities in this conversation. Though we do perhaps play around, this should itself not be regarded as childish…So then, you'll pardon me if I play around with you at first—not for the sake of playing around, but to exercise the mind's strength and sharpness ([1], p. 122).

The clear suggestion is that the various linguistic problems (and even less a full-blown philosophy of language) were not the point of the first half of the dialogue. But what was then?

Students need help to answer this question. My proposal to students is that readers should take seriously a point that Augustine and Adeodatus agreed on earlier in the dialogue. They agreed that there are two ways of teaching: either by communicating something or by exhibiting something, that is, by telling or by displaying. If Augustine fails to tell us much about what is teaching in the first half of *On the Teacher*, does he perhaps nonetheless succeed in displaying for us something about teaching? Thus, I ask my students: what does Augustine display or exhibit for us about teaching in the first half his work?

Students always rise to the occasion with many good answers. One may have to wait for some answers and to prod for others, but students always produce a wonderful array. Here is a sample of their answers.

Answers 1 & 2: As Augustine explicitly says in the previous quotation and also exhibits in the dialogue itself, the pursuit of knowledge must be both serious and playful. It is serious in its ultimate aim but playful along the way with a willingness to try out different ideas and to make mistakes in the course of doing so. Similarly, Augustine explicitly says in the previous quotation and also exhibits that inquiry has to be systematic, beginning with easier problems (like his linguistic problems) first so that the mind gains "strength and sharpness".

Answers 3 & 4: Augustine and Adeodatus display the values of persistence and perseverance in the dialogue. Theirs is a sustained effort to think through various language puzzles, and they return again and again to their topics in spite of difficulties, detours, and dead ends. Augustine and Adeodatus also display the values of humility and docility. Neither grows angry or despondent by the difficulties, detours, and dead ends, and each is willing to be led by the other's questions, insights, and suggestions.

Answer 5: Augustine seems to be working hard in *On the Teacher* to exhibit the need for interest or commitment in intellectual inquiry. The language puzzles in the first half of the work seem to be designed to function as hooks to draw Adeodatus (and, by extension, readers) into the search. They attempt to produce perplexity and thereby interest.

Answer 6: Augustine's work displays the value of conversation. The work is, after all, a dialogue between two people. The form of the work suggests that Augustine thinks human beings advance intellectually in community with others rather than in isolated islands of independence.

Answer 7: Finally and piggy-back on the last point, though *On the Teacher* is a dialogue, the work is written for readers who are not in dialogue with anybody. They are simply reading about a conversation of others. So, although not engaged in conversation with another human being, readers of *On the Teacher* would seemed to be called to an internal dialogue between themselves and the text: "what does Augustine mean here", "why does Adeodatus say this", "is this claim true", "why is this work written the way it is", and the like.

This last point about what Augustine is displaying in *On the Teacher* is most important because it coincides with what he explicitly tells Adeodatus (and readers in general) in the second half of the dialogue. Thus, on to the second half.

The second half of the work begins with more language puzzles. Augustine also explains a few more requirements of rational inquiry (similar to those he displayed earlier in the first half) such as caution before assenting to anything and resistance to misology (a hatred or distrust of reasoning), especially after one's confidence has been shattered a few times. But the main point of the second half (and the main point of the whole dialogue) emerges after Augustine and Adeodatus return to a line of reasoning begun in the first half.

In the first half of the dialogue, Adeodatus maintains that "nothing can be shown without signs", unless it can be exhibited in some fashion. That is, when we want to make something known to somebody else, we always resort to words or some symbolic gesture, or we display what we want others to recognize. After both departing from this position and returning to a modified version of it in the second half of the work, Augustine ends the formal dialogue and begins an extended, twelve-page monologue intended to guide Adeodatus (and readers) to several conclusions.

The first is that "nothing can be shown with signs", the exact opposite of what Adeodatus has maintained throughout the dialogue. If we do not already know what words signify, then words are useless and can show nothing, and if we do already know, then there is nothing new for words to show. Instead of words or other signs doing the showing, the only thing, according to Augustine, that can show us whether something is or is not the case is (1) our senses, (2) our memories, or (3), in the case of conceptual matters, "an inner light of Truth" that we "consult". In the third (the case of conceptual matters) we find Augustine's theory of divine illumination, very briefly sketched and raising many questions that are left unanswered. Is divine illumination the cognitive grasping of objects that have been illumined divinely, or is cognitive grasping simply to be divinely illumined?

Does human knowledge require God's sudden and extraordinary causal appearance in the world, or are human beings always in possession of a piece of the divine which they make use of when they come to know? Is divine illumination intended to explain how we know everything or only some things? Do the mechanics of divine illumination differ from the mechanics of mystical experiences or divine inspiration? All are unanswered.

We also find Augustine harmonizing his Christian faith with his philosophical convictions. Augustine (following the lead of Scripture) identifies the inner light that teaches in the course of an internal dialogue as Christ himself, the second person of the Trinity who came down from heaven and became incarnate, dwelling and operating within human persons ([1], pp. 139, 146). This is an unusual claim, no doubt, and it is perhaps peculiar to Augustine. But it is Augustine's. It is Augustine's Christian philosophy.

The takeaways from *On the Teacher* include at least three things for undergraduates. First and foremost, Augustine presents an account of teaching and learning radically at odds with what students usually think. Augustine both tells and exhibits how genuine teaching consists in an internal dialogue within students. Students have to see things for themselves and make the truth their own. Memorizing, repeating, imitating, and going through the motions in yet some other ways do not suffice. As for the external, conventional teacher, that person can only attempt to occasion the moments of genuine teaching. Thus, genuine education is not dissemination or transferal of information. Dissemination or transferal of information is better called something like *instruction*, and it can only produce belief, not knowledge. Instead, genuine education is an activity in which students are always the primary agents as they see things for themselves and make the truth their own. As Augustine puts this point, "who is so foolishly curious as to send his son to school to learn what the teacher thinks?" ([1], p. 145).

Moreover, coming to know conceptual truths is for human beings a mysterious phenomenon. How people can grasp permanent and unchanging truths as simple as "$3 + 2 = 5$" is deeply puzzling. Either the puzzle has to be explained away, or an adequate account of human cognition has to preserve the puzzle. Augustine's divine illumination (like Plato's theory of recollection, Aristotle's agent intellect, and Descartes' "light of reason") preserves the puzzle, whereas Hume's empiricism and contemporary theories in philosophy of mind like behaviorism, functionalism, and eliminative materialism explain away the puzzle of human knowledge. By taking philosophical chances and identifying the "inner light of Truth" with Christ the God-man, Augustine unites faith and reason in a Christian philosophy that shows why some this-world mysteries permanently surpass understanding. They are bound up with an incomprehensible wisdom before all ages, with God Himself.

Finally, while Augustine's account of human knowledge is in terms of divine illumination, he does not demand that we, his readers, agree with him. Divine illumination is not a doctrine. Rather, the entire movement of the dialogue has been to move from external conversation, to an internal dialogue of asking questions and searching for adequate answers, and finally to seeing and determining for oneself how it is that we come to know. Thus, while Adeodatus ends the dialogue saying "I have learned that it is He [Christ] alone who teaches us whether what is said is true" ([1], p. 146), we may not now (nor ever) see it that way.

At the bare minimum, *On the Teacher* is a good, though less common, introduction to the Christian philosophy of Augustine. When things go well, Augustine's short dialogue can also help students better understand the intellectual journey that they began in elementary school, are continuing in college, and will remain on the whole of their lives. When things go very well, the hope is that students' greater understanding will contribute to their greater success on that journey.

Conflicts of Interest

The author declares no conflict of interests.

Reference

1. Augustine. *Against the Academicians and the Teacher*. Translated by Peter King. Indianapolis: Hackett, 1995, pp. 94–146. Available online: http://netbible.org (accessed on 3 April 2015).

Augustine's *De Musica* in the 21st Century Music Classroom

John MacInnis

Abstract: Augustine's *De musica* is all that remains of his ambitious plan to write a cycle of works describing each of the liberal arts in terms of Christian faith and is actually unfinished; whereas the six books extant today primarily examine rhythm, Augustine intended to write about melody also. The sixth book of *De musica* was better known in late Antiquity and the Middle Ages than the first five, and it takes up philosophical questions of aesthetics related to the proportionate ordering discernable throughout creation. After a brief introduction summarizing *De musica*'s content and its importance in subsequent Christian writings, my presentation outlines and explains how I have used this document in my own music classes. For example, my students learn that a vital notion in Augustine's writings, and in Neoplatonism more broadly, is the spiritual benefit of academic study. That is, through study of music, one gains insight into the created order, but, more importantly, one's soul is strengthened and trained to perceive higher realities of the cosmos such as the ordering of the planetary spheres and the progression of celestial hierarchies, which span the spiritual distance from God to humanity.

Reprinted from *Religions*. Cite as: MacInnis, J. Augustine's *De Musica* in the 21st Century Music Classroom. *Religions* **2015**, *6*, 211–220.

1. Introduction

In his *Retractions* (I.5), Augustine recounts that he began *De musica* [1] as he prepared for baptism in Milan, in 387 CE (see quotation below). Augustine's ambitious plan was to write a cycle of works describing the liberal arts in terms of Christian faith. Sadly, *De musica* is his only surviving educational treatise and is actually unfinished [2]; whereas the six books extant today concern rhythm, Augustine intended to write about melody also. Written as a dialogue between master and student, the majority of the first five books discuss the motions, quantities, and qualities of rhythm, understood generally as a fundamental element employed in musical and poetic art, e.g., the classifications and use of quantitative meter in verse composition [3]. The sixth book of *De musica* was better known in Augustine's day than the first five, and it takes up philosophical questions of aesthetics related to the proportionate ordering discernable throughout creation. In the following, I will briefly summarize *De musica*'s contents and its importance in subsequent Christian writings. Additionally, I will outline how I have used this document in my own music classes at Dordt College, a Christian liberal arts college in the Reformed tradition.

2. Augustine and Music

Music was, of course, an important factor in Augustine's conversion and spiritual formation. At the famous *tolle lege* event, in 386, which Augustine describes in *Confessions* VIII, the child-like voice said "take up and read" in a sing-song fashion (*cum cantu dicentis*) ([4], p. 171). Additionally, in *Confessions* IX, Augustine mentions how singing the Psalms of David moved him profoundly while a catechumen: "What cries I used to send up to Thee in those songs, and how I was enkindled toward Thee by them! I burned to sing them if possible, throughout the whole world, against the pride of the human race" ([4], p. 179). In that same book, Augustine mentions the devotional power of singing hymns and canticles: "The voices flowed into my ears; and the truth was poured forth into my heart, where the tide of my devotion overflowed, and my tears ran down, and I was happy in all these things" ([4], p. 184). At the death of his mother, Monica, in 388, Augustine records how the entire household sang Psalm 101, "I will sing of mercy and judgment unto thee, O Lord", and how, by recalling her favorite hymn, *Deus Creator Omnium*, he was comforted (*Confessions* IX) ([4], p. 195).

Augustine's relationship to music as a liberal art was, in many ways, typical for his day. That is, in late Antiquity, *musica* was largely a mathematical art studied in the philosophical context of Neoplatonism. For example, in *De ordine*, completed in 386, Augustine presents the liberal arts as preparation for philosophical study and explains how numbers are a means by which the unity and coherence of creation can be discerned, with implications for living a well-ordered life. Additionally, it was thought, through the study of physical reality, e.g., via quantitative liberal arts, like music, a soul is trained to reach for the incorporeal. This aphorism is actually a cornerstone in Augustinian aesthetics: Get past the responses of your physical senses to perceive the higher reality; move beyond the created to the Creator. With this justification, derived from Romans 1, Augustine began a Christian textbook on grammar, which he claimed was later lost (*Retractions* I.5.3) [5], as well as a Christian explanation of music, the first six books of which were completed after his return to North Africa from Milan:

> At the very time that I was about to receive baptism in Milan, I also attempted to write books on the liberal arts, questioning those who were with me and who were not adverse to studies of this nature, and desiring by definite steps, so to speak, to reach things incorporeal through things corporeal and to lead others to them. But I was able to complete only the book on grammar—which I lost later from our library—and six books, *On Music*, pertaining to that part which is called rhythm. I wrote these six books, however, only after I was baptized and had returned to Africa from Italy, for I had only begun this art in Milan. Of the other five arts likewise begun there—dialectic, rhetoric, geometry, arithmetic, and philosophy—the beginnings alone remained and I lost even these. However, I think that some people have them ([6], pp. 21–22).

3. *De Musica*, Book VI

In a letter responding to Memorius, Bishop of Capua, in 409 (Letter 101), Augustine acknowledged Memorius's request for a copy of *De musica* ([7], p. 144). Augustine had promised Memorius a revised copy of the treatise, but was apparently unable to get to it. He ended up sending only Book VI and said that this book was actually more important than the first five:

> But I am sending the sixth book to your Charity at once. I have found a revised copy of it and it contains the essence of all the other books. Perhaps your serious mind will find

it worth your while. As for the other five, they will hardly seem worth reading to our son and fellow deacon, Julian… ([7], p. 147).

The difference between the first five books of *De musica* and Book VI is further emphasized by Augustine in his introduction to that book, in which he explains that all his preceding discussions are but childish trifles and that their true worth lies in guiding the enquiring mind to this final culminating portion. Augustine distinguishes four types of rhythm (*numeri*): those in the process of being produced, those that are heard, those residing in memory, and those sounding in the air. These types of rhythm are ordered, in terms of excellence, and a fifth superior category is introduced, those rhythms perceived by natural judgment. The Latin word *numerus*, which Augustine uses throughout *De musica*, can mean either "rhythm" or "number". "Rhythm" is the most common sense for *numerus* in *De musica*, and, for example, this translation is used throughout in Martin Jacobsson's translation of Book VI (*cf.*, [8], p. 7).

In order to rank their types, Augustine explains how rhythms act in relation to the human soul and physical body; he concludes that both soul and body have their own rhythms (respectively superior and inferior) and that the soul cannot be acted upon by the body. Additionally, because it is hard to account for the fact that a physical sound can have any interaction with the non-physical soul, Augustine's proposes that the soul acts first.

For Augustine, the loftiest action one may take with regard to rhythm is its judgment according to reason, the very action necessary to best pursue musical knowledge, according to his definition from *De musica* I.2, derived from Varro: "*Musica est scientia bene modulandi*" ("Music is the science of modulating well"). *Modulor*, in this context, may signify an application of measure to musical quantity, as in rhythm, and not simply musical singing or playing ([9], p. 7).

This preference for theorizing (or philosophizing) to practice is at least as old as Plato; in *Republic* (§597–598), Plato demonstrates that an artist imitates the appearance of a thing but does not necessarily understand the thing's reality or nature. Similarly for Augustine, in *De musica* I.6, performers of music are inferior to those who discern and describe the structure and components of music. Additionally, the fact that performers play for praise or money is an example that they are ethically compromised in their approach to music. Though, it should be said that, on this point, the master and student conversing in *De musica* appear to disagree ([1], pp. 186–87). The student argues for the possibility of a performer who is also educated in the theories of music, and his master does not completely dismiss the idea.

Augustine then explains how the discernment of rhythmic equality and symmetry in music is only one way in which we may identify an order pervasive throughout all creation. For example, the motions of the cosmos demonstrate an appropriate ordering for the soul; the planets move in perfect unity in imitation of eternity, and their rhythms unite earthly things in "the hymn of the universe" (*carmini uniuersitatis*):

> Let us, therefore, not look askance at what is inferior to us, but let us place ourselves between what is below us and what is above us, with the help of our God and Lord, in such a way that we are not offended by what is inferior but enjoy only what is superior. For the pleasure is like a weight for the soul. And so pleasure sets the soul in its place. "For where your treasure is, there your heart will be also" [Luke 12:34]…In this way,

through the rhythmical succession of their times [*numerosa successione*], the orbits unite the terrestrial things, subjected to the heavenly ones to the hymn, as it were, of the universe ([8], pp. 65–67).

Additionally, for Augustine, those rhythms we experience in our earthly life may be beautiful, but they should not be valued inordinately. Rather, pleasing, well-crafted rhythms point us toward an inherent love of order—which the soul needs—and serve as another call to embrace reason as opposed to base sensuality.

In *De musica* VI.14, Augustine proposes that orienting the soul toward God is a matter of properly ordered love, to which all the movements and rhythms of human life are to be directed:

> Now, do you think that I should speak at length about this, when the holy Scriptures in so many volumes and with such authority and sanctity tell us nothing but this, that we shall love our God and Lord with all our heart and with all our soul and with all our mind and love our neighbour as ourselves [Luke 10:27]? Thus, if we direct all these movements and rhythms [*motus numerosque*] of our human activity to this end, we will undoubtedly be purified ([8], p. 91).

In the concluding sections of *De musica* VI, Augustine expounds three final instances of reading rhythmic equality and proportionate ordering into other aspects of creation (VI.17) ([8], p. 111ff.). (1) He references the construction of particles of earth that display "corrationality" (*conrationalitas*, Augustine's translation of ἀναλογία, in Book VI) [10]; (2) The ordering of the elements in terms of excellence displays an overall harmony. For example, air strives for unity with greater facility than earth or water and is, therefore, superior, and the planets display the limit and supreme splendor of unified bodies; (3) The entire process of the soul's journey back to God is also a rhythm entailing equality and order.

In a brief remark at the close of this book, Augustine goes beyond the moving planets and the soul's quest for theosis and comments on the rational and intellectual rhythms of "the blessed and holy souls" (VI.17) ([8], p. 117). As he later clarified in his *Retractions* ([6], p. 48), Augustine is here referring to the angels who mediate as messengers between God and humankind:

> These, which are mobile likewise in the temporal intervals, are preceded and modified by a vital movement which serves the Lord of all things, without having distributed the temporal intervals of its rhythms, but with a power that gives the times, over which power the rational and intellectual rhythms of the blessed and holy souls without any intervening nature receive the law of God—without which not a single leaf falls from a tree and for whom our hairs are counted—and transmit it to the earthly and infernal laws ([8], pp. 115–17).

Throughout *De musica* VI, Augustine refers to the Ambrosian hymn, *Deus Creator Omnium*, his mother's favorite, and this hymn serves as a model for what Augustine intends music to be ([8], p. 111). That is, there are rhythms at play all along the process of someone recalling and singing the chant, to the hearing of it, to the contemplation of it, and, for Augustine, the song is so well crafted that a soul easily moves from the beauty of the music, received by the senses, to contemplation of God's transcendent beauty.

4. *De Musica* in Subsequent Christian Literature

The importance of *De musica* as a music treatise and Augustine's place as an authority on music by the sixth century is confirmed by Cassiodorus in his *Institutiones Divinarum et Saecularium Litterarum* (2.5.10) ([11], p. 222). And, in the ninth century, the Irish polymath, John Scottus Eriugena, cited Augustine's *De musica* in his magisterial *Periphyseon*. Continuing his discussion of place and time as predicates for existence, Eriugena states that "everything that is, except God, subsists after some manner" [12] (*Periphyseon* I, §482B):

> Do you see then that place and time are understood to be prior to all things that are? For the number [*numerus, i.e.*, rhythm] of places and times, as St. Augustine says in chapter six of the "*De musica*", precedes all things that are in them: for the mode [*modus*], that is, measure, of all things that are created is, in the nature of things, logically prior to their creation; and this mode and measure of each is called its place, and so it is ([12], p. 127).

Additionally, in *Periphyseon* III, §630D ([13], p. 53), Eriugena's description of the "natural orders" follows closely Augustine's argument, in *De musica* VI.17 ([8], pp. 109–11). For example, Augustine had described participants in the chain of being as keeping a balanced, proper order. So too, Eriugena advances a constituted order and, like Augustine, sees the chain as communicating grace and goodness to all its parts, goodness in their existence and grace in their beauty. For Augustine and Eriugena, the order of the entire sequence is proportionate and equal, thus producing a concord that encompasses every part.

Not only does Augustine's *De musica* show up in Eriugena's philosophizing in the ninth century, it is also cited in the *Enchiriadis* documents. Throughout *Musica* and *Scholica enchiriadis*, the authors survey theoretical knowledge of the past (e.g., defining the modes, probing connections between music and human nature, and calculating the music of the spheres) and explain issues connected to ninth-century, Carolingian musical praxis (e.g., the improvisation of *organum*). Augustine's definition of music as *scientia bene modulandi* is used to open *Scholica enchiriadis*, and the discussion on rhythm at the end of Part I draws from Augustine's treatise. The relevance of *De musica* in the ninth century is further confirmed by its inclusion in the manuscript, Latin 7200, in the Bibliothèque nationale de France, along with *De institutione musica* by Boethius, the ninth book of Capella's *De nuptiis Philologiae et Mercurii*, and a treatise on the divisions of the monochord.

Augustine's standing as an authority on music, though not to the same degree as Boethius (*cf.*, *De institutione musica*), persisted through the eleventh century; Berno of Reichenau drew on *De musica* in his *Musica Bernonis seu Prologus in Tonorum* ([14], p. 36). As for the twelfth century, William Waite proposes in his book, *The Rhythm of Twelfth-Century Polyphony*, that Augustine's *De musica* may have been a source of the system of modal rhythm formulated at Notre Dame in Paris by Leoninus and Perotinus ([14], pp. 29–39). These rhythmic modes, organized into patterns of long and short durations, provided a workable solution to organizing multiple voices singing together at the same time and spurred new developments in subsequent polyphonic practice [15].

In the thirteenth century, Robert Grosseteste (1175–1253), Bishop of Lincoln, and Bonaventura (1221–1274) employed Augustine's ideas about musical aesthetics, explained in *De musica* VI ([14], p. 36). And Roger Bacon (*ca.* 1214–1294), in his *Opus Tertium* wrote:

> It is necessary that one should thoroughly understand the laws of meters and rhythms…and it is impossible to comprehend these unless one knows the five books of Augustine's "*De Musica*"…Only Augustine reveals the truth of this matter. It is impossible to know what is rhythm or meter or verse truly and properly except through these books ([14], p. 36).

In the fifteenth century, Franchinus Gaffurius, an Italian music theorist, cited Augustine's *De musica* in his *Theorica Musicae*, and it was through Gaffurius that *De musica* was transmitted to Andreas Ornithoparcus, in the sixteenth century (e.g., *Micrologus*) ([16], p. 278).

5. *De Musica* in the 21st Century Classroom

This whirlwind tour of Augustine's *De musica* in past centuries should raise the question, of what benefit could Augustine's insights on music be for music students today? In fact, I have used this treatise in my own music history and literature classes, and found that Augustine's intelligent and speculative words are actually received rather well.

My first attempt at introducing Augustine to my music students was in 2012. In that class, students were assigned Brian Brennan's article, which summarized the entire *De musica* treatise and provided some cultural context [16]. In class, I passed out excerpts, mostly from Book VI, and we talked about the harmony Augustine perceived in all the created order, all the way from the human soul to the steady movement of the firmament. We observed Augustine's view that there is a hierarchy, an order to the cosmos into which we all fit as smaller parts of a larger whole, each contributing to the overall unity and cohesion.

I pointed out that the study of music in late Antiquity was an all-encompassing discipline; that is, I highlighted all the topics brought up in such a short music treatise: memory, education, God, the human soul, the universe, number and rhythm, time, and ethics. My not-so-subtle assertion was that my music students need not worry about their choice of major; if we follow Augustine's lead, the study of music helps us make sense of the world around us and our place in it.

The students, though respectful of Augustine's achievement, did have questions about the apparent division of soul and body in Augustine's dialog. For example, Augustine's assertion that the rhythms of good music point the soul upward away from fleshly desires and entanglements seemed, for my students, to deny the goodness of the material creation in which we are called to live, flourish, and pursue justice. Many of my students, therefore, identified a conversation within the Christian intellectual tradition to which they had something to say, as musicians.

Recently, in 2014, I taught the same music history and literature class and again used Augustine's *De musica*. This time I was audacious and required them to read the entire sixth book. Our conversation was very similar to the previous semester, only I spent more time placing the treatise in the context of Platonism.

Plato himself had connected music to his examinations of both the human soul and the cosmos, and his followers in later eras used musical terminology in similar ways. For example, Plotinus (204/5–270 CE), considered a founder of Neoplatonism and its first systematic writer [17], used musical terms especially in his discussion of the soul's ascension to the One in his *Enneads*, e.g., *harmonia* helps the soul perceive the universe and reality, and the soul's union with the Universal-Soul results in *symphonia*.

In taking up the question of where the human soul comes from and where it goes when our body dies, Neoplatonists elaborated an allegorical journey from the stars to an earthly body, at birth, and back to the stars, at death. For example, Plotinus asserted that there is a spiritual aspect to our humanity that points to that higher, better reality. To a Neoplatonist, therefore, matter really is bad, and mankind, as a mix of body and soul, matter and spirit, requires a purgation of materiality and a return to God through knowledge. For example, in the following excerpt from *Enneads* I.3.1, Plotinus describes the ascent we must make back to the One, via pure philosophy or a liberal art like music, by which the physical and sensible lead us upward towards the intelligible:

> First of all we must distinguish the characteristics of these men: we will begin by describing the nature of the musician. We must consider him as easily moved and excited by beauty, but not quite capable of being moved by absolute beauty; he is however quick to respond to its images when he comes upon them, and, just as nervous people react readily to noises, so does he to articulate sounds and the beauty in them; and he always avoids what is inharmonious and not a unity in songs and verses and seeks eagerly after what is rhythmical and shapely. So, in leading him on, these sounds and rhythms and forms perceived by the senses must be made the starting-point. He must be led and taught to make abstraction of the material element in them and come to the principles from which their proportions and ordering forces derive and to the beauty which is in these principles, and learn that this was what excited him, the intelligible harmony and the beauty in it, and beauty universal, not just some particular beauty, and he must have the doctrines of philosophy implanted in him; by these he must be brought to firm confidence in what he possesses without knowing it ([18], p. 155).

The similarities between Plotinus's and Augustine's description of how one should properly receive music, and beauty more generally, are obvious: It all points to God, if we let it. In addition, acknowledging my students' good impulse to resist separating soul and body, I used this moment in class to stress that Augustine was, of course, a product of his own era, influenced by the intellectual currents of his day. I also noted that the insights music and all the arts provide us really do affect how we live. To this point, Augustine's affirmation of the benefits to liberal learning is profoundly relevant for us today and an example we are wise to follow.

Other valuable lessons include how Augustine's vision for Christian aesthetics integrates his vision for Christian ethics: For Augustine, beauty is related to truth and goodness. That is, one may not separate the judgment of beauty from the other responsibilities of our lived experience, which are to be ordered appropriately (*cf.*, [8], pp. 33–35). The very experience of beauty prompts the search for something more, and to stop at the beautiful object itself, for example, is wrongheaded and unjust.

This same point is taken up by Elaine Scarry in her recent book, *On Beauty and Being Just*:

> Something beautiful fills the mind yet invites the search for something beyond itself, something larger or something of the same scale with which it needs to be brought into relation....One can see why beauty...has been perceived to be bound up with the immortal, for it prompts a search for a precedent, which in turn prompts a search for a still earlier precedent, and the mind keeps tripping backward until it at last reaches something that has no precedent, which may very well be the immortal. And one can see why beauty...has been perceived to be bound up with truth. What is beautiful is in league with what is true because truth abides in the immortal sphere ([19], pp. 29–31).

Finally, and perhaps paradoxically, we observed that Augustine's understanding of art and aesthetics was both objective and subjective. That is, his explanation for beauty includes the object before us, its form and function, but also our perception and reception of it. Objectively, we have a basis for true study and productive discourse about the things we encounter in the world, their structure and order. Subjectively, we are responsible for ordinate enjoyment and use; we should love the right things in the right way. Additionally, if we accept Augustine's understanding of aesthetics as embracing both the objective and subjective, we may, by implication, account for the diversity of artistic expression across human cultures. God's own beauty is infinitely vast, and the created materials at our artistic disposal are various; it only makes sense that beauty be endlessly diverse.

6. Conclusions

I plan to include Augustine's *De musica* in future music classes, in ways similar to those described above. New areas for exploration include tracing with my students how musicians and theorists engaged Augustine's ideas throughout history; if this music treatise was a source of creative inspiration for others, why not us? Additionally, though I have made productive use of Augustine's philosophically oriented sixth book, there are still the first five, which brim with ideas about rhythm as a musical element to be shaped and sounded, faithfully and fruitfully. It would appear that we still have much to learn from Augustine.

Conflicts of Interest

The author declares no conflict of interest.

References and Notes

1. Augustine. "*De musica*." In *The Fathers of the Church*. Translated by Robert Taliaferro. Washington: Catholic University of America Press, 1947, vol. 4.
2. In referring to Augustine's educational treatises, I mean those he intended to write on each liberal art. Augustine stated in his *Retractions* that, as far as his original plan was concerned, he only completed the six books on music and a treatise on grammar, which he lost. In *De ordine* and *De doctrina christiana*, Augustine mentions music as an aspect of academic and theological study, but these treatises are not about music; they do not explicate musical theoretical principles.

3. Augustine's discussion, throughout the first five books of *De musica*, includes rhythmic applications for both music and poetry. For example, Augustine's discussion of "voluntary rests" in *De musica* IV.15 concerns musical practice and not quantitative meter.
4. Augustine. *Confessions*. Translated by Albert Outler. Nashville: Thomas Nelson Publishers, 1999.
5. Cf. Vivien Law. "St. Augustine's '*De grammatica*': Lost or Found?" *Recherches Augustiniennes* 19 (1984): 155–83.
6. Augustine. *Retractions*. In *The Fathers of the Church*. Translated by Mary Bogan. Washington: Catholic University of America Press, 1968, vol. 60.
7. Augustine. *Letters*, Vol. II. In *The Fathers of the Church*. Translated by Wilfrid Parsons. Washington: Catholic University of America Press, 1953, vol. 18.
8. Augustine. *Aurelius Augustinus: De musica Liber VI*. Translated by Martin Jacobsson. Stockholm: Almqvist and Wiksell, 2002.
9. Calvin Bower. *Fundamentals of Music*. New Haven: Yale University Press, 1989. The concept of modulation as transitioning from one key area to another does not apply in this context.
10. To be clear, Augustine had translated ἀναλογία as *proportio* earlier in his treatise, in Book I.
11. Cassiodorus. *Institutions of Divine and Secular Learning*. Translated by James Halporn. Liverpool: Liverpool University Press, 2004.
12. John Scottus Eriugena. *Periphyseon I*. In *Scriptores Latini Hiberniae*. Translated by Inglis Patrick Sheldon-Williams. Dublin: Dublin Institute for Advanced Studies, 1999, vol. 7.
13. John Scottus Eriugena. *Periphyseon III*. In *Scriptores Latini Hiberniae*. Translated by Inglis Patrick Sheldon-Williams. Dublin: Dublin Institute for Advanced Studies, 2005, vol. 11.
14. William Waite. *The Rhythm of Twelfth-Century Polyphony: Its Theory and Practice*. Westport: Greenwood Press, 1973. With regard to the quotation from Bacon's *Opus Tertium*, Chapter 64, Bacon mentions the five books of Augustine's *De music* and intends the *first* five books, since he refers to the sixth book elsewhere, e.g., Chapter 59.
15. It should be noted that Waite's proposed connection between Augustine's *De musica* and the development of Notre Dame polyphony in the twelfth century is not universally accepted.
16. Brian Brennan. "Augustine's *De Musica*." *Vigiliae Christianae* 42 (1988): 267–81.
17. The term Neoplatonism was first used during the nineteenth century to refer to the work of Plotinus and his followers. Cf., Raymond Erickson. "Boethius, Eriugena, and the Neoplatonism of *Musica* and *Scolica Enchiriadis*." In *Musical Humanism and Its Legacy: Essays in Honor of Claude V. Palisca*. Edited by Nancy Baker and Barbara Hanning. Stuyvesant: Pendragon, 1992.
18. Plotinus. *Enneads I.1–9*. In *The Loeb Classical Library*. Translated by Arthur Hilary Armstrong. Cambridge: Harvard University Press, 1966, vol. 440.
19. Elaine Scarry. *On Beauty and Being Just*. Princeton: Princeton University Press, 1999.

Section IV.
Exemplary Assignments

Teaching Augustine's *Confessions* in the Context of Mercer's Great Books Program

Bryan J. Whitfield

Abstract: Students in Mercer University's Great Books program read Augustine's *Confessions* in the third semester of a seven-semester sequence. Their previous reading of Greek and Roman epics and philosophical treatises as well as Biblical material equips them with a solid foundation for reading and discussing Augustine. This essay reflects on that preparation and models ways that instructors can use opening discussion questions related to those earlier readings to guide students into substantive reflection on the *Confessions*.

Reprinted from *Religions*. Cite as: Whitfield, B.J. Teaching Augustine's *Confessions* in the Context of Mercer's Great Books Program. *Religions* **2015**, *6*, 107–112.

1. Introduction

Undergraduate students at Mercer can choose one of two ways to fulfill their general education requirements. All students must fulfill requirements in math, science, and foreign languages. For the balance of their general education requirements, they may elect to follow the seven-course Integrative program (a distributional scheme) or follow a seven-course Great Books sequence emphasizing foundational texts in the Western intellectual tradition. This Great Books sequence moves students sequentially from Homer, Sophocles, and Thucydides to Dostoevsky, Weber, and Camus. Augustine's *Confessions* [1] is a central text in the third semester of the sequence, which students take in the fall semester of their sophomore year.

Mercer's faculty developed this sequence in consultation with Eva Brann, then a tutor at St. John's College in Annapolis, but decentralized faculty groups developed the particular reading lists for each course. The faculty shaped selections for the context of Mercer's College of Liberal Arts and the strengths of its faculty. They chose complete works where possible, considering the accessibility of works for undergraduates as well as the way that texts might speak to each other across the curriculum. The guiding concern, however, was pedagogical. The faculty were less focused on the development of themes or a history of ideas than on choosing texts about which students could think and write as a means to a liberal education [2].

2. Opening Questions

In these Great Books classes, capped at eighteen students per section, students focus on reading and discussing the primary texts. Classroom instruction is not focused on lecture, but on guiding students to form and to engage questions that emerge from the texts themselves. Reflective inquiry on the texts and these questions leads students to engage the texts through discussion and subsequent writing.

As a teacher in these courses, one of my roles is to watch over and guard the discussion. Part of that task is finding ways to launch the discussion well. Often the key to an effective class discussion is an apt generative question that the teacher or a student poses at the beginning of the hour as a basis for discussion, in-class writing, or both. As my colleague Thomas Huber has written, good opening questions are questions upon which the teacher has reflected for a long time, "a question for which the teacher has no final answer yet, but one for which he or she knows, or at least strongly believes, the text has something important to say and probably quite a bit to say." [3]. Huber encourages his students to "sound the depths possible from the opening question", avoiding shallow engagement for a quest that is "intense, involved, and vital." [3]. For me, effective questions must be both wide and deep, capacious and rich. As Gregory the Great once observed of scripture, good discussion questions must be like "a river…broad and deep, shallow enough here for the lamb to go wading, but deep enough there for the elephant to swim" [4]. Such questions have several possible points of entry and operate on multiple levels, so that responses can initially supply textual evidence and then move toward deeper analysis and reflection. The goal, of course, is that all may learn to swim like elephants.

3. *The Confessions* in the Context of Mercer's Great Books Sequence

Mercer students who are in the third semester of this sequence of Great Books are well equipped to read the bishop of Hippo when they encounter Augustine's *Confessions.* Their reading of three of Plato's dialogues (*Euthyphro, Apology,* and *Meno*) as well as all of the *Republic* provides a strong basis for understanding Augustine's Platonism. Their reading of Aristotle's *Nicomachean* Ethics gives them important categories and concepts for discussing friendship, a recurrent theme in Augustine's reflections. Having read the *Aeneid*, these students can appreciate both Augustine's tears at Dido's death and the way Augustine's own journey from Carthage to Rome parallels that of Aeneas.

In addition to their familiarity with these seminal works of the Greco-Roman tradition, the students in Mercer's Great Books III have read significant portions of both the Old Testament and the New Testament, including Genesis, Psalms, the Gospels, and Romans. The Great Books program uses these scriptures as the initial reading for this third semester of study, and students move directly from their reading of the Bible and a brief examination of creeds to two or three weeks spent reading the *Confessions*, usually Books 1–10.

Because they have read seminal texts from the Greco-Roman tradition as well as the biblical texts, these sophomore students have a solid foundation for reading, discussing, and writing about the *Confessions* on a level few contemporary American undergraduates experience. That foundation is one worth celebrating. I have remarked that the purpose of the first two and one-half semesters of the sequence is, after all, to equip students to read Augustine.

However, that jest is a serious one, for *Confessions* models a life of reflection on reading and writing. It is a book about books, a book about a life with and in books, a book in which books are quoted, studied, debated, and cherished. The plot turns on Augustine's reading of books, from Cicero's *Hortensius* to "the books of the Platonists" to Paul's letter to the Romans. The *Confessions* is, in short, a Great Book about the Great Books.

In reflecting on my own initial offering of this course, I realized I had done little to help students engage the "great bookishness" of the *Confessions*, to help them build upon their unique foundation for reading *Confessions* as readers of Plato, Aristotle, Virgil, and the Bible. I had not done the best job helping my students reflect on Augustine's own debt to the classical world or to the traditions of scripture. In my defense, I could raise the excuse that, as a New Testament scholar, Augustine is almost four hundred years later than my field of expertise. However, to be honest, my previous teaching in the Great Books sequence had been in the second semester—reading Plato's *Republic*, Euclid's *Elements*, Aristotle's *Nicomachean Ethics*, and Virgil's *Aeneid*—and my own research has focused on the New Testament's own intertextual use of Hebrew Bible. So while teaching Augustine's *Confessions* might have been a new task, my work with these other texts in the tradition was not.

So I began to develop new opening questions for class discussion or for in-class writing exercises that would engage the *Confessions*' use of these other texts the students had read in ways that would allow them to grasp Augustine's biography and thought more deeply and reflectively. What follows here is a sample of five questions and some initial reflections about them.

4. Sample Questions

Question for Day 1 (Books 1–2): Compare and contrast the opening paragraphs of *The Confessions* (Book 1, Chapters 1–5) with Psalm 139. What similarities do you see, and what differences? What do these texts say about the relationship between God and human beings? Are Augustine and the psalmist writing in the same genre? Why or why not?

Reflection: The goals of this prompt are to open up a conversation about both the ideas and the genre of the *Confessions*. Students in the Great Books program have read epics and philosophical texts, but this is their first exposure to autobiographical writing in the sequence. In the past, some of them have been struck by the connection to the Psalms and their interior focus. This prompt encourages students to engage the rich biblical intertexture of the opening paragraphs of the *Confessions*, which include well over a dozen references to the Psalms as well as allusions to or quotations from Genesis, Exodus, Deuteronomy, Job, Jeremiah, the Gospels, and the letters of Paul. Despite these other allusions, it is the voice of the psalmist that predominates.

Although the allusion to Psalm 139 is not Augustine's first reference to the Psalter, it is a crucial one that leads to a key Augustinian theme, as Augustine begins to reflect on the relationship of his consciousness of God and his consciousness of self: "Not yet am I in hell, after all, but even if I were, you would be there, too; for if I descend to the underworld, you are there." ([1], *Conf.* 1.2.2). The interplay of awareness of God and self lies at the heart of the psalm and the opening paragraphs. Thus the prompt has the potential to generate discussion of a significant Augustinian insight as well as raise questions of Augustine's genre and purpose for writing.

Question for Day 2 (Book 4): Although Augustine finds little profit in reading Aristotle, as he recounts in Book 4 ([1], *Conf.* 4.16.28), he and Aristotle do share a significant common topic: that of friendship. Reflect on your reading of Aristotle's discussion of friendship in *Nicomachean Ethics*. How would Aristotle evaluate Augustine's friendships at Thagaste, particularly with his friend who dies ([1], *Conf.* 4.4.7)?

Reflection: Admittedly, the connections are less apparent than those in the previous example, and Augustine's own understanding of friendship draws more from Cicero than Aristotle. However, this example effectively introduces the theme of permanence and transience as a key Augustinian theme, and the students have read Aristotle rather than Cicero on friendship. The two books that treat friendship are generally the parts of the *Nicomachean Ethics* that generate the most student interest and reflection. That encounter is often the first time they have reflected systematically on friendship. As one student told me, "I never knew you could *think* about friendship." Such reflection occurs at a formative point for these students as they are moving away from their families of origin to establish new relationships with others as independent young adults. Reading Aristotle, they have pondered friendships of use, pleasure, and virtue, friendships between people of unequal status, and the relationship of friendship and happiness or human flourishing. Thus this question provides a way to connect their previous reading with an analysis of Augustine's experiences and may lead to an investigation as well of Augustine's lack of happiness and flourishing.

Question for Day 3 (Book 5): In the first book of *Confessions*, Augustine praises his early lessons in literacy, valuing them more than his later reading of Virgil. He complains that "I was forced to memorize the wanderings of some fellow called Aeneas, while forgetting my own wanderings, and to weep over Dido" ([1], *Conf.* 1.13.20). Does your reading of Books 3 to 5 bear out such a negative assessment of Virgil? Or are there ways that the particular episodes in these books or the shape of Augustine's own story resembles the great Roman epic? What does Augustine's relationship to Virgil's epic suggest?

Reflection: Michael McCarthy, among others, has written about the "Augustine's mixed feeling" with respect to Virgil [5]. The discussion of Books 3 through 5 is an apt point at which to raise that issue. Students can reflect on the opening lines of Book 3, where Augustine speaks of "the din of scandalous love affairs" in his student days at Carthage ([1], *Conf.* 3.1.1). They may note that he, too, establishes an intimate relationship with a woman in Carthage (the mother of Adeodatus). They may also, with some prompting, note the parallels between the grief and cries of Dido and Monica when their loved ones sneak away from Carthage and head to Rome ([6], *Aeneid* IV, lines 403–978; ([1], *Conf.* 5.8.15). At stake in this question is not simply the issue of Augustine rewriting the journey of Aeneas (which itself was a rewriting of the journey of Odysseus). The discussion hopefully opens out onto the deeper issue of Augustine's complex relationship to the values of Rome over against the values of the city of God. Students may reflect on the younger Augustine's attraction to Rome and Milan and his career aspirations in contrast to the later Augustine's assessment of those passions.

Question for Day 4 (Book 7): In Book 7 ([1], *Conf.* 7.9.13), Augustine praises God for leading him to "some books of the Platonists." But as he discusses what he learned from these books, he—not once, but four times—quotes from the opening lines of the Gospel of John to identify what he did and what he did not learn from the Platonists. At first glance, that seems like an odd way of expressing Platonist philosophy. Why does Augustine take that approach? How are the ideas of the Platonists related to the words of the Fourth Gospel?

Reflection: This prompt seeks to lead students to explore the dimensions of Augustine's intellectual conversion that he presents in Book 7, where he discusses the way that he has come to God "from the Gentiles" ([1], *Conf.* 7.9.15), using the "gold of the Egyptians." In Book 7 ([1], *Conf.* 7.10.16), Augustine recounts his vision of "incommutable light" in language that strongly recalls Plato's "Allegory of the Cave" ([7], *Republic*, Book 7, 514a, 2–517a, 7) but at the same time echoes the prologue to John's Gospel that he has quoted earlier. This passage, indeed, most of Book 7 of the *Confessions*, presents both the confluences and the tensions of these two traditions—the classical Greco-Roman tradition and the Christian tradition—which Augustine subsumes and transforms.

Gaining a sense of this Augustinian amalgam—and its significance for the West—is crucial for any reader of the *Confessions*. Another question for this day might focus on the resonances with the "Allegory of the Cave", which students read the previous semester in their time spent with the *Republic*. However, a question focused solely on Platonism would miss the dynamism of Augustine's intellectual conversion in which the books of the Platonists and their advice "to seek for truth beyond corporeal forms" ([1], *Conf.* 7.20.26) lead Augustine toward the reality of the Christian God.

Question for Day 5 (Books 8 and 9): At the end of Book 7, Augustine discovers the writings of Saint Paul. He reports that as he began to read, he found there "every truth I had read in those other books", but also that as he read Paul, "the least of the apostles", he "was filled with dread" ([1], *Conf.* 7.21.27). Why is Paul, both as a convert and as an author, so important for Augustine and his conversion?

Reflection: This prompt seeks to provide several points of entry into a discussion of the conversion, not simply of Augustine's intellect, but of his will. The conversions of Paul and of Antony, as well as those of Victorinus and the friends of Ponticianus at Trier (through their reading of *The Life of Anthony*) form richly textured interlocking conversion narratives. For both Antony and Augustine, the words of scripture are central for conversion. For Antony, it is the Gospel lesson he hears the day he arrives late for worship; for Augustine, it is the words of Paul's letter to the Romans that he takes up and reads ([1], *Conf.* 8.12.29). Thus, Augustine frames his conversion narrative with his reading of Paul. Augustine will go on to become, for good or ill—indeed for good *and* for ill—Paul's most significant interpreter in the West. What is it in Augustine that so resonates with the experiences of and the writings of the apostle to the Gentiles? Plumbing that question is vital for students' understanding of Augustine, but also for their understanding the history of scriptural interpretation and theology in the West.

5. Conclusions

Mercer's Great Books program offers a unique context for reading Augustine's *Confessions*, but instructors of other kinds of undergraduate courses may adapt these opening questions for different contexts. Assigning shorter readings drawn from Plato, Aristotle, Virgil, and the Bible before assigning the *Confessions* may create a context in which these or similar questions can guide students into rich discussion of Augustine's life and thought. Teachers might develop a list of other texts to provide a similar entrée into discussion for *The City of God* or Augustinian texts. One goal of this exercise is to foster thinking and writing about the connections between different texts that students have read across time, with the aim that they will develop the ability to connect past reading to their current reading—in whatever context they find themselves. My ultimate goal, of course, is that my students and I may engage these questions and other substantive ones that will abide with us, trouble us, and guide us as we, like Augustine, seek to find our way to that peaceful homeland, walking "steadily in the way that leads there, along the well-built road opened up by the heavenly emperor" ([1], *Conf.* 7.21.27), knowing that our asking, seeking, and knocking will at last bring our restless hearts to that place of receiving and finding where the door is opened to us ([1], *Conf.* 13.38.53).

Acknowledgments

My thanks to the organizers of Samford's conference on *Teaching the Christian Intellectual Tradition*, to my Mercer colleagues Diana Stege, Thomas Huber, Peter Brown, and Charlotte Thomas, who provided some history of the development of the Great Books program, and to Charles J. Scalise for his valuable suggestions. I am also indebted to the insights of William R. Cook and Ronald B. Herzman [8].

Conflicts of Interest

The author declares no conflict of interest.

References and Notes

1. Augustine. *The Confessions*, 2nd ed. Translated by Maria Boulding. Hyde Park: New City Press, 2012.
2. For a complete list, see Great Books Program. "The Books: What You Will Read." Mercer University. Available online: http://departments.mercer.edu/gbk/books.html (accessed on 15 January 2015).
3. Thomas A Huber. "What is a *Good* Great Books Discussion?" Available online: http://departments.mercer.edu/gbk/essay01.html (accessed on 1 October 2014).
4. Gregory the Great, Expositio in Librum Job, sive Moralium libri xxv.4.
5. Michael C. McCarthy. "Augustine's Mixed Feelings: Vergil's *Aeneid* and the Psalms of David in the *Confessions*." *Harvard Theological Review* 102 (2009): 453–79.
6. Virgil. *The Aeneid*. Translated by Robert Fitzgerald. New York: Vintage, 1983.
7. Plato. *The Republic*. Translated by Joe Sachs. Newburyport: Focus, 2007.
8. William R. Cook, and Ronald B. Herzman, *St. Augustine's Confessions*. Chantilly: The Teaching Company, 2004. DVD.

Augustine and Autobiography: *Confessions* as a Roadmap for Self-Reflection

Mark S. M. Scott

Abstract: In this article, I explore a pedagogical strategy for teaching Augustine's *Confessions* to undergraduate students, which involves a final essay assignment. In the assignment, students compose their own "confessions" at the end of the term that employs Augustine's *Confessions* as a roadmap for rigorous self-reflection. Like Augustine, they must employ a creative literary frame, without duplicating his rhetorical technique of framing his autobiography as a prayer to God. Moreover, they must reflect on the salient questions, key people, pivotal moments that have shaped them, and analyze their shifts in worldviews. The assignment aims to demystify Augustine and to reinforce the evolving nature of the self as it moves through time and absorbs new ideas and experiences, as well as helping students begin to formulate a coherent and constructive life narrative.

Reprinted from *Religions*. Cite as: Scott, M.S.M. Augustine and Autobiography: *Confessions* as a Roadmap for Self-Reflection. *Religions* **2015**, *6*, 139–145.

1. Introduction

As a former teacher of rhetoric and as a bishop, teaching was as instinctive as it was routine for Augustine. Given his pedagogical sophistication and stature in the history of Christianity, Augustine makes an ideal fulcrum for Samford's inaugural conference on "teaching the Christian intellectual tradition". Through his lectures, sermons, and writings, Augustine employs multiple pedagogical techniques to educate his audience in philosophy, theology, and scripture for the purpose of eliciting deeper apprehensions of truth. In his *Confessions*, for instance, Augustine shares his story of spiritual restlessness and wandering for clear pedagogical purposes, not for self-aggrandizement or self-indulgence. They are meant to "arouse [or "stir up"] the human mind and affections toward him [God]" ([1], p. 36). In the ancient world, as Peter Brown notes, autobiographies function as conversion narratives, stories of dramatic transformations from one point of view and way of life to another, with the intent of sowing the seeds of conversion in the readers, and thereby motivating them to action: "Conversion had been the main theme of religious autobiography" ([2], p. 171). Since Augustine's autobiography has deeper didactic designs beyond the surface narrative, we might try to mine them for insights into the reality of the self's transformation throughout life, and the underlying factors that shape that transformation. If, in particular, the *Confessions* evince subtle strategies for self-reflection, then we might explore ways to utilize these strategies to facilitate sophisticated student self-reflection. In my paper, I will discuss an undergraduate essay assignment that invites students to write their own "confessions" using Augustine's *Confessions* as the template for their self-reflection.

2. Context

Let me provide some context before I outline the essay assignment, its aims, and its results thus far. I am an Arthur J. Ennis Postdoctoral Fellow in the Augustine and Culture Seminar Program at Villanova University [3]. I teach three sections per semester of the Augustine and Culture Seminar, known as ACS, a two-semester humanities sequence that examines "great books" from the ancient and modern world. Each section consists of 16 freshmen students. As a seminar, ACS emphasizes critical dialogue on classic texts and their salient themes. As a great books course, it explores classic works of literature for insight into the course's guiding question: *Who am I?* As a writing intensive course, it requires students to write approximately 30 pages per semester. Villanova, as an Augustinian institution, inscribes its Augustinian values of truth, unity, and love into its curriculum through the ACS seminar, where Augustine's *Confessions* serves as the signature text in the fall semester and continues to exert influence in the spring semester as an interlocutor for the modern texts.

3. Assignment

Over the semester, I assign various types of essays, including short reflection papers, longer analytical essays, and creative essays. At the end of the fall semester, I give students two options. They can either write a short research essay (six to eight pages) on Augustine's *Confessions*, in which they analyze a specific person, theme, or movement in its literary context and in the wider context of Augustine's intellectual milieu, or they can write a longer autobiographical essay (8–10 pages) where they compose their own "confessions" in creative interaction with Augustine's *Confessions*. If they choose the latter option, I give them detailed instructions, which I will now delineate before discussing the rationale and some interesting preliminary results.

First, I articulate the basic intent of the essay assignment: to tell their story in their own words using Augustine's *Confessions* as a roadmap or blueprint. I caution against misinterpreting the title of the assignment. *Confessions*, I insist, does not mean share your "deepest, darkest secrets". That is not the point of the assignment. Rather, I ask them to reflect deeply about their past, present, and future as a way of responding to the course's guiding question: *Who am I?* Students generally respond positively to the assignment at first. Most freshmen welcome the opportunity to write about themselves. It comes naturally, especially since they had to write mini-autobiographical essays as part of their university application. As I continue to flesh out the assignment, however, their initial euphoria dampens as they begin to see the complexity and intensity of the essay. Once they see that Option 2 is not an exercise in vanity and self-promotion but an opportunity for rigorous, sophisticated self-reflection, Option 1 seems to many an easier route, and many select it over writing their own confessions.

Second, I instruct the students who select Option 2 to couch their confessions in a distinctive literary frame. It cannot be a straightforward, pedestrian, informational autobiography. Students are tempted to write what amounts to breezy, desultory, date and data-driven journal entries on their life if they are not directed otherwise. I tell them that I am asking for a more reflective account of themselves than the standard journal format allows. Augustine, I remind them, frames his entire

Confessions as a prayer to God, and reinforces that literary frame throughout. Recall his famous lines in the opening paragraph: "You [God] have made us for yourself, and our heart is restless until its rests in you" [4]. Similarly, they must have a literary frame suitable to their narrative (prayer, as a bishop, was obviously well-suited to Augustine). My only restrictions are that it cannot be a prayer, since the assignment asks them to emulate Augustine without duplicating him, and that it has an authentic literary quality. For some students, the literary frame comes easily and fuels their enthusiasm for the essay. For others, it is a struggle that deflates their enthusiasm. I will give some examples below.

Third, I point to Augustine's *Confessions* as a paradigm for their self-reflection [5]. What are the questions he asks? What are the topics he explores? What are the key moments he identifies? Again, the point is not to replicate Augustine—to simply reproduce his story in their autobiography—but for them to tell their own story under his expert guidance, which entails careful attention to multiple facets of the formation of the self, including: key figures (parents, friends, mentors, teachers), pivotal moments (crises, epiphanies, travels), major influences (intellectual, spiritual, literary), worldview (theological, philosophical, ethical), spiritual struggles and shifts, and aspirations for the future. Obviously they are not able to cover all of these topics exhaustively, but it gives them a sense of the intellectual caliber they should strive for and the kinds of questions they should be asking as they explore their interior life within their literary frame, following Augustine's lead.

Finally, I preemptively address the perennial philosophical question asked by students from time immemorial: "How do I get an 'A' on the assignment?" Sometimes when I am asked "what are you looking for in the essay?" I reply Socratically "what are *you* looking for from it? What new existential registers do you hope discover through the process?" After a few moments of awkward silence and blank stares I outline the grading criteria. Thus, in addition to the standard criteria of grammar, style, and substance, I tell them that their grade will be based on the analytical and introspective depth of their self-reflections, the creativity of their literary framing device, the intellectual rigor of their discussion, and the range of topics covered. Many turn away from Option 2 when faced with the full scope of the assignment, although generally most opt to write the confessions assignment over the research essay, despite some trepidation.

4. Pedagogical Objectives and Obstacles

The purpose of the assignment is twofold. In the first place, it helps to overcome their resistance to Augustine and his *Confessions*. When students see his autobiography as a story that speaks to their story rather than as a pious rant, they begin to appreciate it more. Like other ancient texts, students sometimes find it incomprehensible, irrelevant, and even off-putting (think: sinful babies, pears, and concubine), but if they begin to see it as a text that can still illuminate their experience, despite its antiquity (which decidedly counts against it for many students), then they are more willing to discard their chronological prejudices and enter into dialogue with him. When they write their confessions in the light of Augustine's, they sympathize with him more and view him more as a fellow quester after truth rather than as a moralizer telling them not to have any fun and trying to make them feel guilty.

Second, the confessions assignment facilitates the student's engagement with the course's guiding question: *Who am I?* Through their careful deliberations about the complex formation of their identity in interaction with their relationships, experiences, and worldviews, they gain a heightened sense of self-knowledge, first passes at the Delphic oracle, as it were, with which they are better able to evaluate and shape their intellectual and spiritual formation. Ideally, the exercise of charting their interior development over their first 18 years heightens their awareness of the ongoing nature of self-construction and stimulates the desire to revisit these questions throughout their lives. While fully actualized, existentially-aware freshmen are perhaps rare, given the opportunity, many find the assignment foundational to their educational formation.

There are three main pedagogical problems with the assignment. First, it requires sophisticated self-analysis and maturity and some freshmen simply do not have the experiential, emotional, and intellectual capacity to complete it well. Second, on a related point, it is difficult for many students to resist the urge to write a flat-footed, straightforward, virtually unreflective autobiography, especially at the end of the semester with other essays and exams bearing down on them. While some fall into this trap, others do produce dynamic, thoughtful, creative essays. Third, students sometimes share extremely personal and sensitive details in their confessions assignment, despite the persistent caveat that the assignment is not about unburdening their soul. It is imperative not to blur the boundaries between professor and priest or counselor. If students reveal information that indicates the need for specialized spiritual or psychological help, professors should direct them to the appropriate university office rather than venturing beyond their carefully demarcated professional roles.

5. Results

Finally, let me share two anecdotes that show the heuristic potential of the assignment. At first I was very reluctant to offer the essay assignment, primarily because of the three obstacles I enunciated above. I thought that the essay concept would work well in theory, but not in practice. I worried that most freshmen were not equipped to do it well, and that I was setting them up for failure. Additionally, I did not want to force facile self-reflection if they were not willing or able to undertake rigorous introspection. I made the assignment optional to avoid some of my own misgivings about it, so that those who were not comfortable with it or were not competent to engage in that level of introspection could take the more familiar, conventional route.

My first attempt at the assignment was in an upper-level Religious Studies course on Augustine at the University of Missouri. The course consisted of about 25 students, from freshmen to seniors, many of whom I had taught in previous courses. About half the class chose the confessions assignment, and nearly all my returnee students chose it, which signals the level of trust required to make the assignment work. By far, the best essay was written by a student who I had not taught before and, more surprisingly still, was virtually silent for the majority of the course, despite many opportunities for discussion. In contrast to her reticence during the semester, her essay was expressive, extensive, engaging, and even engrossing. She wrote 25 pages for a 10 page assignment, which I would normally penalize, but she did not waste a word. I could not put it down, and that is a rare experience in the trenches of grading. She deftly detailed childhood struggles, relational and vocational crises, developments in her worldview, academic victories and defeats, theological and philosophical questions that she wrestled with, and the ways all these experiences informed her identity. She was clearly more comfortable with the written word than the spoken word. What I realized after putting the paper down was that I would have never encountered her amazing mind if I had not offered the assignment, and that she would not have had the opportunity to display her rich interior life to me and to benefit from the task of thoughtful self-analysis. She appreciated my remarks to her essay and she opened up more afterwards. It seemed to empower her.

Villanova's ACS course gave me the perfect opportunity to revisit the assignment and to refine and enrich it further, given its openness to explore questions of spiritual formation in addition to intellectual and broadly ethical formation. Many students have written insightful, penetrating essays that impressed me artistically and substantively. They write them at the end of the fall semester and it seems to give them confidence for the spring semester, both to solidify their sense of self and to explore the course question in dialogue with modern classics. In other words, it gives them an intellectual foundation from which to grow in the spring semester.

Students employ various framing devices, including the letter format (to parents, grandparents, future spouse, future child, future self, past self), fictional diary entries, song lyrics/titles, poems, seasons, imagery from sports, hobbies, quotations, *etc.* When I taught the course over the summer I had a student compose her entire essay as a poem. While she faltered in the medium of analytical essays, she flourished in the creative medium of poetry, which allowed her to express herself and engage the concepts of the essay assignment more naturally and freely. Because she was a part-time student who took courses at night, I did not expect to see her in the fall, so I wrote her a short e-mail expressing my delight over her essay, my desire for her to find outlets for her poetry, and my affirmation of her academic abilities, which she strongly doubted. I realized the assignment gave her the ability to overcome a lot of self-doubt and to allow her to express herself in the medium that maximized her intellectual potential. So the assignment often has a profound effect on students who appreciate the opportunity to reflect on these big questions in a structured, artistic format. Moreover, it deepens the intimacy in the classroom, since the students open a window into their inner life and since I have students share excerpts from their essays in class, if they are comfortable. It deepens the interpersonal dynamics in the classroom and gives them a memorable takeaway from the course. For institutions utilizing writing portfolios, it works well as literary "artifact" of their work.

6. Conclusions

There are many ways to rework and redeploy a confessions assignment in courses on Augustine, theology, Early Christianity, and various literature courses that read substantially from the *Confessions*. Professors would have to adapt it to their particular institutional sensibilities and course objectives. Some professors might be more open to spiritual reflection than others. Some might permit personal reflections, some might not. Either way, I would recommend making it optional. I find the essay works best in smaller seminar settings where you are able help students tailor it to their distinctive personalities, histories, and academic objectives. Above all, for the assignment to achieve its full potential, you have to establish an atmosphere of trust, encouragement, and confidentiality. If your students know they can trust you with their stories, they will impress you with their ability to write ingenious confessions, many of which would make Augustine proud.

Appendix

Essay Prompt

Confessions and Self-Discovery: Spiritual and Intellectual Autobiography

Write your own *Confessions* (8–10 pages). Model your reflections on Augustine's *Confessions*, but do not attempt to replicate his style, format, and substance. Instead, tell the story of your spiritual and intellectual journey in your own way, employing your own distinctive literary style. Like Augustine's *Confessions*, tell your story by engaging some of the following themes:

- Key figures: family, friends, mentors, teachers.
- Key moments: crises, epiphanies, affiliations, journeys.
- Major influences: intellectual, spiritual, literary.
- Theological views: God, humanity, salvation.
- Philosophical views: knowledge, being, cosmology.
- Ethical views: the nature of the good life.
- Transitions: shifts in your worldview.
- Intellectual and personal struggles.
- Future trajectories: who do you want to become? What are the next steps?

In addition to the standard considerations of grammar, style, and substance, your paper grade will be based on these additional considerations:

- Analytical and introspective depth.
- Creativity: like Augustine, employ a literary framing device (e.g., diary entries, letter (to parent, grandparent, future spouse, child, self), Bible verses, play, dialogue/story, song lyrics/titles, poem, seasons, imagery from sports, hobbies, quotations, *etc.*).
- Level of sophistication/insight/self-reflection. Intellectual quality. Topics covered.

Conflicts of Interest

The author declares no conflict of interest.

References

1. Augustine. "*Revisions* II, 6 (32)." In *Confessions*, 2nd ed. Maria Boulding, trans. New York: New City Press, 2012. (reprint 1997).
2. Peter Brown. *Augustine of Hippo: A Biography*. Berkeley: University of California Press, 2000. (reprint 1967).
3. Augustine and Culture Program at Villanova University. Available online: http://www1.villanova.edu/villanova/artsci/acsp.html (accessed on 1 December 2014).
4. Henry Chadwick, trans. *Confessions*. New York: Oxford University Press, 1992.
5. For a helpful introduction to Augustine's life and thought, see Henry Chadwick. *Augustine of Hippo: A Life*. Oxford: Oxford University Press, 2009.

Augustine, Addiction and Lent: A Pedagogic Exercise

Maria Poggi Johnson

Abstract: The article describes a series of pedagogic exercises developed to help students in a General Education course at a Jesuit university to engage fruitfully with Augustine's Confessions in a way that will facilitate and deepen their understanding of a classic text of the Western tradition and, at the same time, promote their personal formation in keeping with the goals of Ignatian pedagogy.

> Reprinted from *Religions*. Cite as: Johnson, M.P. Augustine, Addiction and Lent: A Pedagogic Exercise. *Religions* **2015**, *6*, 113–121.

Teaching has many great pleasures. However, it also has its share of small but exquisite pains. One of those that has particularly tormented me in recent years, as it has become increasingly popular with my students, is the word "relatable".

Much as I loathe the word itself, I do have sympathy for what my students use it to express. One of the most rewarding facets of teaching at a Jesuit institution like mine is Ignatian pedagogy's embrace of *cura personalis*: the care and education of the whole person, emotional, moral and spiritual as well as intellectual. As faculty we are not only permitted but actively encouraged to form rather than merely to inform our students. This formation, naturally, can best be done—indeed can only be done—with the willing cooperation of the students. Therefore, at least some texts and topics need to be "relatable", to address questions that already engage or preoccupy our students, whether or not they are explicitly aware of it. This, of course, can be managed: the challenge lies in finding texts that are both "relatable" and intellectually serious, that can engage the students without compromising the integrity of classroom or academic discipline.

What could meet this challenge more perfectly than the *Confessions*? In it Augustine tells the story of his long, winding, and often tormented path to the church. He recalls his feelings, motivations and conflicts at every stage and interrogates better to understand the human condition in relation to God, in whom he eventually finds peace. With the *Confessions* in hand, we can stand in front of a classroom of young people who are finding their way, amid uncertainties, distractions, and mistakes, towards their adult selves, reaching for a clear understanding of their desires, their priorities, their motivations, their happiness, the role of love and sex and meaning in their lives, and we can tell them, "Here, guys. This is one of the classics not only of the Christian intellectual tradition, but of all of Western literature. It is about a young man finding his way, amid uncertainties, distractions and mistakes, towards his adult self, reaching for a clear understanding of his desires, his priorities, his motivations, his happiness, the role of love and sex and meaning in his life" Could there be a greater gift to teacher and students both? And yet, the first time I assigned it for "Introduction to Christian Theology" (the course is required of all students at my institution: the second part of a sequence that begins with "Introduction to the Bible"), the response was as unmistakable as it was incomprehensible. Augustine was "not relatable".

After my initial bewilderment and frustration at this response I rallied. I have introduced into the class a series of pedagogic exercises designed to help the students make an explicit personal connection to some sections and topics of the *Confessions*, with the goal of opening them to the text as a whole. This essay will describe these exercises.

The series begins with Augustine's discussion in Book I of his childhood education. "I was not fond of study", he writes, "and hated being driven to it. Driven I was, though and that did me good, though my own attitude was far from good, for I learned only under compulsion" ([1], I 12.19). This, at least, is instantly "relatable", and opens a class discussion of students' own experience of education. Do they enjoy learning? If not, why not, and why, then, are they in college? What internal and what external forces motivate them to study? Unsurprisingly, perhaps, many students are considerably more attuned to the latter than to the former. They are very aware that possession of a college degree is essential for access to the kind of adult life they intend for themselves. However, the conversation draws their attention to topics of which they are less aware. How, beyond the business of "getting a job", might the process of *earning* that degree equip them to live that life? What value might their education might have beyond that of facilitating certain practical goals? We discuss what Augustine says about the enduring value of the lessons he so resented in his youth. "[B]y means of them", he says, "I was gradually being given a power which became mine and still remains with me: the power to read any piece of writing I come across and to write anything I have a mind to myself" ([1], I 13.20). Does the ability to understand and to articulate any point one comes across seem immensely empowering and liberating?

This first conversation is informal. Its goal is simply to initiate, early in the semester (*Confessions* is the first text we read), a conversation that ties reflection on the text to self-reflection on the part of the students. The second stage in the series of exercises is structured more formally and arises from our reading of the episode beginning in ([1], II 4.9)—one of the most famous in the book. As an adolescent Augustine and his friends stole pears from a neighbor's orchard. Years later, the adult Augustine devotes several pages to puzzling over this escapade Why did he do it? He writes that "Those pears were beautiful, but they were not what my miserable soul loved. I had plenty of better ones, and I plucked them only for the sake of stealing, for once I picked them I threw them away" ([1], II 6.12). What could have induced him to sink to such "abysmal depth", to be so "in love with my own ruin"? ([1], II 4.9)

My students' initial response to this passage varies between puzzlement and scorn that Augustine is "beating himself up" so much over so seemingly trivial an incident. To try to make sense of the episode, they offer various strategies, most involving some form of the notion that "back then" people took religion more seriously, or moral standards in society were higher, or people's vision of God was more threatening, with the consequence that they sinned less and felt guiltier about it than we do "nowadays", (nowadays being both laxer and more enlightened.) Their explanations then, focus on the fact that Augustine is different from us: not relatable.

I argue, from the text, that stealing the pears was not in itself a major incident in Augustine's life. It interests him as an occasion to explore the universal question of why we do things we really do not want to do. He initially reflects that he "feasted on the sin, nothing more…it was only the criminal act that lent it savor" ([1], II 6.12) but is convinced that in any human act some good is being sought, however perversely. He concludes that the motivation was the thrill of camaraderie, of friendship, albeit "an exceedingly unfriendly form of friendship" ([1], II 9.17). "I would not have done that deed alone" ([1], II 9.17). However, the explanation meets with limited success: my students are still distracted from Augustine's subtle reflections on motivation by the strangeness of a grown man fretting over a few pieces of pilfered fruit. This is clearly just Augustine being weird.

At this point I hand out 4 × 6 index cards. I tell the students, "write down the last time you made a decision that *you think* was bad. When have you chosen to do something that you thought was wrong or knew wasn't really going to make you happy?" The classroom immediately becomes very quiet. When people have finished, I collect the index cards in a bag, shuffle them, redistribute them randomly, and each student reads aloud the one they have drawn. Many of the "confessions" are about time-management and procrastination. Some involve drugs and alcohol, some sex and relationships. Some are worrying: I always make it clear that I am available to talk. Usually one or two lead to a burst of laughter.

This is one of those rare moments in the classroom when every student is listening with rapt attention. The experience is powerful, I think, as all of the responses are read is a group portrait emerges of the class as a collection of individuals variously flawed, confused, conflicted, prone to act against our own better judgment. When we have illustrated and acknowledged collectively and concretely one of Augustine's central insights—that we are mysteries to ourselves, uncertain about our own motivations, given to flouting our own reason, values, desires—the students are more inclined to give Augustine a hearing. After discussing this, I ask them to apply it to what they wrote earlier: what good were you pursuing when you made the choice that you identify as bad? Why do you say that it is a lesser good? What is the good that you wish you had been pursuing instead? Why do you think that is better? Our previous act of collective self-exposure has generated a feeling of trust, even of intimacy, in the classroom, and there are generally students who are willing to volunteer their own experiences: for instance, the satisfaction of leveling up on the video game *versus* the greater but more distant satisfaction of getting a good grade because of the extra hour spent editing the essay or studying for the test. The effect of this exercise, at least for those students who are ready to engage sincerely with it, is to counteract their defensive tendency to roll their eyes at Augustine for "getting all freaked out about the pears". As we proceed with the book, we refer back to this experience as a reminder that for all the strangeness of his culture, Augustine's story can bring into focus for us aspects of our experience that we might otherwise not notice explicitly.

The next exercise in the series comes with Book VIII and Augustine's treatment of the divided will. By this point Augustine is 32. From the perspective of my students, this looks like extreme old age. Surely, by thirty-two, they will have it all figured out. At all events they will be well launched in life and progressing with their professional lives. In one sense Augustine is very much where they hope to be: has built a very successful career as a rhetorician and teacher, and in worldly terms is thriving. However, he absolutely does not have it all figured out. As an adolescent he read Cicero's *Hortensius* and it turned his life around, kindling in him a passionate love of philosophy and starting him on an ardent search for truth (the episode is recounted in [1], III 4.7–4.8). On this search he has spent a number of years among the Manichees, (a gnostic sect that proclaims good and evil to be divine powers permeating the universe and vying for the souls and fates of humans) but has become disillusioned with them. He has experimented with Platonic mysticism. He has toyed with astrology. And he has, under the influence of Ambrose of Milan, moved closer to Christianity, to the point that he is fully convinced of the truth of the Christian creed and longs to convert.

But he does not convert, and he is miserable. "I was attracted to the Way", he writes, "but the narrowness of the path daunted me, and I still could not walk in it" ([1], VIII 1.1). The daunting narrowness of the path has to do with sex. Augustine had lived for many years with a woman with whom he has a son. He loved her and was devastated when forced to send her away because she was an impediment to the marriage his family had arranged for him. He has had to wait two years until his fiancée is old enough to marry but, as he puts it "I chafed at the delay because I was no lover of marriage but a slave of lust," and in the meantime, although still heartbroken over the rupture with his son's mother, he has taken another concubine, "in no sense a wife" ([1], VI 15.25). He wants, deeply, to be a Christian, but he also wants, urgently, to have sex: the two desires are incompatible. (For reasons of time we pass swiftly over the reasons why Augustine takes it for granted that this is the case—to get too involved with them might derail us for hours, as would discussion of the fact that his fiancée is eleven, or that he praises his mother for holding her tongue so effectively that her husband never beat her. In the classroom, you have to pick your fights, if you possibly can. It is disappointing, in one sense, that my students typically let me get away with that, but it is a relief none the less.)

Augustine, naturally, reflects deeply on his predicament: on the conundrum of harboring two incompatible desires. "I was aligned with both", he says, "but more with the desires I approved than with those I frowned upon, for these latter I was not really the agent, since for the most part I was enduring them against my will rather than acting freely. All the same, the force of habit that fought against me had grown stronger by my own doing, because I had come willingly to this point where I now wished not to be" ([1], VIII 5.10).

Here, as before, students' initial reaction is typically that Augustine is getting all bent out of shape because "back then" people were very uptight about sex whereas nowadays we know not to make such a big deal of it. That sex happens to be Augustine's issue is initially a problem as it distracts the students from getting to the heart of the matter. I have found the best way to help them past it, so that they can engage with the text is to spend some time exploring the nature of addiction. Our translation does not use the term, but students can generally produce it with little prompting. It is a concept that they engage with regularly, as most of them have experience at second or third hand (and generally at least one student in every class at first hand) with some form of chemical addiction, and are well aware of its destructive potential.)

After some discussion, I distribute index cards again, and ask them to write down an addiction they have: a habit whose force routinely overpowers the free exercise of their will, preventing them from acting in ways that they really want to, a pattern of behavior that, like Augustine's, was initially freely chosen, but has since taken on a life of its own, directing their actions while no longer offering significant satisfaction. Essentially, I tell them "think of something you do a lot, that nobody makes you do, and that you really wish you could stop doing". I lead the way by sharing my own addictive pattern of fault-finding and criticizing and its consequences in my personal relationships. Again, the room is silent and intensely focused, both while the students write, and later, when we read aloud all of the shuffled and redistributed notes. Some students write just a word or phrase. There are a few chemical addictions—alcohol, tobacco, pot. A number invariably identify video games, which for many present a significant impediment to their being the kind of students they want to be, and getting the sort of grades that will help them get where they want in life. The most interesting ones, at least to me, are longer, and that describe addictive habits in interpersonal relationships—being jealous, being insecure, picking fights. This activity, like the first, counteracts the students' tendency to keep the *Confessions* at arm's length, to focus on the difference between them and Augustine, and thus to dismiss his reflections on his experience as irrelevant to their own lives and concerns. It helps them to see that, although Augustine's account of his divided will may seem alienating and extreme, it expresses an experience which they all have, and which they, in their own way, find frustrating and troublesome.

The final exercise in the series grows directly out of this and, due to the place of Augustine in my syllabus, occurs early in, or just before, Lent. I have learned over the years that a good number of my students, including those who profess very little in the way of religious belief or practice, habitually take on some sort of Lenten fast. Typically this involves giving up junk food, but junk food is something that very few students mention during the "name your addiction" exercise. In the Lenten Addiction Challenge I ask them to design a fast related to the addiction they mentioned, and to journal about it for the duration of Lent. (The instruction sheet which I give to my students is appended to this article.)

I cannot do justice within this essay to the variety of results this exercise has produced. A few examples, however, may serve to give the reader a sense of the results. A student who began with the fairly conventional goal of quitting smoking failed to do so, but realized through the course of the exercise that she used smoking as a mechanism for coping with stress, and by the end had identified a number of stressors in her life that triggered her reaching for a cigarette, and was taking steps to reduce them. Another student, who named as his addiction a perfectionism that lead to crippling procrastination, came gradually to understand and describe it not as an intellectual or emotional issue but rather as a spiritual one. "God is perfect", he wrote, "and that means I don't have to be". By the end of the exercise this insight had actually won him a considerable degree of freedom from the problem. One young man identified his addiction as picking fights with his girlfriend when they spoke on the phone. His journal showed his growing awareness of his motivations, of the needs and impulses that prompted him to introduce difficulty and drama into these conversations. These are by a large margin the most interesting student work I read all semester—as highly individual as the stacks of essays are undistinguished.

I will conclude this essay with a survey of the strengths and weaknesses of this series of pedagogic exercises as I see it. Let me begin with the latter. On might argue that the exercises constitute an invasion of the students' privacy unwarranted by the educational benefit. Although my Jesuit institution, as I mentioned earlier, actively encourages faculty to engage in formation of the student as a whole person, I am sensitive to the possibility here I might be veering too close to a line that should not be crossed.

I use several strategies to mitigate this. First, if the students are to engage with the exercises in a way that will render them meaningful and useful, they clearly have to feel safe. I have outlined above a number of the steps I take to protect anonymity by ensuring that everybody's "confessions" are treated equally, and that none can be traced back to their author. In addition, I invite students to follow me to the office if they wish, to watch me shred the papers as soon as the in-class exercises are completed. Second, I participate honestly myself. To admit one's weaknesses in private, let alone to expose them in public, is intimidating, and particularly so for people at our students' stage in life, when they are on the brink of the "real world" and anxious about how they will manage when they get there. The least I can do, if I am asking them to do something uncomfortable, is to join in myself, and hopefully to show that not only in the 4th century but also in the 21st one can function successfully as an adult while still vexed with struggles, conflicts and inconsistencies. Third, I make clear that although the Lenten Addiction Challenge grows out of a Christian text, and is linked to the Christian calendar, it is only as "religious" as they want it to be, and that they are free to parse it as an exercise in self-knowledge and self-mastery. Augustine found the end of his struggles in a relationship with God, and the whole text, written in the second person is a testament to that. Naturally, we treat the religious dimensions of the text thoroughly, but I assure them that the last thing I want is for students who do not have a personal faith commitment to fake some sort of piety. Fourth, I offer an alternative assignment that requires a regular practice of silence, and is also designed to encourage them in a discipline of reflection and self-awareness (the syllabus description of this alternative exercise is also appended to this essay.)

The other weakness of the exercise is that there is no way of confirming that students are actually engaging with it. I am open about this. With a view to perhaps defusing the temptation, I tell them that of course if they really want to they can "cheat" and just make something up, both for the in-class exercises and for the Lenten Addiction Challenge but I stress that there is nothing to be gained from it. Both the Challenge and the alternative assignment are pass-fail: students will accomplish nothing by manufacturing the sort of response that they might imagine I, or Augustine, would particularly value, and it is much less trouble, as well as far more useful for them, simply to tell the truth.

As for the strengths of the series of exercises, I see two. First, it exposes students to habits that promote reflection and self-knowledge. This, I believe, is in itself a valuable part of their education. Our students have been formed in a culture that discourages the hard work of genuine introspection: renders it, in fact, extraordinarily difficult by making distraction constantly and intrusively available. Many of them are rarely alone, rarely silent—both valuable if not essential conditions for self-reflection—and many of them will openly confess that they regard solitude and silence as alien and even frightening and are unlikely to undertake self-examination in any sustained way unless they are initially required to.

These exercises provide them with structured and contained opportunities to reflect on some aspects of the human condition: the complexity of our motivations, the weakness and conflicts in our wills. Because these aspects arise out of a text, the experience is a shared one: shared not only with the classroom but also across the centuries. My hope is that this communal aspect will render some of these experiences at least less intimidating, if no less troubling. Students are not alone in their conflicts, inconsistencies and addictions. My hope, further, is that students will find these experiences liberating and enriching, or at the least intriguing, and may be encouraged to continue some habit of self-reflection after the end of the class. Although there is no reliable way of verifying students' sincerity, it is certainly the case that a number of students close their journals by saying that, although they began it grudgingly they have found the habit of writing helpful and would like to continue it.

The first strength of the exercises I have described, then, lies in encouraging students to undertake a valuable personal practice in a context created directly by the reading of a class text. The second strength, I believe, lies in the effect of this experience on the students' reading of the text. The goal of the exercises, as I said at the beginning of this article, is to render Augustine more "relatable". Students are inclined, quite understandably, to find the huge historical and cultural gap between them and Augustine unbridgeably alienating. Someone from such a strange and distant world can surely have little in common with them, and only the most academically-minded among them—those students who find ideas inherently interesting and are eager to encounter them in any context—are inclined to approach the *Confessions* as anything other a hoop they are required to jump through. A lecture on Augustine's pivotal role in the development of the Western understanding of the nature of the self, or professorial assertions to the effect that we have all grown up a world significantly shaped by Augustine and his ideas, will likely interest only the same coterie of students.

The exercises, therefore, are designed to lessen the gap between Augustine and the students, including those not naturally drawn to historical texts in theology, by guiding them while they explore elements of their experience that echo those Augustine recalls and reflects on. If students thereby come to find Augustine more "relatable"—if they find some point of contact between his concerns and their own—they are opened to the possibility that the book as a whole might have something to offer them. Moreover, if Augustine, who articulates conflicts and perplexities they also experience, finds in theology a useful tool for addressing those conflicts and perplexities perhaps it might have something to offer them too.

I have not collected quantifiable assessment data on these pedagogic exercises—I do not know how one would do so. However, my experience has certainly been that since I have implemented them, this section of the class has gone much better. My students have been less likely to dismiss Augustine as coming from a world so utterly different from theirs that his concerns can have no possible bearing on theirs. They have been more open to discussing the issues he raises, and they have even been somewhat more ready to consider theology as a dynamic enterprise, worth engaging in. As distasteful as the term "relatable" may be, it indicates what can be a powerful pedagogic tool. A little classroom time devoted to these simple exercises has the potential, at least, to draw students into a fruitful engagement with one of the great texts of the Western tradition and even with the discipline of theology.

Appendix: Syllabus Description

Spiritual Exercises. Read Instructions Carefully, and Choose ONE.

Lenten Addiction Challenge

While discussing Augustine, you identified a personal addiction: a habit that regularly keeps you from making the choices that you really want to and pursuing the goals where you believe your true happiness lies.

Your assignment during the season of Lent, is to design a "fast" related to this addiction. Set a goal that is realistic, but will be genuinely challenging, and that will force you regularly to confront your addiction. The purpose is to help you to understand what feeds and energizes your addiction, to come to greater understanding of its role in your life, and to lessen its hold on you.

If you are a Christian, or understand yourself to be in a relationship with God, you should approach this prayerfully, asking for help and support. If you are not, it will be a useful exercise in self-knowledge and self-mastery.

You should keep a journal for the duration of the exercise. This can be no more than a few lines, noting how you did in relation to your goal, though you may find it useful to write more. Once a week (pick a day and stick to it), your journal entry should be a little longer and should review and analyze the past week.

Silence

You will engage in a regular practice of silence. You will begin with a minimum (you can do more) of 3 min, 5 times a week. By week 3, you should be up to a minimum of 5 min, 6 times a week.

During this time, you are to be silent and in silence. Go somewhere where you can be by yourself and turn everything off. No phone, texts, iPod, book, pen, paper, tv, no conversation, no nothing. Your goal during this period is simply to be in your own skin, and to come to know where your mind and emotions go when they are alone with themselves with no external stimuli or distractions. What thoughts, feelings, memories, anxieties, daydreams float to the surface?

You should keep a journal. At the very minimum, keep a record of when and where you practiced silence, and write a few words for each session, noting what your primary thoughts or concerns were during that time. Once a week (pick a day and stick to it), your journal entry should be a little longer and should review and analyze the past week.

For BOTH OPTIONS you will show me your journal, and turn in an 1–2 page informal essay, describing your experience during the exercise and discussing what, if anything, you learned from it.

Acknowledgments

This paper was given at the conference on Teaching that Christian Intellectual Tradition at Samford University, October, 2014. My thanks are due to the organizers of the conference.

Conflicts of Interest

The author declares no conflict of interest.

References

1. Saint Augustine. *The Confessions*. Translated by Maria Boulding. New York: New City Press, 2012.

Section V.

Augustine in the Core Curriculum and Beyond

Augustine's *Confessions*: Interiority at the Core of the Core Curriculum [1]

Michael Chiariello

Abstract: When St. Bonaventure University decided to redesign its core curriculum, we turned to Bonaventure's account of the mind's journey to God in the *Itinerarium Mentis in Deum* as a paradigm by which to give coherence to the undergraduate experience consistent with our mission and tradition. Bonaventure was himself an Augustinian philosopher and thus Augustine's *Confessions* holds a place of great significance in our first year seminar where it is studied in conjunction with Bonaventure's inward turn to find God imprinted on his soul. This paper is an account of the original rationale for including Augustine's *Confessions* in our curriculum and a report of continuing faculty and student attitudes towards that text nearly two decades later.

Reprinted from *Religions*. Cite as: Chiariello, M. Augustine's *Confessions*: Interiority at the Core of the Core Curriculum. *Religions* **2015**, *6*, 755–762.

When I learned that the conference theme was "Augustine Across the Curriculum", I saw an opportunity to contribute to this discussion from my experience developing, teaching, and administering our university's core curriculum. My remarks are directed to the place of the *Confessions* within the curriculum rather than the substance of Augustine's thought or writings. I decided to write from the point of view of academic leadership, wanting to share whatever lessons from my experience might serve those who commit to a similar process of change and curricular development. But I also want to use the opportunity to discuss the importance of curriculum development in institutions whose mission includes teaching the Christian intellectual tradition and, further, I want to put this work of curriculum-building within an even more global area of concern: the assault on liberal learning and the fragmentation of our common intellectual life.

Here is the role Augustine plays in our curriculum. Our freshmen take a first-year seminar in which they are required to read several excerpts from St. Augustine's *Confessions* ([1], pp. 157–76). The selections comprise Book I, chapter 1 where Augustine expresses the paradox of faith and knowledge—"who can invoke thee knowing thee not?"—and a more extended selection from Chapter 9 wherein he discusses the difficulties he encounters, and the punishment he receives, as a student. Moreover, in Book VII, chapters 7–13, we trace his intellectual formation, particularly his rejection of Manichaeism with his treatment of the problem of evil, his study of the Platonists, and his rejection of materialism. Finally, in Book VIII, we explore his conversion process and his struggle to overcome his sexual appetites, as well as his theory of free will and of the possibility of sin.

Although I regularly teach this freshman seminar, I was not party to the writing of the original common syllabus. Thus, I was most curious to see whether the inspiration for choosing Augustine's *Confessions* in the first place had survived almost two decades since its implementation.

---

[1] Paper presented at *Teaching the Christian Intellectual Tradition Conference* held at Samford University, 2–4 October 2014.

Having played an early role in the curriculum's genesis, I was interested in the question of continuity as new faculty joined the program and early participants moved on. In order to compare what had originally inspired our choice of the *Confessions* with the understanding of the faculty who currently teach in the core, I conducted an informal inquiry into the reasoning behind the selection. Unfortunately, I was not satisfied with the information I had collected, feeling that it was fragmentary and anecdotal rather than sufficiently representative and unbiased. Although I will share some observations related to my informal inquiry, I will focus instead on a more global hypothesis regarding the condition of higher education today and the special intellectual responsibility borne by institutions whose mission encompasses teaching the Christian intellectual tradition.

But first I want to tell the more local story regarding the development of St. Bonaventure University's core curriculum. In the mid-nineteen-nineties, we undertook a thorough review of our core, or general education curriculum, requirements. The then-current curriculum was a set of required courses in philosophy and theology, with distribution requirements in the humanities, as well as the natural and social sciences—in other words, a conventional Catholic undergraduate program. One of the challenges to the review process was to provide "coherence" to the curriculum. This mandate was taken loosely to mean that the curriculum should have a rationale justifying the set of required courses. That rationale, in turn, was to serve as the basis for ongoing curricular assessment, while maintaining a consistency with our institution's mission.

The key to meeting this challenge involved the retrieval of a medieval metaphysical framework to provide an organizing schema for a new curriculum. The consequence of this move was radical, suggesting an academic counter-culture of sorts, while rejecting both the positivism and post-modernism of our current intellectual culture. Moreover, borrowing such a framework meant deemphasizing academic specialization while stressing the unity and interdisciplinary nature of knowledge. This shift in emphasis away from specialization was not, however, consciously advanced by the creators of the curriculum. Still, the pursuit of coherence was real, even if the metaphysical turn was the result of a coincidental process.

This metaphysical turn was fostered by a fortuitous movement among a group of lay faculty who had taken up the study of the classics of the Franciscan intellectual tradition. What resulted was a new interest in the thought of our patron and namesake, St. Bonaventure, and his classic work, *Itinerarium Mentis in Deum*, or *The Mind's Journey to God* [2]. This work describes a spiritual and philosophical journey to God through three stages of reflection, preceded by a stage of mental and spiritual preparation, and followed by a concluding account of the soul's union with God. The stages comprise: (1) reflection on the natural world without, or what we might call "the external world"; (2) reflection on the human world within, *i.e.*, the mind, the soul, or the person; and (3) reflection "upward" to the 2.

Each of these stages of reflection divides into two steps. In the first step, the mind reflects simply by use of its natural powers or reason, and finds God through his "traces" or the marks of His creative encounter in the world outside, inside and above. In the second step, the power of reason is enhanced by divine illumination through faith, grace and God's word. What unfolds is a progressive schema, literally an itinerary of the mind's journey to God, which follows the six steps thereby formed. Many will recognize in Bonaventure's schema the monumental achievement of Augustine synthesizing Athens and Jerusalem, philosophy and theology, faith and reason. We adopted Bonaventure's account of the mind's six-step journey to God as a paradigm by which to give coherence to the undergraduate experience at an institution with our specific mission and tradition.

Using this Bonaventurean framework to shape our entire core curriculum was never seen as a feasible option, but we adopted this model to create a syllabus and textbook for a required freshman seminar entitled "The Intellectual Journey" [1]. Each of these steps suggested an area of study and a wide range of related texts and themes. This yielded a course with widely diverse readings encompassing classic and contemporary writers, prominently including the *Confessions*, and addressing questions suggested by Bonaventure's steps (see Appendix). For instance, selections from the *Confessions* are incorporated into the textbook chapter corresponding to Bonaventure's third step, which is described by Bonaventure in the *Itinerarium* chapter entitled "Of the reflection of God in his Image stamped upon our natural powers" ([1], p. 153). The unit of the course was designated by the title "The Nature of the Person", and here we find Augustine proceeded by Francis of Assisi's "Fifth Admonition", and followed by Marcus Aurelius' *Meditations*, Montaigne's "*Why I paint my own portrait*", Maxine Hong Kingston's "A song for a Barbarian Reed Pipe", and Sartre's "Existentialism as a Humanism" ([1], pp. 153–208).

Currently there is a review of the curriculum and newer faculty are unfamiliar with the wide-ranging discussions that preceded its adoption twenty years past, and therefore less aware of its rationale. Many are unconvinced that we need a common core of required courses at all. Most will recognize this last point as part of a familiar trend away from liberal education. Addressing this trend, I believe that a curriculum committed to the transmission of the Christian intellectual tradition has a special rationale for liberal education, and that Augustine has a role to play in this effort.

In my attempt to understand Augustine's place in our curriculum, I asked a member of the original curriculum committee, "why Augustine?" His answer was the latter's initiation of what he referred to as the "method of interiority", which he characterized as "an attempt to experience God in the very depths of the conscious mind". He cited a portion of Book VII, chapter x, "And being admonished by these books to return to myself, as I entered into my own inward soul, guided by thee…" ([1], p. 163). I wondered whether this view was well understood by faculty currently teaching the course, so I solicited comments from them in an open-ended way. Although none mentioned "interiority", my earliest respondents were positive regarding this text, with several claiming that the *Confessions* was among the most important readings of the course and at least one claiming that it is their students' favorite as well. Many saw this reading, or Augustine generally, as key to understanding Bonaventure, and at least one respondent, with good reason, considered the readings by Plato, Augustine and Bonaventure as a set.

However, I was somewhat skeptical that this response was more widely shared. I knew from casual conversations that more than a few colleagues skip this reading altogether or give it limited time and somewhat less enthusiastic response. One respondent admitted that he only taught Augustine because it was designated as required. He added his preference, Descartes, as a supplemental reading. (Several colleagues were quick to point out that Descartes was himself an Augustinian!) Others were happy to teach Augustine, but found the editing of the textbook selection less than helpful. For example, the textbook passages do not include the story of

Augustine's theft of his neighbor's pears, or the earliest accounts of language acquisition. The former is seen as a way to have undergraduates more readily see the relevance of this text in the accounts of his troubled youth. The latter is for those who are familiar with Augustine only through the famous reference in Wittgenstein's *Philosophical Investigations* ([3], pp. 2–4).

Regarding student reactions to Augustine, information was very scant. I might generalize that I found that faculty who considered *the Confessions* among the most important readings in the course tended, understandably, to spend the most time on it. They also were the most concerned with students' sometime negative reception of this text, in terms of both understanding and appreciation. As one colleague commented, "The more I stress its importance, the less they read it!" Some made an effort to show students that Augustine's struggles to "find himself" were not unlike their own youthful concerns. Another colleague went so far as to read much of the selections aloud during class time. He explained that it was important to make his students cover the text, whether or not they had read it themselves, adding "this triggers pretty good response…"

Part of the current review of the curriculum is an assessment of the Intellectual Journey course, and I expect there will be proposals to change the "canon" of this class. It is unclear how the *Confessions* will fare. I found two evenly divided sectors within the community of Intellectual Journey instructors. One treats the Bonaventurean framework as part of the substance of the course and therefore privileges those authors, such as Augustine, who directly illuminate Bonaventure's thought. For others, Bonaventure suggests the framework that organizes a collection of texts, a mere editorial strategy, while the independence of the separate texts, including the *Confessions*, is stressed. This polarity raises the question: is the text canonical, privileged and required, or do we promote the autonomy of texts, faculty and students in our curriculum design?

Most telling of all was the remark of one colleague who covered the text reluctantly and admitted, without elaboration, that his approach "now differs significantly from the views of those who originally shaped the course". I suspect that this drift of understanding is unavoidable unless provision is made, through continuous dialogue, to assess the aim and goals of the course. For this to be fully realized, a core curriculum must be seen as the ongoing work of a living community of colleagues, rather than a mere list of course descriptions and sections to be staffed.

We may be tempted to expand on a waggish remark often attributed to Bismarck, and compare the creation of a curriculum to the making of laws and sausages. No doubt the give and take among disparate disciplines in this process may seem more like a political negotiation. Yet what I have reported is a more positive idealization of the process, but no less correct. Disciplines are not political parties, but rather modes of inquiry to which academics commit. What might appear to be horse-trading or turf-protecting in the collective shaping of a common core is better viewed as the pursuit of academic goals to which our colleagues are committed, sometimes passionately and almost always for good and respect-worthy reasons. So rather than succumb to this somewhat cynical sausage-making analogy, it is most important to see the curriculum as a living institution fostered by an ongoing faculty conversation of ideas rather than interests.

Perhaps a more apt political analogy for the process of curriculum building is a revolution, or a successful democratic movement for large-scale reform. How do we maintain a continuity of ideals through succeeding generations? The discouraging reality is that change is easier to effect than to maintain. While making a curricular revolution may depend on the enthusiasm of volunteers, maintaining it requires consistent support from senior administration for the institutionalization of such a change through hiring, promotion, and resources for faculty development.

A core curriculum, particularly one that stands in contrast to normal academic compartmentalization, needs to cultivate its own community of support, including a core cadre of dedicated and self-renewing faculty and an independent internal administration. Where such change entails crossing disciplinary boundaries in course content and faculty training, many colleagues will be understandably cautious. Advocates who are committed to such a contrary vision of the academy need to address questions regarding the quality of programs and the qualifications of faculty. Indeed, in my experience many colleagues simply assumed that courses and faculty that transgress disciplinary boundaries are substandard and resist the hiring of committed generalists. Younger faculty, in particular, see teaching general education as a professional risk. The consequence, in many institutions, is staffing by the involuntary assignment of regular faculty and/or the widespread use of adjunct faculty. Of course, this not only fulfills the suspicions of many faculty skeptics, but it also invites discontinuity and drift in the transmission of the core's originating vision.

To avoid this sort of breakdown, institutional leadership's whole-hearted commitment is needed. This is practically axiomatic: passive or half-hearted support not only dooms efforts at reform, it signals the failure of such efforts to express clearly the institution's mission.

Finally, I suggest that we must address a much larger context in curriculum development, particularly in schools whose mission includes teaching the Christian intellectual tradition. A crucial, but unacknowledged, element of this work addresses what I see as an ongoing crisis: the increasing incoherence of our academic and intellectual culture. The outlines are well known: (1) Higher education has become increasingly professionalized, challenging the significance of the liberal arts, particularly regarding traditional requirements, among both students and administrators; and (2) Knowledge has become increasingly fragmented among disparate disciplines, with positivist rejection of metaphysics and post-modern skepticism regarding meta-narratives. How should a curriculum address this situation? Or, more to the point, how should a curriculum which conveys the Christian intellectual tradition, or in the case of my university, the Catholic and Franciscan intellectual tradition, address this post-modern condition?

The privileging of liberal education, by requiring it of our students, is a step forward. Through the collaborative development and delivery of a liberal arts core of the sort I have in mind, students see masters of different disciplines in dialogue, respecting the diversity of intellectual life, and most importantly, seeking a sense of a coherent whole intellectually, personally, and for our institution and others like it, spiritually. The fact that this precedes the inevitable move into their specialized major fields and non-liberal areas of professional preparation is most important. What we have to offer is an education that gives our students much more than either a collection of unrelated choices, or a too highly specialized, and thus incomplete, instrumental education.

I believe that institutions responsible for the transmission of the Christian intellectual tradition serve a purpose that runs counter to the prevailing intellectual culture, perhaps as a corrective, or simply to preserve the possibility of an alternative. And there is no doubt that institutions of other faith traditions, or with some other coherent set of values and worldview, may also serve that purpose. Such mission-focused institutions provide a rationale, perhaps an imperative, for liberal education and the values it embodies.

But for institutions with a specific commitment to teaching the Christian intellectual tradition, the retrieval and transmission of Augustine's project, the quest for personal, intellectual and spiritual integrity for himself and for a unified theological/philosophical foundation for Christian civilization is of immeasurable value, and indeed, unavoidable.

Conflicts of Interest

The author declares no conflict of interest.

Appendix

1. The Structure of Bonaventure's Itinerarium

Prologue – preparation of the mind/nature of learning

	natural knowledge THROUGH	aided by grace/revelation IN
Outward: natural world Vestiges of God	Step 1 sense	Step 2 imagination
Inward: human mind Image of God	Step 3 mind	Step 4 will
Upward: God's names Names of God	Step 5 Being	Step 6 Goodness

Repose: Completion of the Journey; Mystical Union w/ God

2. Common Texts for the Freshman Seminar, The Intellectual Journey

The Intellectual Journey, John Apczynski, Editor

Prologue. The Life of Learning
Bonaventure, "The Prologue" from *Itinerarium mentis in Deum*.
Cicero, *Pro Archia poeta (In Defense of Archias)*.
Annie Dillard, "Library Card Incident".
J. H. Newman, "Knowledge Viewed in Relation to Professional Skill".
Richard Rodriguez, *The Hunger of Memory*.
Thomas Wolfe, "Young Faustus".
Richard Wright, "The Library Card".

Step 1. Inquiry and the Universe
Bonaventure, *Itinerarium* I.
Bonaventure, *Life of Francis*.
Genesis, "The Story of Creation".

Paul Colinvaux, "The Succession Affair".
Paul Davies, "Did God Create the Universe?"
June Goodfield, "A Diversion and a Failure".
Aldo Leopold, "Reading the Forest Landscape".

Step 2. Imaginative Perspectives on the Natural World
Bonaventure, *Itinerarium*. II.
St. Francis of Assisi, *Canticle of the Sun*.
Matthew Arnold, "In Harmony with Nature".
Gerard Manley Hopkins, "God's Grandeur".
Barbara Novak, "The Nationalist Garden and the Holy Book".
H. D. Thoreau, "Up the West Branch".
William Wordsworth, "Lines Composed a Few Miles above Tintern Abbey".

Step 3. The Nature of the Person
Bonaventure, *Itinerarium*, III.
St. Francis of Assisi, "The Fifth Admonition".
Augustine, *Confessions*.
Marcus Aurelius. *Meditations*.
Maxine Hong Kingston, "A Song for a Barbarian Reed Pipe".
Michel de Montaigne, "Why I Paint My Own Portrait".
Jean-Paul Sartre, "Existentialism as a Humanism".

Step 4. The Person in Society: Reconciliation and Transformation
Bonaventure, *Itinerarium*, IV.
Simone de Beauvoir, *The Second Sex*.
Lord Byron, *Childe Harold's Pilgrimage*.
Sigmund Freud, *Civilization and Its Discontents*.
Martin Luther King, Jr., "Letter from Birmingham Jail".
Karl Marx and Friedrich Engels, *The Communist Manifesto*.
Vatican Council II, "Pastoral Constitution on the Church in the Modern World" (*Gaudium et Spes*).

Step 5. Images of Ultimate Reality
Bonaventure, *Itinerarium* V.
Chandogya Upanishad.
John Donne, *Sermon 23. Holy Sonnets 4 & 10*.
Elizabeth Johnson, *She Who Is*.
Ursula K. Le Guin, "Schrödinger's Cat".
John Milton, *Paradise Lost* (Book 3).
Plato, "The Allegory of the Cave".
Huston Smith, "The Beyond Within".

Step 6. The Search for Value and Meaning
Bonaventure, *Itinerarium*, VI.
Aristotle, *Nicomachean Ethics* I.
Clare of Assisi, *Testament*.
Don DeLillo, "Waves and Radiation".
Emily Dickinson, "Apparently with No Surprise", "Because I Could Not Stop for Death", and "I Heard a Fly Buzz".
T.S. Eliot, "Journey of the Magi".
Homer, *Iliad*, Book XXIV.
Matthew, "The Sermon on the Mount".

Step 7. "Let Us Begin Again": The Joy of Discovery
Bonaventure, *Itinerarium*. VII.
Dante Aleghieri, *The Divine Comedy* [*Inferno* canto 1 and *Paradiso*, canto 33].
Euripides, *Bacchae*.
John Keats, "On First Looking into Chapman's Homer".
Luke, "Paul's speech at the Areopagus".
Thomas Merton, "The Sleeping Volcano".
Francesco Petrarca, "The Ascent of Mont Ventoux".

References

1. John Apcynski, ed. *The Intellectual Journey*, 2nd ed. Boston: Pearson Custom Publishing, 2002
2. Bonaventure. *Itinerarium Mentis in Deum*. Translated by Philotheus Boehner, OFM. St. New York: The Franciscan Institute, 1956.
3. Ludwig Wittgenstein. *Philosophical Investigations*. Translated by G.E.M. Anscombe. Oxford: Basil Blackwell, 1958.

The Physics of Augustine: The Matter of Time, Change and an Unchanging God

Thomas Nordlund

Abstract: Scientific questions posed by St. Augustine, early father of the Christian church, are presented as a part of a proposed undergraduate course for religion and philosophy students. Augustine regularly seasons his religious, philosophical and moral investigations with analysis focused on the physical nature of the universe and how it can be quantified: "And yet, O Lord, we do perceive intervals of time, and we compare them with each other, and we say that some are longer and others are shorter" (*Confessions*, Book 11). The physical analysis is sometimes extended, pressing the attention and grasp of the unsuspecting student of religion or philosophy. Though Augustine emphasizes that true knowledge comes from faith and revelation, his physical inquiries imply that he values such analysis as a way toward truth. In contrast, Master of Divinity programs, which train the majority of Western Christian ministers, require little science experience and usually no physics. Serious investigation of Augustine's physical explorations reveal an alternative way of understanding scripture, especially Jesus' sayings: could the master engineer who created the universe sometimes be speaking in straightforward scientific terms?

Reprinted from *Religions*. Cite as: Nordlund, T. The Physics of Augustine: The Matter of Time, Change and an Unchanging God. *Religions* **2015**, *6*, 221–244.

1. Introduction to Augustine, the Physicist

> What, then, is time? If no one asks me, I know what it is. If I wish to explain it to him who asks me, I do not know…

> But, then, how is it that there are the two times, past and future, when even the past is now no longer and the future is now not yet? But if the present were always present, and did not pass into past time, it obviously would not be time but eternity…

> …And yet, O Lord, we do perceive intervals of time, and we compare them with each other, and we say that some are longer and others are shorter. We even measure how much longer or shorter this time may be than that time…But we measure the passage of time when we measure the intervals of perception… (Augustine, *Confessions* 11:XIV–XVI).

St. Augustine is recognized as one of the most important early church fathers. He is said to be an expert in rhetoric (though he later despised this vocation), persuasive writing, theology and philosophy. However, an experienced physicist, reading Augustine's most well-known book, *Confessions*, is startled by his sudden shift from descriptions of personal failings and his relationship with his father and mother, to a physicist's discussion of the nature of time, how it is measured and time's relation to past, present, future and "eternity". He proceeds to question how a "changeless" God could possibly *do* anything, if time can only be defined in terms of change. The unsuspecting physicist, coming upon the above passage as an isolated quote, would, if "O Lord" were removed, assume a quote from a fellow physicist, perhaps writing for a popular audience. While a philosopher might also be proposed as the source, the impulse to *measure* and compare the magnitude of one interval with another is a primary feature of physics, the most fundamental quantitative science. Of course, the scientific method did not exist till long after Augustine's death. Though Archimedes, Eratosthenes, Hero, Ptolemy and others before Augustine may be called physicists, Physics, as a formal discipline, began in the tenth century AD and later. Nevertheless, Augustine's apparent tendency to think in terms of physical quantities and their measurement should qualify him as at least an honorary physicist.

Augustine's scientific capabilities and fixation on time, eternity, creation and the nature of God and His relation to man, is further amplified in his other writings, and suggests that he often thinks *as a true early physicist*. At the same time, Augustine is suspicious of natural reason, emphasizing that the source of true knowledge is faith:

> But since the mind itself, though naturally capable of reason and intelligence is disabled by besotting and inveterate vices not merely from delighting and abiding in, but even from tolerating His unchangeable light, until it has been gradually healed, and renewed, and made capable of such felicity, it had, in the first place, to be impregnated with faith, and so purified...Now the only way that is infallibly secured against all mistakes, is when the very same person is at once God and man, God our end, man our way [1].

Augustine's attitude toward his own scientific explorations seems to be one of simultaneous wariness and expectation of revelations, after renewal of his (scientific) reason through faith.

This paper focuses on a few scientific questions raised by Augustine, related to time: how a simple, but hard to grasp, physical model of time(s) offers simple, but hard to grasp, answers to some of Augustine's questions. The approach is physical, designed as part of an undergraduate physics course for students of religion, philosophy, divinity, and physics, with an insistence that,

(i) arguments must be quantified,
(ii) that models and theories must be tested, both with experimental evidence from the natural world *and* from the Bible and
(iii) that scripture be interpreted, at least initially, in its most straightforward, physical, literal sense.

The biggest challenge seems to be conveying an understanding of the dimensions—spatial and temporal—of our normal universe, how the laws of physics require smooth connections between one, and a subsequent, instant of time, and how reality is affected if an additional space or time dimension is added. St. Augustine's contemplations of time and space can be viewed as an early attempt to formulate these quantitative laws, explicitly demanding that Biblical descriptions ("faith") of an unchanging and all-powerful God[1] simultaneously fit with these formulations. In a sense,

---

[1] Use of the descriptor "all-powerful" will be briefly explored in this paper. The author does not believe that Augustine explicitly asserts that God is "all-powerful" in the commonly (mis)understood sense of "He can do anything we can imagine".

Augustine was an early theologian and scientist who believed that religion and science do not occupy separate spheres of understanding, but should fit smoothly together.

By necessity, a physics course designed for undergraduate religion or philosophy majors must be introductory. Like all standard introductory physics courses, it cannot be technically correct when it deals with "real life"; to do so would overwhelm the new student. While complicated and cutting-edge information is often transferred to students in other disciplines, physics focuses on a student's ability to use fundamental, quantitative principles to generate his or her own answers. Examples of technically incorrect treatments of physical phenomena in physics courses abound. The treatment of projectile trajectories, assuming only the force of gravity were relevant, would have gotten a 17th-century artillery advisor imprisoned for incompetence, yet this is how we still teach undergraduate physics. This is justifiable because (i) to include the other relevant forces would overwhelm the new student; and (ii) the simple treatment points the student in the right direction for understanding. The ideas presented in this paper ignore relevant advanced physics topics, such as general relativity and cosmology theory, in favor of a simpler approach that allows students, on their own, to both *calculate important quantities* related to some biblical statements, and to interpret scripture from a physics point of view. A second, more advanced course on physics and theology might include important topics such as cosmology, quantum gravity and general relativity [2], but the treatment would still need to be at a "factual" level. Such advanced physics material is usually only mastered by physics graduate students specializing in theoretical or mathematical physics. The reader can make a useful connection between the current paper and these more advanced treatments by examining the chapter in the just-cited reference entitled "The Debate Over the Block Universe". (This paper falls mostly on the "block-universe" side of the debate.)

Why does the issue of time play a central role in Augustine's physics? The laws of physics, as currently understood, all relate fundamental measures of mass, position, activity, and capability to the passage of time. For example, Conservation of Energy, asserts that the total amount of energy in a defined, isolated system remains constant with time. This would initially seem to correlate with the biblical idea that God is unchanging:

> Every good gift and every perfect gift is from above, coming down from the Father of lights with whom there is no variation or shadow due to change. (James 1:17, English Standard Version).

> "For I the Lord do not change; therefore you, O children of Jacob, are not consumed." (Mal. 3:6, ESV).

Augustine seems to have noted the difficulty that a truly *unchanging* God could *do* nothing, since *doing* is defined by change with time:...*time does not exist without motion or change*...Religious or philosophical treatments of these passages usually resort to interpretations of "change", "changeless" and time in specialized senses: "changeless" refers to some inherent nature or properties of God, such as His goodness or holiness, but not to inactivity.

In physics, the connection between *action* and *change* is clear. Forces cause a change in motion, as in Newton's Second Law of motion:

$$F = ma = m\frac{\Delta v}{\Delta t} = m\frac{\Delta\left(\frac{\Delta x}{\Delta t}\right)}{\Delta t} \qquad (1)$$

where F, m, a, v, x, and t stand for force, mass, acceleration, velocity, position and time. We interpret force as the cause of changes in motion or in stored energy. The multiple occurrence of the symbol Δ, representing "change in", shows that the principle of change is deeply embedded in the laws of physics. Even the principle of conservation of energy—that total energy of an isolated system does not change—contains implicit time dependence, since kinetic (motional) energy is defined in terms of a velocity, $\mathbf{v} = \frac{\Delta x}{\Delta t}$, and since various forms of energy making up the constant total can interconvert as time proceeds. While some might argue that God's unchanging nature may be the equivalent of total energy, with a myriad of changes and conversions going on beneath the surface, Augustine's writings on time show that he considers our time to be inapplicable or irrelevant to God's nature and action.

One can propose to focus a program of study solely on the nature of time and of God's unchanging character. The track of such a study typically leads to philosophical explorations of the definition(s) of time and their evolution over history. We propose a different track: to start with the known laws of physics, view them in terms of the mathematically-required continuity and smoothness of trajectories as time proceeds, with no explicit "definition" of our dimension of time outside of this requirement that the arrangement of objects at one instant of time must fit smoothly with arrangements at previous and subsequent instants. If God is to fit into this model, but remain unchanging but active, the simplest way is to propose a second dimension of time; not a second "type" or "meaning" of time, but a second dimension. The test of such a model involves checks on (i) whether and how an existence can make any sense with two time (or time-like) coordinates; (ii) agreement with known laws of physics in our normal world; and (iii) agreement with descriptions in the Bible. All three of these requirements work toward eliminating the freedom to redefine and adjust meanings to better conform reality to one's personal notions. In short, we seek to maintain a scientific approach. The ultimate objectives of this effort are to develop a flexible (expandable) course or course module that could either be taught as a standalone course or as a "module" in a core course in natural science, physics, religion or philosophy at the junior/senior undergraduate or graduate (masters) level. Such a course or course module might be called "Physical Theology".

2. The Student

The number of 21st-century people who are interested in, and might need to better understand the connections between, the physical laws of the universe and theological ideas of a supreme being is presumably large, at least in comparison to the number of physicists in the world. A new course that aims to be of value to that large number of people can approach this educational goal in one of two ways: (i) prepare a course or educational materials for this large group or (ii) educate the natural teachers of this large group—the ministers who serve local religious congregations. Approach (i) suffers from the tendency to produce a work (e.g., a book) that will attract popular attention and can be digested in a relatively short amount of time. This is difficult in the case of physics, because physics insists on understanding specific questions and observations from fundamental principles—an arduous process—and because these principles do not seem terribly spectacular. For example, to understand how an iron axe-head might float[2], a physicist would need to start from elementary principles of force (Newton's Laws) and buoyancy, using calculations to back up assertions. This would take a large amount of time for the meager goal of understanding one recorded statement in the Bible. Approach (ii), which aims to train those ministers who will teach much larger audiences on a weekly basis, seems more hopeful. These ministers would rarely teach physics *per se*, but would incorporate a mindset of the boundaries of physical laws into their messages.

The majority of future ministers in the Christian western world train in Master of Divinity (M.Div.) programs. Most such programs are professional, with specified student courses and experience required for accreditation. A recent (2011) survey by the author and Philip Markham, then a M.Div. student at the Beeson Divinity School of Samford University, on the physical science background of M. Div. students in schools accredited by the Association of Theological Schools (ATS), revealed virtually no physical science expected of M.Div. students. See Figure 1. (More details can be found online [3])at Of the one hundred seventy survey invitations sent to deans, associate deans or directors of academic programs of ATS-accredited schools, 45 responses were obtained—a response rate of 26%). When asked the percentage of students who study physical science while enrolled in their M.Div. program, 54% of program directors responded, 0% of students; 40% responded, 1%–10% of their students. Two directors stated that more than 20% of their students study physical science while enrolled.

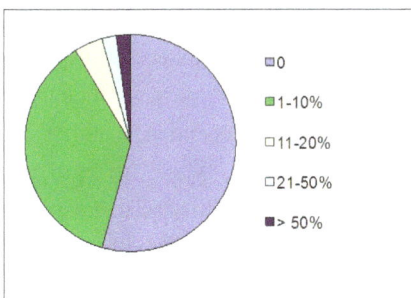

Figure 1. Percentage of students who study physical science while enrolled in one of 45 M. Div. programs.

When asked to rank the importance of new course material in their program, additional physical science course work ranked sixth (last), behind international cultures, psychology, music, management/business, and law. Considering the professional status of M.Div. schools, it is perhaps understandable that training their students to manage a church, with its expected daily tasks and

---

[2] So the man of God said, "Where did it fall?" And he showed him the place. So he cut off a stick, and threw it in there; and he made the iron float. II Kings 6:6 (New King James Version).

problems, comes out ahead of a gaining a better ability to (scientifically) comprehend the physical laws of existence and the relation to heaven. One conclusion from this information is that an attempt to insert a significant amount of additional physical science into a professional M.Div. program will likely fail. A comment from one survey respondent, that their program expects incoming students to have the needed science background from their undergraduate degree program, suggest that an attempt to insert a "Physical Theology" course into an undergraduate religion or philosophy curriculum might be more successful.

M.Div. students have a variety of undergraduate backgrounds, but commonly graduate from B.A. degree programs in religion and/or philosophy. Proposing a standalone Physical Theology course that fulfills a core science requirement is not a viable option in many universities, but a full course or course module on this subject might well fit into upper-level electives in religion and philosophy programs. Such a course module might also be considered in interdisciplinary or liberal-arts majors in the sciences.

3. What Is Time and How Does It Govern Physical Laws?

We cannot and will not attempt to answer the question "What is time?" other than to indicate that the precise nature of time is not well understood. Augustine argues that the "time" we humans have some intuitive feeling for came into existence with the creation of the universe [1]. This would seem to make sense, since the primary (perhaps only) use of time in physics theory relates changes and movements of matter and energy to a time variable. There would, then, be no time if there were no matter/energy. In the model presented in this paper, this understanding would remain, with the revision that our normal time forms the linkages between instants of existence. One has only to look at the proliferation of recent books and review articles about time and whether it exists at all to know that this topic is still actively discussed, at least in the popular, scientific press [4–11]. In fact, the primary laws of physics have been applied for hundreds of years without knowing the precise physical nature of time at all, beyond its occurrence as a fundamental independent mathematical variable, upon which many physical quantities depend. The author, like typical practicing physicists, was never bothered about the question, "What is time?", in spite of nine years of formal university education in physics and decades of experience with precise measurement of time from 1 picosecond (10^{-12} s) to hours or more. The one exception to "never bothered" occurred in an advanced quantum mechanics course, in which the state of an elementary particle at a time, t, required the inclusion of interactions at other times, both before *and after t*. Causality thus became an issue of discussion for a short time. Nevertheless, physicists and non-physicists alike constantly rely on measurement of time and of quantities that depend upon time: age, position, velocity, force, energy, chemical reactions, biological metabolism…If we could not use measures of time in a practical way, the world would make no sense.

We are, in fact, more and more dependent upon increasingly precise measurements of time, an aspect of life that Augustine commented on (See previous quotes). The world standard measure of time is partly maintained by the National Institute of Standards and Technology (NIST) in the United States, consists of a cesium fountain atomic clock, and is one of an international group of atomic clocks that define Coordinated Universal Time (UTC), the official world time.

The uncertainty of this atomic clock, as of January 2013, was about 3×10^{-16} second: this clock would neither gain nor lose a second in more than 100 million years. This precision may seem a bit extreme, but some aspects of our lives, such as GPS systems, depend on precise time measurement. Unlike our understanding of atoms, protons, neutrons, and other particles, where fundamental theories and experiments have predicted and confirmed substructure in these particles, we have no theory of time that proposes that it might consist of more fundamental entities.[3]

3.1. The Nature of Time

A clear distinction should be made between how the physicist employs measurements of time to understand and predict phenomena, using laws of physics, and human, intuitive perception of time. Except to point out the most common view, we leave the latter field to students of psychology.

3.1.1. The Math

The physicist writes that the position, x, of a car, starting from position x_0, moving with an initial speed, v_0 (speed at some initial *time*, defined specifically for the phenomenon at hand to be time = 0), and a constant (independent of *time*) acceleration, a, depends upon *time* in the following mathematical way:

$$x = x_0 + v_0 t + \frac{1}{2} a t^2 \qquad (2)$$

Actually, this equation does not represent any fundamental principle; rather, it results from the fundamental principles and physical definitions:

$$\begin{aligned} \mathbf{a} &\equiv \Delta_t \mathbf{v} \\ \mathbf{v} &\equiv \Delta_t \mathbf{x} \end{aligned} \qquad (3)$$

where Δ_t represents a mathematical time derivative of the quantity that follows it. Most of us learned the simple version of the second equation in Equation (3) in grade or high school as "distance = rate × time", where "rate" is "v". Underlying all these relationships are basic laws:

$$\begin{aligned} &\textbf{Newton's Second Law: } \mathbf{F} = \mathbf{ma} \\ &\textbf{Conservation of Energy: } E_{final} = E_{initial} \end{aligned} \qquad (4)$$

where F = force, m = mass, a = acceleration, and E = total energy. We will not belabor any mathematical points. The primary take-home message for scientists and non-scientists alike is that we do not have to specify the precise nature of time in order to employ the great laws of physics to understand or predict most of the universe's behavior, from atoms, to galaxies, to iPhones. We physicists only need to know that position, velocity, energy and other physical quantities depend "smoothly" on a measure called "time", which seems to always increase in the positive direction.

---

[3] This also applies to the *x*, *y* and *z* coordinates of space, though we know time is a different sort of entity.

3.1.2. The Perception of Time

The term "river of time", or some expression reflecting the notion that time flows in the forward direction, is often used to convey how the world behaves as time goes by. When asked in a scientific context, we 21st-century citizens usually go a bit further and claim that time flows constantly, inexorably in a forward direction, and that this flow pays no attention to what happens to be going on in our world or in his or her life. Even the expressions, *as time goes by*, or *as time passes*, reflect the intuitive idea that some mysterious quantity we refer to as time, is somehow moving. However, when asked simple, standard questions, like "Moving in what?" or "Moving with respect to what?", we are confounded, moving from statements like, "Well, it depends on what you mean…" to, "Why does it really matter?", to "Oh, just shut up!". The more thoughtful would perhaps reply,

> What… is time? If no one asks me, I know what it is. If I wish to explain it to him who asks me, I do not know. (Augustine, *op. cit.*)

One thing is perfectly clear: as long as we leave time—an independent quantity, essential to all physical laws, laws that describe our universe in as much detail as we normally ask; whose extent can be measured as precisely as we might desire; whose passage is tied to virtually all important, human experience (like our jobs and our lifespan)—as a murky and unspecific, but unique and fundamental, quantity that individuals are free to interpret as they prefer, and that physicists have no need to interpret, we will not make much progress on Augustine's most fundamental questions:

> But how didst Thou make the heaven and the earth? and what is the engine of Thy so mighty fabric? …
>
> [they] strive to comprehend things eternal, whilst their heart fluttereth between the motions of things past and to come, and is still unstable. Who shall hold it, and fix it, that it be settled awhile, and awhile catch the glory of that ever fixed Eternity, and compare it with the times which are never fixed, and see that it cannot be compared; and that a long time cannot become long, but out of many motions passing …but that in the Eternal nothing passeth, but the whole is present… [12].
>
> …time does not exist without motion or change…[13].

We could redefine the meaning of words like "unchanging" to refer to only a restricted set of characteristics, like "character" or "knowledge", when describing the Christian God. We may also be unable to resist the invention of new words, like *supralapsarianism, eisegesis, a- and b-series of time*,[4] with the claim that we cannot expect usual human words to correctly describe God or the entirety of our reality. (See, for example, dictionaries of philosophy or religion, [14,15]) Physicists, Augustine included, would respond with, "Words are fine, but tell me how to calculate something that I can compare with reality."

---

[4] This last pair of philosophical definitions, pointed out to the author in 2007 by Rev. Dr. Rodney Holder, former Course Director of the Faraday Institute of the University of Cambridge, led, by a circuitous route to the simpler, more "physical" view of times discussed in this paper and the proposed Physical Theology course.

3.1.3. A "Fearful" Proposition about Time

> The fear of the Lord is the beginning of wisdom. (Proverbs 9:10).

While refined philosophical/religious definitions and words can be explained and justified, they seem to have little connection to the "fear of the Lord" that is said to be the beginning of wisdom. Such wisdom would seem to be a fundamental goal of religious philosophers. Augustine seemed quite fearful of the Lord, and wrote of it in connection with his questions related to "What is time?" This author is not thoroughly read in Augustine, but it seems that Augustine is not very concerned with applied physics issues like "What determines the range of a projectile?" or "How can we store energy for use later?"—questions that were favorites of physicists of the 17th century and later. His main concerns relate to the operation of the universe and God's relation to it. The intensity of his desire to understand emerge soon after declaring his questions about how time works:

> My soul is on fire to know this most intricate enigma. Shut it not up, O Lord my God, good Father;…This is my hope, for this do I live, that I may contemplate the delights of the Lord.
>
> Behold, Thou hast made my days old, and they pass away, and how, I know not. And we talk of time, and time, and times, and times…(Augustine *Confessions, op. cit.*).

Augustine thought about many deep, unsettled, and unsettling moral issues, but when he wrote of his soul being *on fire*, he had just described his attempts to understand the enigma of time and how God and the universe fit together. How can we comprehend this fire in his soul? We could minimize the scope of his blazing concern by supposing Augustine was worried about his own eternal destiny. However, his use of the words "hope", "live", and "delights" suggest that his soul-fire was more akin to the feelings of Christian and Hopeful, in *Pilgrim's Progress*, as they approached their goal:

> …drawing near to the city, they had yet a more perfect view thereof…by reason of the natural glory of the city, and the reflection of the sunbeams upon it, Christian with desire fell sick; Hopeful also had a fit or two of the same disease…[16].

What ideas about time might instill a deep sense of "fire", "fear" and "delight" in Augustine? Perhaps he had some inkling that the fundamental question of how God and our physical universe fit together focuses on the single question: "What is time?" A Physical Theology course would fail its main purpose utterly, if it did not address the fundamental physical principles that underlie the relationship between God and His creation, without resorting to a simple segregation of the "earthly" from the "heavenly". After all, God did not segregate himself from our world. Physical Theology, in the tradition of Saint Augustine, can and should freely admit its shortcomings and questions, but it cannot simply assert that the physical world obeys laws of physics and the theological world, the laws of theology (or religion or philosophy). A clear biblical reason for a required intimate connection between physics and theology can be found in the Bible:

> In the beginning was the Word, and the Word was with God, and the Word was God. He was with God in the beginning. Through him all things were made; without him nothing was made that has been made. (John 1:1–3, NIV).

The meaning of the "Word" is described later in this passage as being the person of Jesus, the Son of God and one "member" of the trinity: God, the Father, Son and Holy Spirit. Jesus is later described as being born as a human being, but still being God, the Son. Physical Theology should seek to understand these rather simple[5] statements with a simple, enlightening, non-obfuscatory model that integrates Jesus' material qualities with His eternity and ability to create all things. How can we possibly accomplish this integration, and how might this involve Augustine's questions about time?

To introduce a possible model of time, to be evaluated by students of Physical Theology, we appropriate in Figure 2 a graphic created by NASA:

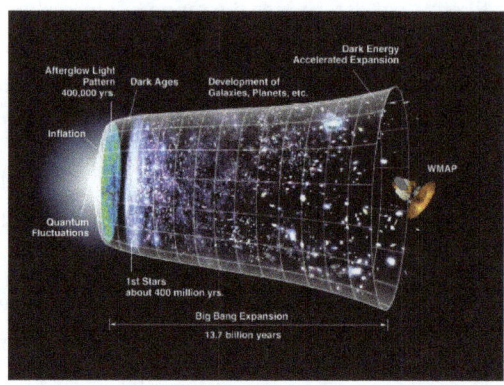

Figure 1. "Time Line of the Universe" The time-dependent structure of the universe in four dimensions—three spatial (x,y,z) and one time (t)—is expressed in a pseudo-3D image by ignoring one spatial dimension and replacing the horizontal spatial coordinate by the time coordinate. Graphic courtesy of NASA: may be freely used for educational and informational purposes [17].

Such a picture of the development of the physical universe was earlier used by Brian Greene, in his 2004 book *The Fabric of the Cosmos*, and was described as a "view from nowhere" [18]. The implication of Greene's statement was that this Figure 2 view of physical reality did not reflect what any human or imaging device could "see" from any point in the universe. The author (TN) has used the simplified picture shown in Figure 3 in several special university courses since 2003 to illustrate the ideas that (i) our real universe can be viewed in terms of time "slices" of the 3D structure of the universe; and (ii) that the laws of physics can be viewed pictorially as requiring a smooth, continuous path of an object. In Figure 3a, an object's path can be tracked with no abrupt changes in direction and no discontinuities in the track. In Figure 3b, the object's track changes direction suddenly, corresponding to the application of a large force. This track may be consistent with laws of physics (e.g., Equations (1)–(4)), but if the discontinuity is abrupt enough, the force may correspond to a concentration of power large enough to create matter-antimatter pairs, which could then create a large explosion. Such matter-antimatter creation has been done with high-power, pulsed lasers [19,20]. Figure 3c shows an object following a discontinuous track. Such discontinuity implies the application of an infinite force and power, which violates the laws of physics and could, if the

---

[5] "Simple", in the sense of uncomplicated, not necessarily "easy to understand".

displacement were just "almost" instantaneous, create conditions required for the generation of a "bubble universe" [21]. Such events may not be welcome to any human that happened to be near.

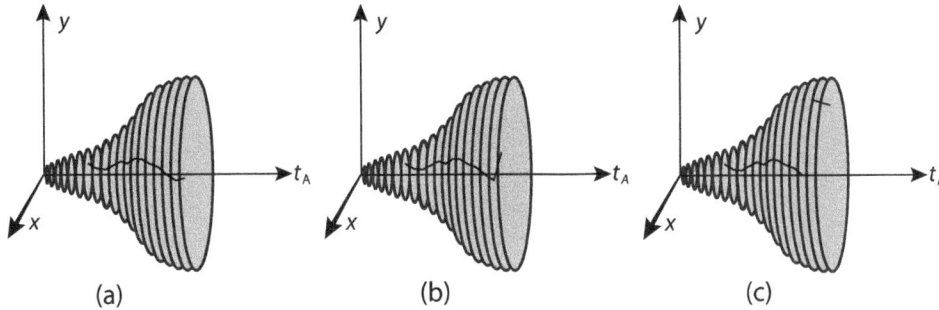

Figure 2. Two of the three spatial dimensions (x, y), with the one normal time dimension plotted horizontally in place of the z dimension. The entire spatial structure of the universe at a given time along the t_A axis is represented by the corresponding time "slice". (**a**) the path of a normal object, obeying the laws of physics, follows a smooth, continuous path as time increases. (**b**) an object subject to a sudden, very large force. (**c**) an object violating the laws of physics.

Though some of the mathematics of path continuity in Figures 2 and 3 should be presented in a physical theology course, this pictorial representation of laws of physics gives the less mathematically-inclined student a visual handle on the main issue, that laws of physics prevent disruptions and discontinuities in physical processes, and that extreme discontinuities (miracles?) can be accompanied by extreme, and perhaps destructive, energetic events.

A quick response of some religious readers to Figures 2 and 3 might be that this is "God's view" of a reality, which includes more than just what we humans can see. There are, however, several problems that this interpretation. First, Figure 2 has introduced an additional dimension, beyond our normal four dimensions, without any description of its properties and evidence for its existence. Second, the introduction of additional dimensions to existence must satisfy constraints of predictability and stability, described by Max Tegmark (Figure 4) [22]. In a Physical Theology course, this issue would be investigated at a simple level. One of the possible conclusions resulting from Figure 4 is that our normal, human existence can *only* explore three spatial and one time dimension. If the universe has 7–8 more spatial dimensions, as in string theory, those extra dimensions must be tiny and "curled-up", preventing humans from personally exploring them. The next course exploration would be to consider whether an additional time (or time-like) dimension could exist. In spite of dozens of time-travel novels and movies, such a possibility would incur the "unpredictable" stamp of Figure 4.

"Unpredictable" does not just mean that we may get some surprises along the way; rather, nothing would make sense and normal materials would not hold together. Cause and effect would take a holiday, depending upon exactly what rules might govern processes involving both time dimensions. Taking a breath might not result in air entering one's lungs. Our bodies that are constructed of flexible, constantly-moving chemical and mechanical parts could not sustain their stable life.

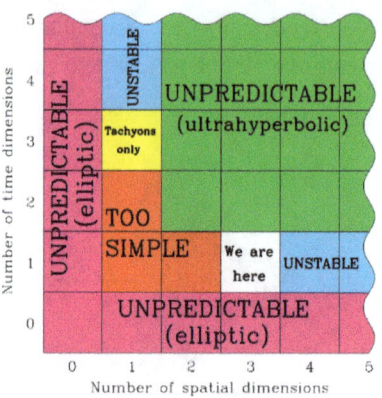

Figure 3. Graphic "On the dimensionality of spacetime", by Max Tegmark (No implied endorsement of the present work) [23]. Licensed under the Creative Commons Attribution-Share Alike 3.0 Unported license.

Going back to the possibility of Figures 2 and 3 being "God's view", the next question to be investigated might be whether a being like God could navigate in a world with 3 (or more) spatial dimensions and two time-like dimensions, t_A and t_B. Note that these times have no connection to the "A- and B-series times" of McTaggart, who postulated those two types of time to correlated with either past/present/future or before/after distinctions, concluding that time did not exist [24]. Some inferences that come out in a fairly straightforward manner are that if God is to navigate this "universe" and interact with our universe without destroying it, there would/could probably be a need for several "forms" of God.[6] If one form with some "substance" could navigate in all dimensions, but resided primarily in t_B, he would risk the introduction of extremely large amounts of energy if he were to step into t_A. The reason for this is that an entity in the t_B realm, interacting with the t_A realm, could not lose any energy in the t_A realm, because no time (t_B) would have passed, so that entity could not change. If he "stuck his finger" into world A, a large or infinite amount of energy (perhaps like a column of fire?) might be discharged into A, though he would not change at all in his world, B. A second, natural and "useful" form for God might be "non-substantial" and able to travel freely in all the dimensions: a "spirit". The "non-substantial" qualifier could be explored further through examination of the math behind Figure 4, but a non-material quality would certainly apply, because all materials we know about are constructed of atoms, which are held together by electric forces, operating in three spatial and one time dimension, that result in extremely stable orbits of electrons around a nucleus. Finally, at least in the Christian religion Augustine believed in, a form of God that could enter and interact with our world without much physical disruption (operating in the normal x, y, z, and t_A dimensions) would be needed, since the other two forms could not fulfill this

---

[6] There is a risk here of being accused of heresy, in attempting to answer questions like, "Why is there a Trinity? Why not a duality, or tetrality?", rather than simply quoting scripture and saying, "That's what is written; don't ask anything further." The author's preference is for a collaborative search by science and religion scholars for answers to these obvious questions that even children ask. From some personal experience, there is also a danger in these investigations of time and our relation to the "expanded" universe, that one encounters a "fear of the Lord" that is rather suffocating. Perhaps this is not a bad thing.

role. Since we require that our physical description of God also encompass biblical writings, e.g., those in John 1 quoted above, this third and last form of God must also have two states: one who can create our universe (probably move independently in both the t_A and t_B time dimensions) and one who operates more like a normal human being in t_A. We find we are approaching the conclusion that a Trinity much like that described in the Bible might well be the ideal, perhaps the *only*, form for God who interacts with our world.

We have reached these quite specific inferences (or perhaps justified speculations) about the nature of God by examining the same question—"What is time?"—that caused the fire in Augustine's soul. Augustine may not have had the mathematical sophistication of modern-day physicists, but he seemed to have an instinctual sense that the transcendence and "otherness" of God had to be connected to the nature of time and time's governing nature in our normal universe.

3.2. Original Sin: Quantifying the Possible Outcomes of Human "Free Will"

A physics course targeted toward students of religion, philosophy and other major fields that commonly lead toward careers in Christian ministry has two major goals: (i) to provide basic understanding of the physical world around us; and (ii) to illustrate how physical principles can be applied to theological questions. The first goal provides the basic tools a future minister needs to more clearly see and explain the difference between unusual events and "miracles". A minister leading a congregation must apply these scientific tools judiciously, as the fragile faith of some religious believers relies on the classification of some experiences as miraculous. The main issue here is two understandings of the word "miraculous". The first meaning is connected to an event that did not and could not have occurred via normal physical processes, a meaning that seems to directly conflict with science. The second meaning less radically states that God was involved in the event. To some, both scientists and non-scientists alike, these two meanings are virtually the same, but the statement that "God was involved" does not necessarily imply that laws of physics were broken. These two meanings of "miraculous" provide the subject for endless debates, but when considered from the primary physical aspect that perplexed St. Augustine—time—some quite new issues come to the fore. These new issues can still be debated, but they first provide at least three profound questions for the science and religion students, as well as their teachers, to ponder.

(i) What is the difference between a highly-unlikely event and a miracle?
(ii) What are the limits on science's ability to project the future course of events?
(iii) Can God change what we consider the "past"?

The second question is likely to cause a good deal of unwarranted confusion, as the physics student would think of the laws of physics and their ability to predict, for example, the parabolic path of a cannonball. The liberal-arts student may, in contrast, imagine a physicist trying to predict the course of human events or the career of a new-born baby. These differing conceptions of unlikely events, past, and future, can be woven together by Augustine's questions about time.

If we provisionally accept the proposals that God operates in a second time-like dimension, independent of our own, and that our world might be viewed by God as in Figures 2 and 3, some clear physical questions present themselves. First, is there some fixed separation in time between the time "slices" of Figure 3? Second, what are the rules governing an object's trajectory from one time slice to the next. We will see that the first question focuses on whether time might be quantized and the second, on whether time might be quite different from the "flowing river" we often conceive of.

3.2.1. Quantization of Time[7]

The *simplest* interpretation of the time coordinate of Figure 3 is that time slices are separated by a constant amount, as science interprets time separations. This implies that time is quantized. The student should recall Augustine's question about the smallest-possible interval of time that can be imagined or proposed, and what that implies about actions. Current physics textbooks state that the normal laws of physics operate only for times longer than the Planck Time, about 10^{-43} s [25]. Since physical laws enforce the continuity and smoothness of the paths of objects, and these laws (probably) do not operate on times shorter than the Planck Time, we propose that the time separation between slices is 10^{-43} s. This time is *incredibly small*. Recall that we can measure times precisely to about $\pm 10^{-16}$ s, so 10^{27} of these Planck Time intervals would fit into our *very small* time-measurement uncertainty. Note that an academic class or two would have to be spent on powers of ten—scientific notation—so that liberal arts majors could easily manage the arithmetic, which, we will see, becomes a bit intense:

$$\text{Scientific Notation: } \left(10^{27}\right) \times \left(10^{-43}\right) = 10^{27-43} = 10^{-16} \qquad (5)$$

Students will and should question this model for time and physical reality, but we almost have the minimum we need to proceed to some "theological" questions.

3.2.2. What Is the World That GOD Created?

The proposal for discussion is that God's creation is not merely the initial "Big Bang" of creation, the infinitesimal leftmost point in Figure 2 or 3, but rather the entire set of coordinates—x, y, z and t—for the entire history of our universe. He constructed the beginning, the end, and everything in the middle, from one edge of the universe to the other edge, as it exists at all times (all times, t_A, since we must distinguish it from the other time or time-like dimension, t_B, that God also operates in). Many objections will be raised at this point, but we try to postpose them and make a connection to Genesis 1:25, 31 and Genesis 2:1, where God declared that His creation was "good" and rested from His work. Note that our scientific understanding of work, involving forces, distances and times, can also apply to God, but that His work involved the t_B dimension.

Let us clarify our model for how God did His creation. In Figure 3, we see that the physical universe fits together according to physical laws, which require that the paths of objects in (x,y,z) space cannot change discontinuously from one time slice to the next. More carefully stated, the discontinuity in position from one time slice to the next cannot be larger than a very small distance.

---

[7] We are initially avoiding the direct question of what, exactly, is this second "time-like" dimension that God operates in, but this evasion of the question is not essentially different than science has done for many years with the nature of our "normal" time.

This model is difficult to comprehend clearly, but we can recall a building experience many of us had as children or as parents of children: building structures using Lego-like blocks. Again, we have to remember we are ignoring one of the three spatial dimensions, in order to incorporate the time (t_A) dimension into out model. When we build structures using such blocks, we start with the first layer. Let's refer to this layer as the first time slice. The thickness of this time slice, as well as all subsequent slices, is constant, enforced by the thickness of the blocks, and corresponds to 10^{-43} s, the Planck Time. (Ignore the thinner plate-blocks that sometimes come in a Lego set.) We note that in putting together a structure, the raised disks and cylindrical slots on the two sides of each block enforce construction rules when we pass from one layer (time slice) to the next (Figure 5).

(a) (b)

Figure 5. (a) a pile of Lego-like blocks; (b) a structure created from the blocks.

Blocks in the second layer must fit with those in the first layer: we cannot place them at an arbitrary position, or the structure will not hold together. Such positioning rules correspond to the laws of physics that describe the universe. Now, suppose we carefully follow the instruction sheet to create a panda bear, Figure 5. After hours of work, we might look at our panda and declare it a *good* structure.

It would be advisable to stop at this point to deflect some accusations of heresy and disrespect to God. The Lego model of creation is intended to allow us humans to comprehend a creation that involves all space and all time, not to assert that God is like a child playing with blocks. Even the briefest musing on the model shows that this childish creation involves numbers that bewilder even the experienced mathematician and cosmologist. How many 10^{-43}-second layers are needed to complete the universe at its present age, about 14 billion years, or $(14 \times 10^9 \text{yr}) \left(\dfrac{3.15 \times 10^7 \text{s}}{1 \text{yr}} \right) \cong 4 \times 10^{17} \text{s}$? If the (horizontal) distance between the raised disks on the blocks corresponds to the Planck Distance, about 10^{-35} meters, how many blocks are needed to stretch across the entire know universe, which is something like a sphere of diameter 100 billion light years (ly): **100 billion ly**$= (10^{11} \text{ly}) \left(\dfrac{10^{16} \text{m}}{\text{ly}} \right) = 10^{27} \text{m}$?

This computation involves four dimensions, but dealing with lengths and volumes in four dimensions is common to mathematicians and can be managed by undergraduates. The numbers are staggering and incomprehensible. Even more difficult to comprehend is the implication of the model that all of the history of the universe is presented "at the same time". There is no uncertainty of the "future"; it is already there, in some sense. If God has managed to create the universe (for all time t_A), using an incomprehensibly large number of building blocks, He will certainly know every detail, to a resolution of 10^{-35} m in distance and 10^{-43} s in time. These distances and times are incredibly smaller than the size of the nuclei of atoms and the time it takes an electron to orbit in an atom. Even if one proposed God could not remember all these details, He could find out anything He wanted, at His leisure in time t_B. In any case, we start to get a handle on why God might be so formidable and so "fearful", rather than blithely thinking that God is, well, some super being. *The fear of the Lord is the beginning of wisdom.* (Proverbs 9:10).

3.2.3. Free Will and the Tree

We strive to make a connection of the above model of creation to free will and original sin. These are quite formidable topics and have been the source for endless debate and countless essays, sermons, and books. The connection of the physical model to free will and original sin cannot be made with absolute certainty and precision—we must leave some questions for the developing ministers and physicists—but we can start.

Suppose the "panda" in Figure 5 is the creation that God declared "good". What happened in the book of Genesis after chapters 1 and 2? Genesis 3 describes the fall of man. This "fall" involves the human desire for the ability to distinguish the difference between good and evil:

> The woman [Eve] said to the serpent, "We may eat fruit from the trees in the garden", but God did say, "You must not eat from the fruit of the tree that is in the middle of the garden…or you will die.".…"You will not surely die", the serpent said to the woman. "For God knows that when you eat of it, your eyes will be opened, and you will be like God, knowing good and evil." (Genesis 3:2–5).

We are usually taught that the serpent, Satan, is the great liar, and that he lied here to Eve. Most good liars know that outright lies are often unconvincing and difficult to maintain. The best lies are truths, with some subtle, essential facts left out. In the model of Figure 3, Eve's existence in our normal universe could be traced as a path or trajectory in space and time. (Consider this as before "the fall", when neither she nor Adam seemed to age and did not need to reproduce, to replace themselves if they died.) If all of existence were already in place for all times (t_A), she would have no way of knowing (experiencing) what is "good" and "evil". Her existence would naturally follow what God created and declared "good", like the panda. Note also that good is now defined as something that conforms to the *entire* creation or structure that God made, as illustrated in Figure 5, not to some debatable moral issues, like, "Should you pay taxes that support a cause you oppose?" Satan asks what could be a higher good than to be more like God and to understand why one option might be evil, while the other is good? Shouldn't Eve want to know and understand? Does God want intelligent companions or robots? If she has no ability to actually see and accept either of two choices, Eve could not truly understand "good" and "evil", right?

We read that both Eve and Adam ate of the *tree of knowledge of good and evil*.[8] What might this tree be? It is pretty clear that after "eating the fruit", these humans could now see two (or more) options for how they might proceed. They did not blindly follow a specific path. In some way, they now had "free will": they could see two options. From a physics or mathematical point of view, this freedom of choice directly implies decision points and mathematical probabilities (likelihoods) for following a given path. If one decision offers two possible paths, and our likelihood for choosing the "correct" path were 1/2, the probability for following a particular path is $\left(\frac{1}{2}\right)^1$, or one half. A second decision point would result in an overall probability of $\left(\frac{1}{2}\right)^2 = \frac{1}{4}$ for following a specified path.

Pause. In this simplest model, we treat Adam and Eve choosing randomly, but even if they consulted experts for each decision, and each decision had a 99%, or even 99.999%, probability of being right, it would make no difference after all decision points were taken into account. This directly leads to consideration of Jesus' assertion that a camel is more likely to pass through the eye of a needle than a rich man is to enter the kingdom of heaven. In terms of the rich man's choices in life, probabilities can be calculated. Likewise, the camel's probability (real camel, passing through a real needle's eye of size less than one millimeter) can be calculated using quantum-mechanical tunneling theory. A rich man, employing many wise advisors, might have a higher probability for making right decisions. Jesus says it makes no difference. In fact, when we calculate the probability as described later in this section, we find that the camel's probability is about one chance in $10^{10^{37}}$, while the rich man's probability is one chance in $10^{10^{40}}$ (or less). The numbers in the topmost exponent may be off by plus or minus 2, but it makes no difference: the camel wins by much more than a landslide. Though no camel could pass through the eye of a needle, even if 100,000,000,000,000 camels try all their lives in each of 1,000,000,000,000,000,000,000,000 different universes, the rich man has an even smaller probability. In fact the ratio of the two probabilities is

$$\frac{10^{10^{40}}}{10^{10^{37}}} = 10^{10^{40}} \qquad (6)$$

This calculation seems like it cannot be right. How can dividing one number by another huge number not matter? If I have $1000 and you have one one-hundredth as much, could you possibly have $1000? No, but when numbers go from familiar ranges like 1000 to incredibly large ranges like those above, dividing $10^{10^{40}}\ 10^{10^{40}}$ by $10^{10^{37}}\ 10^{10^{37}}$ is little different than dividing by 1.0001. Technically the "equals" sign in Equation (6) above should be an "approximately equal to", but the exact answer, $10^{10^{39.999999\ldots}}\ 10^{10^{39.999999\ldots}}$, could not be entirely written on this or 100,000,000,000,000 pages of paper.[9] Our conclusion about the camel *vs.* rich man story? Jesus might be literally stating

---

[8] Note that the issue of times t_A and t_B, how Adam and Eve relate to them, and how they seem to have been expelled from the freedom of t_B (the Garden of Eden), are questions that must also be faced.

[9] In contrast to Equations (7) and (8), these numbers result from considering the decision points to correspond to the characteristic vibration time of each molecule making up a human body. Each molecule in the body must then

a mathematical fact that He would be quite familiar with, from His experience as the Engineer Who designed and constructed the universe.

So, one decision, ½ chance of success; two decisions, ¼ chance to successfully follow any pre-specified path. How many choices must we consider? We humans like to consider that what determines "good" and "evil" involves decisions we have to make over the period of a day or our lifetime. We think we have, perhaps, 10, 100, or even 1000 decisions to make per day. But this analysis has little connection to physical reality, to the intrinsic nature of our universe. It is an analysis we concoct in our minds, because it is easy to comprehend and manage. Suppose we accept the statement that the creation in Figure 5 is "good". This would imply that a particular object in that creation, which has some path that, after the fall of Adam and Eve, follows a path illustrated in Figure 3, would have a *calculable probability* of following that specific path within the overall structure of Figure 5, that God declared "good".

How many "decision points", in terms of the physical nature of our existence, does this involve? If the universe is constructed of 10^{-43}-s slices of time, the lifetime of a person would consist of about:

$$n \cong \frac{(70\text{yr})(3 \times 10^7 \text{ s/yr})}{10^{-43} \text{s}} \cong 10^{52} \tag{7}$$

time slices. If this is the number of decision points, then the simplest estimate for the probability for following a particular path is:

$$\left(\frac{1}{2}\right)^n \cong 10^{-10^{52}} \tag{8}$$

where $n = 10^{52}$. (Note again the unexpected mathematical results. This expression treats a human as one "object", where perhaps the reality of a human is more correctly expressed in terms of the number of individual atoms or molecules making up one's body. Since conclusions do not really depend on these details, we ignore these and other details.)

There will be many protests that we cannot be blamed for things that we have no control over, things that take place on an incomprehensibly short timescale that humans can do nothing about. But if "good", "evil", and "sin" have to do with actual structure and reality in our universe, and not just our human conception of what seems "good enough" or "not so good, but who can blame him", the comparison of the world resulting from Adam and Eve's choice to eat the fruit of the tree, to that God declared "good" is not even close. (Think of a chance in $10^{10^{40}} \, 10^{10^{40}}$.) It does not matter if 99.999% of everyone's decisions are "good", after the entirety of history, the universe we will have "created", as well as the individual life each of us will have created, will look like the left side of Figure 5, not the right side. This conclusion follows from consideration of the nature of our universe, not from a man's perceived ability to resist taking a too-long look at the woman walking in front of him. According to our model, this is the result of Eve's and Adam's choice. This is "original sin": there is "zero" chance in a million universes, with 10 billion people in each, that even one person

---

follow a specific path, in order to correspond to a given collective path. If Equations (7) and (8) are closer to reality, the camel would beat the rich man by a factor of $10^{10^{52}}$.

could follow the path that God created. It's as hopeless for the "good" person (99% correct) as for the "bad" (50% or less correct). This is what Satan failed to disclose in his proposition to Eve. There is no hope at all…unless God decided to do something.

Pause. Have we now postulated two different universes, the one God initially created (the "good" one) and the one that seems to be in the process of being created as time passes? This deserves more discussion than we have time for here, but one must be careful about asserting that our (fallen) universe is being created as our time passes. From God's perspective (Figures 2 and 3), all of t_A, from time zero to the end of time, may already be evident, so any apparent, ongoing "creation" of the universe as t_A passes may only be the view from the human perspective. We will leave to the biblical scholars whether there is written evidence for a second creation in the book of Genesis. As Julian Barbour has suggested [26], an alternative view of time (t_A), as a connecting link between the configuration of the universe at one instant to that in the next, may be a more profitable way of thinking about time.

Adam and Eve's existence before the fall is, of course, mysterious, and we cannot seek to probe the depths. If time were somehow not passing in the pre-fall Garden of Eden, or they somehow operated with some sort of "access" to both times t_A and t_B—after all, Adam walked in the Garden of Eden with the eternal God—their world must have had quite different rules of operation (laws of physics). It would seem that they would not have to eat food in order to stay alive. It appears from the account in Genesis that their bodies were not subject to the processes of decay that would lead to death. Most details cannot clearly be deciphered. However, we can make an attempt to further understand one entity: the tree of knowledge of good and evil. Why might this have been called a tree?

Figure 6 shows what mathematicians call a *decision tree*. Starting from the bottom, initial state, the object (person) encounters the first decision point. We assume two possible choices at each decision point. The probability for making a *left* or *right* decision can be specified, but we assume ½ for simplicity. A pre-selected path is shown in red. The calculations we have been doing correspond to finding the likelihood that an object (person) starts at the bottom and follows the selected path all the way to the top. Each time (vertical line segment) in the tree corresponds to the Planck Time.

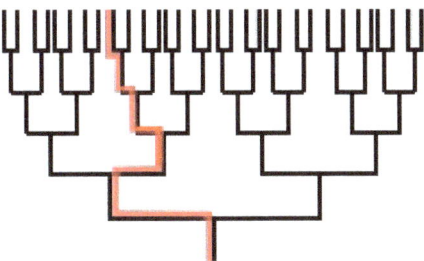

Figure 4. Decision tree. Time starts at the bottom and increases in the vertical direction. Two possible choices are assumed for each decision.

We will not try to defend this view of the *tree of knowledge of good and evil*—it is a bit speculative—except to say that it incorporates the ability to choose good or evil, allows one to actually calculate probabilities, and conveys more understanding than a picture of a common apple tree.

By this point, the author expects that the majority of science, religion and philosophy students, as well as faculty, will be powerfully offended by this model for God, creation, and existence. However, the downfall of a scientific model cannot be based on our sensibilities being offended, but on shortcomings of *simplicity and clarity*, *explanatory and predictive power*, and on *experiment and observation*. We do not have time to explore these issues here, but note that already, we have produced a calculation of the likelihood of a rich man "entering the kingdom of God", and compared it to the likelihood of a camel passing through the eye of a needle, and found that Jesus' comparison of the camel and rich man just might have been a literal statement about the physical operation of the fallen universe and humans, by the person who created it all. If we consider Jesus' statement as a legitimate experimental observation, then this model satisfies the primary requirements of science. The many issues that remain to be clarified require the collaboration of scientists and theologians. Imagine: not a debate between scientists and theologians who are each convinced of their position, but a collaboration of scientists and theologians, none of whom sees how the details of science and theology quite fit together, all of whom are disoriented, but know they need the help of the other side. Augustine might not have been surprised at such an intersection of interests, but collaborations in mainstream science and religion are not common today.

4. Power, Miracles and Changing the Past (?)

Power is a standard subject that both physicists and religious ministers teach in elementary educational courses or sermon series. In the context of the nature of God, Christian ministers and believers may state, "God can do anything He wants", when questioned about the rarity of obvious miracles such as those recorded in the Bible. The statement is usually accompanied by assertions that there are many miracles we don't even notice, like life itself, or a radical change in the health, lifestyle, or attitude of a friend or relative. There may be comments about God dealing with humanity in different ways during different periods of time (dispensations?), or an emphasis on "anything *He* wants", as opposed to what human onlookers might want to see. What people mean by "miracles" is also usually limited to phenomena or situations they have encountered or read about.

One example of God's ability to do miracles, but refusal to do something He does not want to do, can be found in the biblical description of Jesus' temptation by Satan, after Jesus had fasted for 40 days and nights (Matt. 4). Satan first challenges the very hungry Jesus to change stones into bread. Jesus waves away the challenge, quoting scripture, "…man does not live on bread alone…" The obvious implication is that such a miracle is not anything that Jesus or God particularly wants. In his second temptation, Satan transports Jesus to the highest point of the temple, and, after quoting scripture (Ps. 91:11ff), challenges Him to jump off, asserting that God will command angels to rescue Him. Jesus replies with, "Do not put the Lord your God to the test." (Matt. 4:7, NIV) Some translators have offered "tempt" as an alternative for the word "test". The author is not a competent translator, but consideration of the possible limitations on what God may do, in the context of the above model of time and existence, points a clear finger of preference to the "testing" translation.

Why does Jesus invoke a prohibition on "testing" God, when challenged to jump off the top of the temple? The drop would have been about 100 feet, according to a note on Luke 4:9 in my 1985 Zondervan NIV Study Bible. In any ten-year period, most of us would have heard of cases where people have fallen out of high windows and survived almost uninjured. Perhaps Jesus is simply brushing off Satan's challenge as trivial: such a miracle would not seem to be a major test of what God could do. However, if Satan is really as wily as described in the Bible, there may be more to the "test" than appears.

Figure 3 provides us with a tool to analyze at least certain types of "miracles". A miraculous event occurs in the right-most diagram of the figure, where an object is at one position at one time, and at a distant location in the next time slice. This violates the laws of physics, and movement even approaching such a rapid translocation would require the input of a near-infinite power that would tear the universe apart at the point of application. This is not something God would likely want to do. We have arrived at an initial example of what might "limit" God's actions: He will (probably) not do certain miracles, if the result of the miracle would be the destruction of our universe. God could, however, accomplish a rapid-enough translocation of an object to accomplish the goal, which may be to move a child out of the way of a speeding bus, without the need to apply a huge power that would destroy the universe. Given enough forewarning, God could even use a nearby pedestrian to knock the child out of the bus' path.

We have just used a critical phrase that Augustine has already considered: "…compare it with the times which are never fixed, and see that it cannot be compared; and that a long time cannot become long, but out of many motions passing…but that in the Eternal nothing passeth, but the whole is present." (See Introduction). "Enough forewarning" implies that God needs a certain amount of time to do certain things, and that if He intervenes too late, explosive results might occur. An obvious way out of this apparent dilemma is to say that God is never taken by surprise, so He will never be in a position to intervene too late. Is the issue then at its end?

If we take Figures 2 and 3 as a possible way God might "see" our universe, we reinforce our conclusion that God is never taken by surprise: He can, at an instant in time t_B, "see" any event that takes place from the beginning until the end of our time, t_A. He could then intervene at precisely the right time (t_A) and place. In fact, He could intervene at a time 1 second before a possible desired translocation of the object in Figure 3c. This would mean He would have to adjust a few times 10^{43} of the 10^{-43}-second time slices, in order not to produce a discontinuity that would disrupt the universe. This is not so startling, if we have accepted the idea that God can manage $10^{10^{50}}$ objects without a problem.

However, there is another possibility, one that may have lurked behind some of St. Augustine's fiery desire to understand God, time, past, present, future, and eternity. We present this possibility, and then end this paper. If God truly constructed our universe from building blocks that correspond to small intervals of x, y, z, and t, He could intervene and change the local structure of our universe in a manner that would not disrupt its stability. For example, a cancer-ridden ovary could be somehow modified in a way that the cancer would not be there a week later. The intervention by God might be over a period (t_A) of two weeks. Many Christians would have no problem with these statements, except to wonder about the "two weeks", vs. the "a week later". This apparent discrepancy is intentional. What if one of the two "modified" weeks is in what we consider the past? *Can God change something in our universe that we consider "past"?* Note that this is not the same as proposing time travel of an object or person in our universe. God is simply rearranging building blocks. Is there a problem? Is God limited to changing the future? Is this question part of the fire in Augustine's soul?

5. Conclusions

This paper presents a proposed physics course curriculum related to time and eternity as described by St. Augustine in several of his works, as part of a physical theology course or educational module designed for upper-division undergraduate religion, philosophy, and science students. The course could satisfy a core science requirement. The focus is on physical reality, as dealt with by most physicists, and on the nature of God, not on religion, religious practice or morality. The objective of such a course is to provide students with physics tools capable of quantitatively addressing questions relating to common observations in our normal world and to the interaction of eternal God with our world, as described in the Bible. Quantitative tools include those of numerical calculations. The level of the physics is that of an introductory college physics course, but the presentation of the laws of physics focuses on a pictorial/graphical description of the laws in terms of model diagrams in x, y and t coordinates, with the z spatial dimension suppressed for convenience. An object following the laws of physics follows a smooth, continuous path. The proposal to bring God into the same model via the simplest assumption that allows His "activity" and "unchanging" nature, along with unchanged physical laws in our universe, introduces a second time or time-like dimension, t_B, in addition to our normal time, t_A. Like our normal time dimension, the detailed nature of this second time need not yet be specified, other than to note that "free" access to both time dimensions is restricted by considerations of predictability and stability. As with any legitimate physical model, the one proposed enables quantitative predictions and explanations of common, but difficult, biblical issues like original sin, free will, the camel/rich man story, *etc.* The model treats experiments and observations in the normal world, as well as biblical writings as valid "data" that model predictions must conform to. This results in an alternative way to read and interpret scripture in a very literal sense. The approach can produce quantitative explanations (not physical analogies) but should be considered a hermeneutical method, to be added to those already available to students of biblical, philosophical and theological literature.

While presentation of the normal laws of physics is slightly unorthodox compared to mainstream "College Physics" textbooks, the principles are the same and should not be controversial. The proposed second time dimension is not part of conventional physics, and should be carefully dealt with, as should the view that our normal time is simply the directional "glue" that stitches one instant of existence to the next and previous. Physicists should take issue with the proposed presentation of time(s), though no violation of normal physical laws results. Theologians and philosophers may take issue with the model's restrictions on their freedom to interpret scripture, God and reality as they see fit, but such restriction is the purpose of a physical model. Physical laws restrict assertions of "Anything goes". A course goal is to engage both scientists and theologians in exploration, not debate, of some of the model's suggestions, a few of which follow.

- Interpretation of scriptures (e.g., the camel *vs.* rich man comparison) can be done in a literal, simple, physical way that produces additional quantitative understanding.
- God may have freedom to alter the past, with no violation of physical law.

- A "miracle" should be not be defined as a phenomenon that violates laws of physics, but rather as series of events that would not and could not have occurred without the activity of God (e.g., see previous suggestion).
- "Possible" and "impossible" should be considered from a probability perspective: should one chance in 1,000,000 be considered "possible"? One chance in $10^{10^{50}}$?

Acknowledgments

The author acknowledges the work of Philip Markham in the production of Figure 1, as well as the freedom the Department of Physics at the University of Alabama at Birmingham allowed the author to pursue preparation of physics curricula for non-traditional students.

Conflicts of Interest

The author declares no conflict of interest.

Abbreviations

3D: 3-dimensional;
2D: 2-dimensional;
m: meter;
s: second;
yr: year;
ly: light year.

References

1. St. Augustine. *The City of God*. In *The Complete Works of Augustine*. Seattle: Amazon Digital Services, 1887, 10536–49. Kindle edition.
2. Christopher J. Isham, and John C. Polkinghorne. "The Debate over the Block Universe." In *Quantum Cosmology and the Laws of Nature: Scientific Perspectives on Divine Action*, 2nd ed. Edited by R.J. Russell, N.C. Murphy and C.J. Isham. Vatican City State and Berkeley: Vatican Observatory and The Center for Theology and the Natural Sciences, 1996, pp. 139–47.
3. Thomas Nordlund University Faculty. Available online: http://people.cas.uab.edu/~nordlund/ (accessed on 11 March 2015).
4. Sean Carroll. *From Eternity to Here: The Quest for the Ultimate Theory of Time*. New York: Plume, Penguin Publishing, 2010, p. 448. Kindle edition.
5. Craig Callender. *The Oxford Handbook of Philosophy of Time*. Oxford: Oxford University Press, 2011.
6. Brian Greene. *The Hidden Reality*. New York: Vintage Books, 2011.
7. Marc Wittman. "The Inner Sense of Time: How the Brain Creates a Representation of Duration." *Nature Reviews Neuroscience* 14 (2013): 217–23. Available online: http://www.ncbi.nlm.nih.gov/pubmed/23403747 (accessed on 11 March 2015).

8. Mariette DiChristina, ed. *A Question of Time: The Ultimate Paradox*. New York: Scientific American Press, 2012, p. 190. Kindle edition.
9. Ulrich Meyer. *The Nature of Time*, 1st ed. Oxford: Clarendon Press, 2013.
10. Stephen Hawking, and Roger Penrose. *The Nature of Time*. Princeton: Princeton University Press, 2010.
11. Lee Smolin. *Time Reborn: From the Crisis in Physics to the Future of the Universe*. Boston: Mariner Books, 2014.
12. St. Augustine. "The Confessions of Saint Augustine." Edited by R.S. Munday. Salt Lake City: Project Gutenberg, p. 401. Available online: http://www.gutenberg.org/files/3296/3296-h/3296-h.htm - link2H_4_0011 (accessed on 11 March 2015).
13. St. Augustine. *The Literal Meaning of Genesis, Vol I, Books 1–6*. Edited by Johannes Quasten, Walter J. Burghardt and Thomas C. Lawler. New York: Newman Press, 1982.
14. Simon Blackburn. *The Oxford Dictionary of Philosophy*, 2nd revised ed. Oxford: Oxford University Press, 2008.
15. Sinclair B. Ferguson, David F. Wright, and J.I. Packer. *New Dictionary of Theology*. Westmont: Intervarsity Press, 1988, p. 757.
16. John Bunyan. *The Pilgrim's Progress*. Salt Lake City: Project Gutenberg, 2008, section 383.
17. NASA. "Ringside Seat to the Universe's First Split Second." Available online: www.nasa.gov/vision/universe/starsgalaxies/wmap_pol.html (accessed on 11 March 2015).
18. Brian Greene. *The Fabric of the Cosmos: Space, Time, and the Texture of Reality*, 1st ed. New York: Alfred A. Knopf, 2004, p. 130 (Figure 5.1).
19. T. Tajima, and G. Mourou. "Zettawatt-Exawatt Lasers and Their Applications in Ultrastrong-Field Physics." *Physical Review Special Topics—Accelerators and Beams* 5 (2002): 031301-1–9.
20. Hui Chen, Scott Wilks, James Bonlie, Edison Liang, Jason Myatt, Dwight Price, David Meyerhofer, and Peter Beiersdorfer. "Relativistic Positron Creation Using Ultraintense Short Pulse Lasers." *Physical Review Letters* 102 (2009): 105001-1–4. Available online: http://link.aps.org/doi/10.1103/PhysRevLett.102.105001 (accessed on 11 March 2015).
21. Edward Farhi, Alan H. Guth, and Jemal Guven. "Is It Possible to Create a Universe in the Laboratory by Quantum Tunneling?" *Nuclear Physics B* 339 (1990): 417–90.
22. Max Tegmark. "On the Dimensionality of Spacetime." *Classical and Quantum Gravity* 14 (1997): L69–L75. Available online: http://iopscience.iop.org/0264-9381/14/4/002/pdf/0264-9381_14_4_002.pdf (accessed on 11 March 2015).
23. Max Tegmark. "Spacetime dimensionality." Available online: http://en.wikipedia.org/w/index.php?title=File:Spacetime_dimensionality.svg&page=1 (accessed on 11 March 2015).
24. John McTaggart Ellis McTaggart. "The Unreality of Time." *Mind: A Quarterly Review of Psychology and Philosophy* 17 (1908): 456–73. Available online: http://en.wikisource.org/wiki/The_Unreality_of_Time (accessed on 11 March 2015).
25. Stephen T. Thornton, and Andrew Rex. *Modern Physics for Scientists and Engineers*, 4th ed. Boston: Cengage Learning, 2013, Chapter 16.3.
26. Julian Barbour. *The End of Time: The Next Revolution in Physics*. New York: Oxford University Press, 2000.

MDPI AG
Klybeckstrasse 64
4057 Basel, Switzerland
Tel. +41 61 683 77 34
Fax +41 61 302 89 18
http://www.mdpi.com/

Religions Editorial Office
E-mail: religions@mdpi.com
http://www.mdpi.com/journal/religions

www.ingramcontent.com/pod-product-compliance
Lightning Source LLC
Chambersburg PA
CBHW060412010526
44107CB00006B/659